STANLEY KUBRICK

A Narrative and Stylistic Analysis

New and Expanded
Second Edition

MARIO FALSETTO

 PRAEGER

Westport, Connecticut
London

Library of Congress Cataloging-in-Publication Data

Falsetto, Mario.
    Stanley Kubrick : a narrative and stylistic analysis / Mario Falsetto.—New and
expanded 2nd ed.
        p. cm.
    Includes bibliographical references and index.
    ISBN 0–275–96974–6 (alk. paper).—ISBN 0–275–97291–7 (pbk. : alk. paper)
    1. Kubrick, Stanley—Criticism and interpretation.   I. Title.
PN1998.3.K83F35   2001
791.43'0233'092—dc21   00–052863

British Library Cataloguing in Publication Data is available.

Library of Congress Catalog Card Number: 00–052863
ISBN: 0–275–96974–6
      0–275–97291–7 (pbk.)

First published in 2001

Praeger Publishers, 88 Post Road West, Westport, CT 06881
An imprint of Greenwood Publishing Group, Inc.
www.praeger.com

Printed in the United States of America

(∞)™

The paper used in this book complies with the
Permanent Paper Standard issued by the National
Information Standards Organization (Z39.48–1984).

10 9 8 7 6 5 4 3 2 1

For Carole

Contents

A photographic essay follows page 84.

Acknowledgments

Many of the ideas contained in this book developed from a course on the films of Stanley Kubrick that I regularly teach at Concordia University in Montreal. My students have always been a source of inspiration to me, and this book owes a great deal to them. I would like to acknowledge the continued support of Dean Christopher Jackson at Concordia. I would also like to mention the important contribution made by André Caron, who offered me a detailed analysis of the first edition of this book. André pointed out some errors in my descriptions and offered many excellent suggestions for improving the original analysis. His critique was extremely valuable and I thank him for it. All stills are courtesy of the Museum of Modern Art/Film Stills Archive. To Kristian Moen who made invaluable suggestions to improve the manuscript, a huge note of thanks.

Above all, I want to thank Carole Zucker for all the ways in which she has supported and encouraged the writing of this book, in both its incarnations. I dedicate this book to her with much love.

Introduction to the Second Edition

> I have no fixed ideas about wanting to make films in particular cate-
> gories—Westerns, war films and so on. I know I would like to make a film
> that gave a feeling of the times—a contemporary story that really gave a
> feeling of the times, psychologically, sexually, politically, personally. I
> would like to make that more than anything else. And it's probably going
> to be the hardest film to make.[1]
>
> —Stanley Kubrick

It would be almost forty years before Stanley Kubrick realized his ambition to
make a film that, on its surface at least, "really gave a feeling of the times."
When Kubrick spoke those words in 1960, he had no way of knowing that
virtually every film he would go on to direct would reflect the moment of its
making and the times we lived in. It's now clear that all of the director's films
were contemporary, although perhaps not in the way he intended in that particular interview.

   With the release of *Eyes Wide Shut* in the summer of 1999 four months after
Kubrick's untimely death that March, the world finally saw his "contemporary
story." The irony is that *Eyes Wide Shut* may have been the one Kubrick film
with the least to say about the decade in which it was made. The film seemed
decidedly out of time. Its notoriously long shooting and production schedule—
about four years in total—created an enormous amount of anticipation since
Kubrick was finally exploring the sexual and psychological realities of a contemporary marriage in crisis. Had he lived, however, he would surely have
been disappointed by the film's reception. Although the film had its support-
ers, more often than not the reception was a somewhat mystified lack of comprehension. What was surprising among the many reactions to the film was
how divided many critics were and, most surprisingly, just how literally certain

people interpreted the film. There was little discussion of the blurring of objective reality and the subjective presentation of the film's universe. The possibility that the film's protagonist, played by Tom Cruise, might be experiencing the world in some kind of a dream state or, at the very least, that the filmic events were being filtered, heightened and distorted by the characters was not mentioned in many of the reviews.

The hype surrounding the release of *Eyes Wide Shut* that summer may have been the film's own undoing. It's doubtful that Kubrick's examination of marital infidelity involving a rich New York doctor and his wife caught up in a dance of sexual jealousy and suspicion could ever satisfy a large mainstream audience, no matter how compelling. The audiences that came to see what many thought would be the most sexually explicit film of the summer were instead confronted with a magisterial, feverish dream movie that summed up the director's views on love and death, and, in a strange way, cinema at the close of the century. The film's slow editing patterns and ambiguous narrative were simply too strange for a large audience expecting to see the latest Tom Cruise vehicle. The events of the film seemed to exist in a state of perpetual uncertainty. Audiences expecting to be titillated were instead confronted with a serious, autumnal work from a director tackling the issues of human sexuality and mortality in a form unlike anything else in his body of work. Although many Kubrick fans saw *Eyes Wide Shut* as proof positive that the director was still capable of fashioning a complex, multilayered drama, and the film did respectably in terms of worldwide box-office, the overall response was decidedly lukewarm.

Kubrick's miscalculation—and he was not often wrong about his audience—was in clinging to the belief that a large mainstream audience would go along with a clearly serious film that offered some kind of meditation on love and death, from an artist who had been promising to offer such a film for most of his life. The late work of Akira Kurosawa, Ingmar Bergman, Robert Bresson, Jean-Luc Godard and Alfred Hitchcock had also been greeted with a similar kind of disappointment and derision. Yet, the initial reaction to Kubrick's final film was not really all that different from the reaction to other Kubrick films such as *Barry Lyndon* (1975), *The Shining* (1980) and *2001: A Space Odyssey* (1968), which had also surprised and confused many viewers upon their first release.

With *Eyes Wide Shut*, Kubrick continued his life-long pattern of creating art cinema in the guise of popular entertainment. For many viewers, the art simply overwhelmed the entertainment in his latest film. It is difficult to say, at this early stage, whether Kubrick's self-imposed exile in Britain for almost forty years had caused him to lose touch with many contemporary notions of sexuality. We can only speculate since no one can really say what kind of private life he lived and how much contact he had with people. The latest film biographies argue that his life was a rich one, filled with the emotional and intellectual rewards of family, friends and work. His last film was certainly far removed from the preoccupations of most recent commercial movies.

But the re-evaluation and recuperation of *Eyes Wide Shut* has been swifter than usual for a Kubrick film. In less than a year there have been eloquent arguments in the film's defense by such writers as Michael Herr,[2] Kubrick's collaborator on *Full Metal Jacket* and the author of *Dispatches*, still one of the most brilliant and disturbing books to come out of the Vietnam conflict. Critic Jonathan Rosenbaum and filmmaker Martin Scorsese both listed Kubrick's final film as one of the ten best films of the decade. Personally, I have no doubt that thirty years from now people will be discussing *Eyes Wide Shut* with the same seriousness they now bring to the discussion of *2001*, *A Clockwork Orange* (1971) and *Barry Lyndon*. It will take its place as a key cinematic work of the latter part of the twentieth century.

Eyes Wide Shut is a remarkable film on many levels. It moves with the elegance and sureness of style that has characterized most of the director's late work. Yet, it is so unlike most commercial films released in the 1990s that one is forced to rethink much of what we thought we knew about mainstream filmmaking and Kubrick's artistry, despite the fact that it shares many preoccupations with *A Clockwork Orange*, *The Shining* and *Barry Lyndon*. The complexity of its conception of filmic subjectivity is so radical that it represents a major aesthetic statement about the untapped possibilities of cinema. *Eyes Wide Shut* is a film that, on its surface, presents a narrative filled with certainties and banalities when in fact it is full of ambiguity and profundity. It continually shifts its articulation between the obvious and the hidden, the superficial and the profound, the private and the public. The meanings of the film are deeply embedded in what we generally call "subtext."

Eyes Wide Shut argues for a kind of cinema that in the 1950s André Bazin termed "total cinema." Its complex web of meaning resides in every aspect of its construction: the subtle performances, artful decor, extraordinary lighting, unusual shot composition and framing, fluid camera movement, the subtle use of the zoom, a complex narrative structure, complex shot-to-shot editing patterns, and the emotional use of music and sound. Kubrick has always been the consummate filmmaker, but in his final film he has taken great artistic risks that can only be perceived if we abandon many of our preconceptions about the way narrative film functions and also the way we understand Kubrick as an artist. One can only hope that with the passage of time, audiences will revisit the film in the hope of finally seeing and hearing what he was trying so nobly to articulate.

STANLEY KUBRICK: AN OVERVIEW

Stanley Kubrick began his career in the early 1950s making several documentaries and two independent features, *Fear and Desire* (1953) and *Killer's Kiss* (1955). Although he would eventually become a key artist within the studio system, the lack of early studio support proved crucial in shaping the pattern of creative autonomy that characterized his subsequent career.

Kubrick created an impressive body of work that spanned almost fifty years, and his place in contemporary film history is assured. Despite this independence and secure reputation, however, Kubrick's films have often proved difficult for film reviewers and scholars.

Beginning with the release of *2001: A Space Odyssey*, Kubrick's work has generated strong defense from his admirers and equally hostile attack from his critics. Also, the critical standing of a Kubrick film seems to undergo extensive revision over the course of time. It has now become a consistent pattern that the initial response to a Kubrick film is generally an *unreliable* barometer of how the film will be perceived years after its first release.

The Kubrick filmography consists of three short films and 13 features, the first two of which he considered apprentice works. Kubrick's reputation rests essentially on eleven feature films beginning with *The Killing* (1956) and ending with *Eyes Wide Shut*. Stanley Kubrick enjoyed perhaps the most autonomous and commodious arrangement with the studios of any major filmmaker. He freely chose whatever project interested him, and apparently took as much time and money to complete his films as he needed. Despite this remarkable studio support, Kubrick made only five films after *2001*. His approach was always careful and methodical. He was, of course, involved in every stage of production. This not only included the expected writing, producing and directing chores, but also working closely with his fellow artists such as cinematographers, editors and art directors, and even helping to plan the film's release and ad campaigns. This involvement inevitably made the production process longer than those of his contemporaries. There is no denying the fact, however, that Kubrick spent an awfully long time shooting his films. He exemplified a rare strain in commercial cinema: the filmmaker who kept searching for what he was looking for in take after take until something resonated in him and confirmed that he had made his creative discovery. His notoriety for perfectionism and technical mastery of the medium might initially lead viewers to believe that he was always prepared, knew exactly *what* he was going to shoot and *how* it would be shot. In fact, he worked in the opposite way. He often tried to create *in the moment* and always wanted to be surprised by what his actors could deliver. Despite his reputation for technical brilliance, Kubrick respected actors and loved their creativity and imaginative powers.

The need to control all aspects of his productions has contributed to a certain mythology about Stanley Kubrick, the individual. Those who have worked with him, however, seem to agree that his perfectionism was a positive, if occasionally trying quality. Ken Adam, set designer on several Kubrick films, stated in a 1964 interview that "Stanley is an extremely difficult and talented person. We developed an extremely close relationship and as a result I had to live almost completely on tranquillizers."[3] Kubrick seemed genuinely open to other people's contributions, though, and seems to have instilled a high degree of loyalty among his collaborators. All reports indicate that he was not dictatorial on the set and was endlessly patient with his collaborators. He had a reputation for making actors do numerous retakes (as many as 50, we are told, for a simple scene), yet most actors who worked with him speak highly of the experience, appreciative, no doubt, of the opportunity to work closely with a director sensitive to film performance. In a 1975 interview, Malcolm McDowell stated:

This is why Stanley is such a great director. He can create an atmosphere where you're not inhibited in the least. You'll do anything. Try it out. Experiment. Stanley gives you freedom and he is the most marvelous audience. I used to see him behind the camera with the handkerchief stuffed in his mouth because he was laughing so much. It gave me enormous confidence.[4]

The myths associated with Kubrick, of course, extend beyond the film set. And like most film directors, he has contributed to these myths by some of his printed remarks. Tim Cahill summarizes some of the more extreme myths in a 1987 interview:

Tim Cahill: Stanley Kubrick is a perfectionist. He is consumed by mindless anxiety over every aspect of every film he makes. Kubrick is a hermit, an expatriate, a neurotic who is terrified of automobiles and who won't let his chauffeur drive more than thirty miles an hour.

Stanley Kubrick: Part of my problem is that I cannot dispel the myths that have somehow accumulated over the years. . . . In fact, I don't have a chauffeur. I drive a Porsche 928S, and I sometimes drive it at eighty or ninety miles an hour on the motorway.

TC: I've heard rumors that you'll do a hundred takes for one scene.

SK: It happens when actors are unprepared. You cannot act without knowing dialogue. If actors have to think about the words, they cannot work on the emotion. So you end up doing thirty takes of something. And still you can see the concentration in their eyes; they don't know their lines. So you just shoot it and shoot it and hope you can get something out of it in pieces. Now, if the actor is a nice guy, he goes home, he says, "Stanley's such a perfectionist, he does a hundred takes on every scene." So my thirty takes become a hundred. If I did a hundred takes on every scene, I'd never finish a film.[5]

The major events in Kubrick's biography are well documented. Born in the Bronx in 1928, he went directly from high school—where his passions included still photography, jazz drumming and chess—to a job at *Look* magazine at the age of sixteen. He stayed for five years, working as a photo-journalist, before leaving to make his first short film. In an interview with Joseph Gelmis, Kubrick said, "I'd keep seeing lousy films and saying to myself, 'I don't know anything about moviemaking but I *couldn't* do anything worse than this.' "[6] His first film, a documentary entitled *Day of the Fight* (1951), was a profile of the boxer Walter Cartier, the subject of an earlier photo-layout by Kubrick. A second film,

Flying Padre (1951) concerned a priest in New Mexico who flew from one end of his parish to the other in a Piper Cub airplane. This was followed in 1953 by a final documentary, *The Seafarers*.

Though these films did not make Kubrick any money, he felt encouraged enough to embark on his first feature, *Fear and Desire*, an anti-war allegory made for less than $10,000 with funds borrowed mainly from his family. The film was not a financial success. Although it is decidedly awkward in places, it also contains several genuinely poetic scenes. The film garnered some critical attention, and in 1955 Kubrick made a second feature, *Killer's Kiss*, a highly atmospheric film noir. *Killer's Kiss* marked the end of the apprentice phase of Kubrick's career.

These initial experiences proved to be a perfect training ground since Kubrick had no background in theater, television or film school. He learned every aspect of the mechanics of filmmaking, handling virtually every major task on the films himself, including the photography. Apart from this practical experience, Kubrick's aesthetic sense was shaped by frequent film screenings, including many at the Museum of Modern Art, which acted as a kind of film school for the young, aspiring artist. He read books about film by such people as Eisenstein and Pudovkin, decidedly preferring the latter to the former.

With this particular background, it is not surprising that early on Kubrick viewed editing as the most creative aspect of filmmaking: "It's the nearest thing to some reasonable environment in which to do creative work. . . . Editing is the only aspect of the cinematic art that is unique. It shares no connection with any other art form: writing, acting, photography, things like that are major aspects of the cinema, are still not unique to it, but editing is."[7]

After *Killer's Kiss*, Kubrick directed *The Killing*, a highly inventive heist film made in partnership with James B. Harris—an association that lasted through the making of *Lolita* (1962). The complexities of *The Killing* are primarily revealed in its innovative narrative structure. It also features fine performances by character actors generally not given the chance to display their craft. Around this time, Kubrick began to attract the attention of the film world. In a 1957 *Newsweek* article, Kubrick is referred to as the latest Hollywood "boy wonder,"[8] a description amply confirmed by the release of his next film, *Paths of Glory* (1957), still regarded as one of the best anti-war films ever made. *Paths of Glory* announced that Kubrick was indeed a world-class filmmaker. The film displayed a bold stylistic system, especially in its use of moving camera and complicated spatial strategies, as well as a depth of characterization not apparent in Kubrick's earlier work. The handling of sensitive moral issues and involving dramatics elevated Kubrick to the front ranks of Hollywood directors.

After an unproductive period in Hollywood working on several projects, including *One-Eyed Jacks* (1961) for Marlon Brando, Kubrick was hired to replace Anthony Mann on *Spartacus* (1960), a film that proved Kubrick could handle the complicated logistics of a massive Hollywood epic. Although remarkable in many ways, the film is viewed as something of an exception in the director's *oeuvre*. Kubrick did not write any part of the screenplay, had no input in the film's casting, and has referred to himself as a "hired hand" on the film. Although he has complained of the experience, *Spartacus* is an intelligent, if somewhat conventional, epic and was generally well received. Perhaps more than any other experience, the making of *Spartacus* highlighted to the director the importance of being involved in every stage of production.

Spartacus was followed by *Lolita* (1962), the first Kubrick film to be shot in England, where the director continued to work until his death. The adaptation of Nabokov's controversial novel received a somewhat mixed reception, although it was almost universally praised for its fine performances. Most of the negative reaction centered on the differences between the film and the book. The film's (understandable) differences with the novel did not seem to bother Vladimir Nabokov, who, nevertheless, was surprised to discover that most of the script he had written for the film had not been used. He has commented on the film:

A few days before, at a private screening, I had discovered that Kubrick was a great director, that his *Lolita* was a first-rate film with magnificent actors, and that only ragged odds and ends of my script had been used. The modifications, the garbling of my best little finds, the omission of entire scenes, the addition of new ones, and all sorts of other changes may not have been sufficient to erase my name from the credit titles but they certainly made the picture as unfaithful to the original script as an American poet's translation from Rimbaud or Pasternak. I hasten to add that my present comments should definitely not be construed as reflecting any belated grudge, any high-pitched deprecation of Kubrick's creative approach.[9]

As with most other Kubrick films, *Lolita*'s status continues to rise with the passage of time. *Lolita* was followed by one of Kubrick's greatest commercial and critical successes, *Dr. Strangelove, or How I Learned to Stop Worrying and Love the Bomb* (1964). This nihilistic satire, based on the novel *Red Alert*, was originally intended to be a straightforward drama about the cold war, but it eventually evolved into what Kubrick calls a "nightmare comedy." Here is the director discussing the evolution of the film's tone in a 1963 article that appeared in *Films and Filming*:

Now *Red Alert* is a completely serious suspense story. My idea of doing it as a nightmare comedy came when I was trying to work on it. I found that in trying to put meat on the bones and to imagine the scenes fully one had to keep leaving things out of it which were either absurd or paradoxical, in order to keep it from being funny, and these things seemed to be very real. Then I decided that the perfect tone to adopt for the film would be what I now call nightmare comedy, because it most truthfully presents the picture.[10]

Most reviewers thought *Dr. Strangelove* had admirably achieved its ambitions, and reacted favorably to the film. Typical of the positive evaluation of the film was director Bryan Forbes' review in *Films and Filming*, which described the film as "a tragic-comic masterpiece—the first truly moral film of our time: courageous, outrageous, borrowing nothing, admitting of no compromise, very naked and very unashamed: a shattering, womb-trembler of a film."[11] The film was extensively debated, often by commentators who generally did not write film reviews. Robert Brustein, writing in the *New York Review of Books*, described *Dr. Strangelove* as

a work of comic anarchy, fashioned by a totally disaffected and disaffiliated imagination: it is thus the first American movie to speak truly for our generation. . . . For although *Dr. Strangelove* is about a political subject, its only politics is outrage against malevolence of officialdom. Conservatives will find it subversive, liberals will find it irresponsible, utopians will find it bleak, humanitarians will find it inhuman—*Dr. Strangelove* is all these things. But it also releases, through comic poetry, those feelings of impotence and frustration that are consuming us all; and I can't think of anything more important for an imaginative work to do.[12]

Kubrick's next film, *2001*, was something of a watershed in the director's career. The film is now generally acknowledged as a great masterpiece of modernism, but its acceptance was by no means universal or immediate. With the reception accorded *2001*, there is a clear shift in critical response to Kubrick's work. Many of the initial reviews were short-sighted and hostile, and the film proved baffling to a number of reviewers.[13]

In many ways, *2001* is a key film for Kubrick, especially in its radical narrative experimentation. Additionally, the film again exemplified the director's ability to tap into the most important issues of the time, something he had already done with *Dr. Strangelove*. *2001* also illustrated another aspect of Kubrick's talent that we now take for granted: his interest in technology. The film's exhilarating special effects, which Kubrick designed and conceived, remain a standard to which films are still compared. Current big-budget spectacular films may be technically more sophisticated, but they are by no means more aesthetically interesting or accomplished.

2001 also highlighted, as never before, Kubrick's conceptual talent and the fact that he was an artist very much interested in ideas. This intellectual curiosity always found its way into Kubrick's films, and at their most speculative, as in *2001*, his films are embedded with intricate meaning and formal elegance. *2001* represents Kubrick at his most ambitious and curious. It constitutes the director's greatest meditation on the self and individual consciousness. The film creates an involving subjective experience that strains not only the limits of narrative cinema, but our understanding of filmic subjectivity. More than any other Kubrick film, *2001* attempts to create a nonverbal, cinematic experience. Kubrick has stated that he thought the experience of watching a film was something akin to dreaming, and this idea is well illustrated in *2001*: "I think an audience watching a film or a play is in a state very similar to dreaming, and that the dramatic experience becomes a kind of controlled dream. . . . the important point here is that the film communicates on a subconscious level, and the audience responds to the basic shape of the story on a subconscious level, as it responds to a dream."[14] This idea would, of course, resonate in several other films, especially *Eyes Wide Shut,* which more than any other of his films feels like a waking dream.

The nonverbal nature of *2001* is most apparent in the way it foregrounds the sense of sight—at the expense of language. The film's 141-minute running time contains little more than forty minutes of dialogue. As Kubrick stated: "Film operates on a level much closer to music and to painting than to the printed word, and, of course, movies present the opportunity to convey complex concepts and abstractions without the traditional reliance on words."[15] In a more theoretical vein, Annette Michelson situates this aspect of *2001* within a phenomenological reading: "Experience as vision ends in the exploration of seeing. The film's reflexive strategy assumes the eye as ultimate agent of consciousness, reminding us, as every phenomenological esthetic from that of Ortega to that of Merleau-Ponty has, that art develops from the concern with 'things seen to that of seeing itself.' "[16]

Though the radical nature of Kubrick's accomplishment was not apparent to everyone, the film's spiritual and metaphysical aspirations seemed to be precisely what attracted young audiences to it. There has rarely been a film that seemed so perfectly attuned to its historical moment. The film would probably have been unthinkable ten years earlier or ten years later, but in 1968 all the elements seemed to converge in an ideal confluence of perfect timing and artful creation. The cerebral nature of Kubrick's achievement, combined with an intensely involving cinematic experience, distinguished *2001* from other recognizable "art" films of the period. *2001* exhibits another quality central to Kubrick's complex, late work: the gap between the surface meaning of a scene and its deeper, subtextual meaning. The formal intricacies and complex organization of his late films contain rich layers of meaning that may not always be apparent to casual viewers. Despite these intellectual aspirations, the films always contain a strong emotional resonance.

2001 was to have been followed by a film about Napoleon that was never made. Instead, Kubrick followed up his science-fiction epic with his 1971 adaptation of Anthony Burgess' novel, *A Clockwork Orange,* one of his most brilliant and controversial films. The exaggerated, stylized decor and experiments with a first-person point of view contribute to the film's highly determined, theatrically distanced stylistic system.

Although *A Clockwork Orange* received a high degree of praise and numerous awards, it was unfortunately caught in the debate about on-screen violence raging at the time. Most critics who came to the film's defense understood that its stylized presentation formed an argument about violence, but some reviewers claimed that the presentation of Alex (Malcolm McDowell) was too sympathetic for the argument to be effective. In the film's defense, Kubrick has compared Alex to literary characters such as Shakespeare's Richard III: "Alex, like Richard, is a character whom you should dislike and fear, and yet you find yourself drawn very quickly into his world and find yourself seeing things through his eyes."[17] It is true that Alex is presented with a degree of charm absent in the film's other characters, but this kind of negative characterization is not unusual in Kubrick's work. Alex is not presented with complete sympathy, of course, but the film does argue that there is something admirable in the way he channels his creativity. Kubrick has stated that "what we respond to subconsciously is Alex's guiltless sense of freedom to kill and rape, and to be our savage natural selves, and it is in this glimpse of the true nature of man that the power of the story derives."[18] In the same interview, Kubrick claimed that

One of the most dangerous fallacies which has influenced a great deal of political and philosophical thinking is that man is essentially good, and that it is society which makes him bad. . . . Rousseau transferred original sin from man to society, and this view has importantly contributed to what I believe has become a crucially incorrect premise on which to base moral and political philosophy.[19]

A Clockwork Orange earned generally positive reviews, as well as the approval of Anthony Burgess, who called it "very much a Kubrick movie, technically brilliant, poetic, mind-opening."[20] Despite some major differences between novel and film, Burgess concurred that the film communicated much the same moral point as his novel: "What my, and Kubrick's, parable tries to state is that it is preferable to have a world of violence undertaken in full awareness—violence chosen as an act of will—than a world conditioned to be good or harmless."[21]

Kubrick followed the critical and commercial success of *A Clockwork Orange* with what I believe is his most ambitious film, *Barry Lyndon*. This historical epic set in the eighteenth century is one of his most personal films. True to form, the film divided critics once again, with the most negative reviewers arguing that the film was visually stunning but "undramatic," or, more disparagingly, something akin to a three-hour slide show. Certainly the film was slowly paced, detached and painterly. But the dedramatized presentation was a crucial aspect of the film's ambition. Once again, the complex stylistic system of *Barry Lyndon* went unappreciated by many of the same critics who were perfectly capable of appreciating difficult work by Bresson or Michelangelo Antonioni. *Barry Lyndon* contains a new depth of feeling and approach to character, and its painterly world is revealed to be shallow and ephemeral. The seemingly rational, ordered universe masks a chaotic, cruel world beneath. The film contains further experiments with visual style (especially in Kubrick's use of the zoom lens), characterization and voice-over commentary. It relies on complex spatial strategies of camera movement, slow zooms, long takes, camera position, long shots, rhythmical editing and character placement within the frame for much of its impact. Such strategies call attention to the spatial and temporal rigidity and orderliness of the world of the film ensnaring the characters within the two-dimensional space of the image.

Barry Lyndon contains one of the most sympathetic portrayals of character in all of Kubrick's work. There is a depth of feeling for the flawed but noble Barry (Ryan O'Neal) that contrasts markedly with the unemotional style of the film. It is a remarkable accomplishment that Kubrick achieved this high degree of character sympathy within one of the most stylized and distanced presentations of his entire *oeuvre*.

Barry Lyndon's view of the eighteenth century, beneath the surface beauty of the image, is ultimately a negative one. The film paints a portrait of a society that values wealth, position, marriages of convenience, philosophy, art, music, fine clothes, grand architecture and good breeding. But while achieving what many consider an apogee of civilization, this society has lost its energy, passion and intensity. It has been aestheticized into numbness and atrophy. The film seems to argue that it matters little what an era may accomplish, if in the process we lose such essential components of humanity as emotion and free will.

Barry Lyndon is Kubrick's most profound statement on art and human relationships. It is his most fully rounded work, matched only by the very human concerns of his final film, *Eyes Wide Shut*. As much as it is about the eighteenth century, it is also about contemporary society, and offers a sustained analysis of male/female relationships, aesthetics, morality and social institutions.

One of the most striking features of Kubrick's next film, a screen adaptation of Stephen King's *The Shining*, is its visual style. This is achieved in part by the innovative use of Steadicam photography, which facilitates the extensive choreography of character and camera movement. The film may be an instance of an innovative technological development determining a film's style. What is also of interest is the relatively objective way many subjective encounters are presented—the film is a horror tale with many ghostly encounters. The line between objective reality and the subjective, interior life of the characters becomes blurred. *The Shining* raises intriguing questions about character subjectivity and is one of the director's most open filmic texts, offering the spectator an almost endless array of interpretive possibilities.

The Shining is also notable for the wildly inventive and emotionally charged performance of Jack Nicholson in the leading role. The performance is striking for its physicality and expressiveness. Nicholson's performance is wild and extreme, verging on the hysterical. At times, the actor gives the impression of being out of control. The performance relies heavily on the physical and the comic for its effect. It's not a very "respectable" performance and may strike some as overbearing, vulgar and just plain "too much." In fact, it is precisely these risky, over-the-edge qualities that make the performance and the film so invigorating.

Full Metal Jacket (1987), Kubrick's long-awaited follow-up to *The Shining*, is an emotionally distanced, ironic and unsentimental work. As in Kubrick's earlier forays into the combat-film genre, it is concerned with the irrationality of war. Despite its attention to accurate details of presentation, it offers a somewhat abstracted view of war. Although it concentrates specifically on the Vietnam experience, its primary concern is to examine aspects of human behavior that any war or conflict might generate.

Full Metal Jacket contains a meticulously detailed recreation of war-ravaged Vietnam. An unusual aspect of the film's look makes the locale seem like a realistic portrayal of Vietnam, yet it also feels unreal. An abandoned concrete city (Beckton-on-Thames) and gasworks were demolished to lend verisimilitude to the film. The set had previously been used by Michael Radford for his adaptation of George Orwell's *Nineteen Eighty-Four* (1984). Beyond this accuracy, *Full Metal Jacket* achieves a kind of hyperrealism through an almost over-aestheticized decor and production design. The inferno of war has never seemed at once so accurate yet so removed and distant.

THE ANALYSIS

There is a telling moment in *Full Metal Jacket* (1987) when Private Joker (Matthew Modine) tries to explain to an aggressive officer why he wears a peace-symbol button and has the words "Born to Kill" scrawled on his helmet. Joker tells him that "it's something about the duality of man, sir!" The notion that opposite traits make up human nature is not an insight original to either Kubrick or the character, but it is central to Kubrick's world view.

My contention throughout this study is that Kubrick's work revolves around particular dualities of meaning. Most narrative, stylistic or thematic issues in the films relate, in some way, to the following polarities: subjective/objective, classical/modernist, rational/irrational, empathy/distance, clarity/ambiguity, order/chaos, symmetry/asymmetry, conventional/subversive, surface/depth, what we know and what remains hidden. The analysis attempts to describe, with some precision, how I believe Stanley Kubrick's films function and how they generate meaning. What sorts of narrative, stylistic and thematic concerns do they set out to explore? What are the components that make up Kubrick's style? Naturally, with such a rich body of work, the notion that one analysis could adequately cover every significant aspect of how the films operate is absurd. My goal is to deal with as many key questions as can reasonably be attempted in one study. My approach will generally be a formal one. Major issues that I will leave to other scholars include Kubrick's brilliant use of sound and art direction, two areas that each merit a book-length study of their own.

The analysis focuses on various strategies related to the construction of narrative and meaning, including point of view, editing relations, camera-related strategies, performance and the creation of character, and narrative

structure. The project is primarily descriptive and interpretive in nature. I
have chosen to concentrate on the major films over which Kubrick had the
most artistic control: *The Killing, Paths of Glory, Lolita, Dr. Strangelove,
2001, A Clockwork Orange, Barry Lyndon, The Shining, Full Metal Jacket,*
and *Eyes Wide Shut.*

Chapter 1 explores some consistent narrative patterns in several of the director's films. My method includes breaking down the films into sequences
in order to better perceive how structural patterning helps organize narrative. To further illustrate this discussion, several narrative segmentations have
been placed in the Appendix. I begin the discussion by examining the nonlinear temporal structure and impersonal commentary in *The Killing.* The
fragmenting of narrative information is one of the film's most radical elements, although it does not detract from narrative momentum or intelligi-
bility. *The Killing* illustrates the tension in Kubrick's work between the
conventional and the unconventional, between classical story telling techniques and a more modernist narrative mode. I then discuss the issue of narrative gaps in *Lolita,* including the major structuring absence of the character
of Quilty. The first chapter concludes with a discussion of several strategies
of repetition and variation of narrative incident in *A Clockwork Orange,
Barry Lyndon* and *Eyes Wide Shut.*

Chapters 2 and 3 examine how temporal and spatial strategies are key elements in any understanding of Kubrick's stylistics. My underlying argument is that thematic and stylistic considerations are so interconnected that
questions of meaning cannot be restricted to purely formal or thematic discussions. The relationship between style and theme is most clearly apparent
in the films' visuals and patterns of shot-to-shot editing. I begin with
Kubrick's use of the static long take, a key stylistic element. Then I examine
various image and editing strategies in *Paths of Glory,* in particular, the creation of contrasting spaces, point-of-view editing and use of the zoom. I
then discuss how editing in *Dr. Strangelove* tends to frustrate closure and
continually propels the narrative forward. I go on to explore the concept of
cinematic rhythm in several sequences from that film. A detailed shot description from *Dr. Strangelove* can be found in the Appendix. The chapter
continues with a discussion of how image and editing strategies in *2001* create ambiguity in time and space. Several sequences that incorporate rhythmical editing to communicate narrative information without language are
examined.

In Chapter 3, the analysis of *A Clockwork Orange* focuses on the creation
of a theatrical space and how visual and temporal distortion creates a subjective rendering of the world. The tension between the film's subjective
presentation and distanced stylistics, as well as the formal play between fantasy and reality, is explored. The discussion of *Barry Lyndon* concentrates on
various image strategies that are crucial in creating the film's complicated
aesthetic system. More than any other Kubrick film, *Barry Lyndon* reveals

how its thematics are tied to its formal operation and rigorous stylistics. I discuss how rhythmical editing is achieved in several scenes and how classical narrative rhetoric, such as shot/counter-shot and eye-line matches, can be reinvigorated. I then explore an idea that I call "metaphorical space" in *The Shining*. The film's unique look and exploration of space, to a great extent, account for its complicated thematics. It is one of the director's most ironic and distanced presentations. The discussion of *Full Metal Jacket*, a film that achieves a brutal realism through a predominantly distancing aesthetic system, illustrates how camera strategies contribute to an unreal, abstract rendering of Vietnam. The chapter concludes with a consideration of the complicated visuals and shot-to-shot editing patterns in *Eyes Wide Shut*, Kubrick's final masterpiece. This final work contains all that we have come to expect from Kubrick in terms of image construction, and its careful attention to camera and editing strategies confirms the claim that Stanley Kubrick's films contain the most careful construction and attention to cinematic detail of any contemporary film director.

Chapters 4 and 5 shift to an examination of narrative construction and point of view, central to any understanding of the director's aesthetic. I explore the use of voice-over in Kubrick's work, both in first-person and third-person modes. First-person commentary in *A Clockwork Orange* and *Lolita* is examined by focusing on the relationship between each film's narrating voice and the viewer as well as the disparity between what the audience sees in the image and the protagonist/narrator's view of himself. The discussion centers on the self-conscious nature of first-person commentary and how it communicates meaning. I then examine other examples of filmic subjectivity in key Kubrick films. For example, I look at the editing and image strategies in the "Star-Gate" sequence in *2001*, and the use of perceptual point of view to communicate character subjectivity. I also consider the final sequence in *2001* and how point of view is constructed around a subversion of the perceptual point-of-view shot and other rules of classical continuity. I discuss how Kubrick uses visual distortion to communicate a character's experience, especially in *A Clockwork Orange*. I then analyze in some detail aspects of filmic subjectivity in *A Clockwork Orange*, *2001*, and *The Shining*. The discussion of filmic subjectivity in *Eyes Wide Shut* focuses on several strategies that help create the idea that the film's universe may be a projection of its main character. I conclude with a brief discussion of some differences between cinematic renderings of subjectivity and objectivity.

The creation of performance and character is the subject of Chapter 6; in particular, I will examine how the leading characterizations in *A Clockwork Orange*, *Barry Lyndon* and *The Shining* function with respect to other aspects of the films' construction. *Barry Lyndon*, for example, creates character through presentation devices such as placement within the frame, use of the zoom, deep-focus photography, static long takes and other editing and camera strategies. *A Clockwork Orange* presents its leading character, Alex (Malcolm McDowell), as a performer and his violent actions as a theatrical "act." Jack Nicholson's performance in *The Shining* is one of the most ironic, stylized pieces of acting in recent decades and is intimately connected to other aspects of the film's aesthetic system. Kubrick has always been a remarkable director of actors. The performances in these films illustrate how complicated his conception of character is and how interconnected these performance strategies are with other aesthetic ideas at work in the films.

Finally, Chapter 7 speculates on some thematic motifs to demonstrate that the director's world view is coherent and interconnected on thematic as well as formal and stylistic levels. This chapter concludes with a final consideration of Kubrick's achievement.

Films are unique, privileged works of art as well as powerful commodities of popular culture. Even though writing about films and experiencing them are distinctly different operations, I hope that the following analysis, even at its most detailed, does not lose sight of the qualities of wonder, pleasure and curiosity that I associate with viewing films. I have tried to strike a balance between saying something meaningful about the films and being as specific as I can about why I am saying it. I believe passionately in the notion that criticism must never lose sight of the object in its view. The skill with which one illuminates a work of art should never take precedence over the work itself. Perhaps it is that belief that drives my analysis and the conviction that the precise and elegant construction of Kubrick's films deserves careful, thoughtful analysis. The idea that films need to be closely analyzed and carefully examined is not the most fashionable critical methodology at present, especially in a climate where film reviewers can cavalierly dismiss work that has been painstakingly created over many years. I have tried to give the films their due and to focus on issues that I feel have been neglected in much of the Kubrick scholarship.

Stanley Kubrick created some of the most powerful cinematic artworks in contemporary cinema. The director was always intensely concerned with finding the appropriate cinematic shape for his artistic and human concerns. Consistent and strongly recognizable elements define his style—you always know when you are watching a Kubrick film. Many filmic elements contribute to the *Kubrickian* landscape. The mastery of technique and complexity of form in Kubrick's films is impressive, but this formal mastery was always at the service of intricate thematics and organizational coherence. The director used the medium of film to express many ideas about the world and what it means to be human. But he was only interested in communicating those ideas in forceful, serious and inventive ways that made full use of the medium. An attractive aspect of Kubrick's work is that it achieves this complexity while remaining relatively accessible. His films are both entertaining and intellectually stimulating. Kubrick was always able to reconcile his position as an artist of complex *and* popular work. Perhaps that is what makes his films so unique and worthy of close attention.

NOTES

1. Stanley Kubrick, "Director's Notes: Stanley Kubrick Movie Maker," *The Observer*, December 4, 1960, reprinted in Mario Falsetto, *Perspectives on Stanley Kubrick* (New York: G. K. Hall, 1996), 25.

2. Michael Herr, *Kubrick* (New York: Grove Press, 2000). The bulk of this book originally appeared in two *Vanity Fair* articles, one in the August 1999 issue and the other in April 2000.

3. Quoted in Michel Ciment, *Kubrick*, trans. Gilbert Adair (London: Collins, 1983), 38.

4. Ibid., 38.

5. Tim Cahill, "The Rolling Stone Interview: Stanley Kubrick," reprinted in Falsetto, *Perspectives on Stanley Kubrick*, 80–81.

6. Joseph Gelmis, "Stanley Kubrick," reprinted in Falsetto, *Perspectives on Stanley Kubrick*, 45.

7. Stanley Kubrick, quoted in "Interview with Stanley Kubrick" by Philip Strick and Penelope Houston, *Sight and Sound* (Spring 1972), 65.

8. "Twenty-Nine and Running: The Director with Hollywood by the Horns . . . Dissects the Movies," *Newsweek* (2 December 1957), 96.

9. Vladimir Nabokov, Foreword to *Lolita: A Screenplay* (New York: McGraw-Hill, 1974), xii–xiii.

10. Stanley Kubrick, "How I Learned to Stop Worrying and Love the Cinema," *Films and Filming* 9:9 (June 1963), 12.

11. Bryan Forbes, *Films and Filming* 10:5 (February 1964), 26.

12. Robert Brustein, "Out of this World," reprinted in Falsetto, *Perspectives on Stanley Kubrick*, 140.

13. As if to make amends for some of the initial hostile reviews, *2001* was named to the 1992 *Sight and Sound* poll as one of the ten best films of all time.

14. Bernard Weinraub, "Kubrick Tells What Makes *Clockwork* Tick," *New York Times* (4 January 1972), 26.

15. Gelmis, "Stanley Kubrick," 34.

16. Annette Michelson, "Bodies in Space: Film as Carnal Knowledge," *Artforum* (February 1969), 60.

17. Penelope Houston, "Kubrick Country," *Saturday Review* (25 December 1971), 42.

18. Weinraub, "Kubrick Tells," 26.

19. Ibid.

20. Anthony Burgess, *The Listener* (17 February 1972), 197.

21. Ibid., 198.

1

Patterns of Narrative Organization

This initial discussion examines various organizational strategies found in the narrative construction of Stanley Kubrick's work. The chapter explores narrative patterning in *The Killing, Lolita, A Clockwork Orange, Barry Lyndon* and *Eyes Wide Shut*. By beginning this analysis with a discussion of narrative patterns, I will provide a kind of overview before proceeding to the more detailed analysis of later chapters. When scrutinizing strategies related to a film's style and thematics, one can easily overlook the overarching ideas, structures and relations within the work. In the attempt to (re)construct a film's meanings, one can often miss important narrational patterns and structures.

The accepted wisdom is that a film builds meaning by adding partial information from shot to shot. When surveying an entire film and the relations among its various components, one is often left with more information than was seemingly contained within each shot. This effect occurs partly because meaning can reside between shots (even between frames) and in the relation of one shot to another. This chapter will focus on various strategies that help structure filmic narration. Tzvetan Todorov has defined "structure," in its simplest formulation, as "the particular arrangement of two forms in relation to each other."[1] The more forms and relations a work contains, the more complex its structure. Edward Branigan argues that narrative is

a perceptual activity that organizes data into a special pattern which represents and explains experience. More specifically, narrative is a way of organizing spatial and temporal data into a cause-effect chain of events with a beginning, middle, and end that embodies a judgment about the nature of the events as well as demonstrates how it is possible to know, and hence to narrate, the events.[2]

Seymour Chatman claims the following specific elements are necessary for narrative to exist:

> The *signifiés* or signifieds are exactly three—event, character, and detail of setting; the *signifiants* or signifiers are those elements in the narrative statement (whatever the medium) that can stand for one of these three, thus any kind of physical or mental action for the first, any person (or, indeed, any entity that can be personalized) for the second, and any evocation of place for the third.[3]

The notion of anchoring a film's narrative progression to several relations or arrangements of narrative material is obviously not unique to Kubrick, nor is the placement of this discussion here intended to argue that narrational patterning is the most important element in these films. To facilitate our discussions, we will break down each film's narrative action into units. Again, as Todorov has stated, "to study the structure of a narrative's plot, we must first present this plot in summary form in which each distinct action of the story has a corresponding proposition."[4] Narrational patterning is an issue that has received little critical attention in the Kubrick literature, yet it is an important feature of the work. It illuminates many aspects of scene construction and other concerns that can potentially elude close analysis.

NONLINEAR TIME: *THE KILLING*

Although *The Killing*, adapted from Lionel White's novel *Clean Break*, was only Kubrick's third feature-length film, it represents his most radical experiment in constructing a nonlinear time structure. In my analysis, I have determined that *The Killing* can be segmented into thirty-five narrative units (see Appendix). A narrative unit, for present purposes, involves a character or characters performing a distinct action in one location.

The first few sequences of *The Killing* are particularly illuminating in terms of the film's structure. Not only do they serve to introduce the main characters, but we are quickly made aware of the film's nonlinear temporal structure. The device of the off-screen, omniscient voice-over commentary is immediately emphasized. Kubrick also introduces many elements of character motivation in the first fifteen minutes of screen time. The gang members are presented as somewhat atypical criminals. As Johnny Clay (Sterling Hayden) mentions in his scene with Fay (Coleen Gray), they are not criminals in the ordinary sense of the word. We learn of Mike's (Joe Sawyer) devotion to his bedridden wife, Officer Kennan's (Ted de Corsia) money problems, George's (Elisha Cook) subservient relationship to his wife, Sherry (Marie Windsor), and Johnny's history as a small-time crook and his five-year prison stretch. And, in a typical *film noir* opposition, we are presented with Fay's intense devotion to Johnny, in stark contrast to Sherry's *femme fatale*. The character who remains least defined is Marv Unger (Jay C.

Flippen), due, in part, to the delicacy of the homosexual subtext in his un-requited relationship with Johnny.

The idea of presenting the main characters' motivations in the first fifteen or twenty minutes of screen time was a convention of the (late) classical Hollywood model of the time (mid-1950s). Where *The Killing* is unusual is in the way it organizes its presentation. It is in the precise nature of its discourse that the film breaks with convention.

The opening scenes incorporate an omniscient commentary that always specifies the exact time of the actions. The use of a voice-over in itself was obviously not radical in Hollywood fiction film, but its use in *The Killing* is somewhat atypical and represents the reworking of a well-worn narrative convention. The "voice of God" commentary is used primarily to organize the film's nonlinear temporal structure.[5] Using a conventional device in an unconventional way remained a consistent and coherent strategy for the director throughout his career.

The specific characteristics of the voice in *The Killing* would likely have been familiar to American audiences of the mid-fifties from numerous other filmic sources, such as the Louis de Rochemont productions of the 1940s and *March of Time* documentaries. The voice in *The Killing* is not necessarily the same voice, but it has similar expressive qualities, particularly its masculine, authoritative tone.

In *The Killing,* the voice-over performs several functions. Most obviously, it transmits narrative information and organizes the complicated time structure of the film. It also functions as a distancing device, putting the audience at a remove from the film's drama. It prefigures the kind of emotional distance found in Kubrick's later work. The film's major characters do not elicit much sympathy from the viewer, and there is little emotional involvement with their plight. Kubrick's films, however, tend not to operate within the framework of conventional notions of emotional involvement.

Thus, while the voice-over functions in a somewhat distancing way, it is familiar and reassuring as a result of its frequent use in other films. Although its primary function is to pinpoint the exact time of each action and transmit expository information, viewers are also reminded of those other, often nameless films. Through its familiarity, the voice carries with it an element of its own cinematic history; it bears traces of those other films.

The film's narrative events are arranged in nonchronological order. The unusual arrangement of the narrative events is a key characteristic of *The Killing* and sets it apart from most other narrative films. To use Chatman's terminology, the film's story time is substantially different from its discourse time.[6] The film exhibits its most unconventional strategy in the radicality of its ordering of narrative events.

The complete scene breakdown of the film indicates that the pattern of the first few narrative units is sustained throughout. Each time the voice-over is heard, it informs the audience of the precise time of the action. When the voice is not heard, the time is unclear—although in some sequences without voice-over, it is possible to have a general idea of the time of the action. For example, viewers do not know the exact time of the final sequence at the airport, but they know that it is the same evening as the robbery and massacre. Likewise in unit 29, when they see Johnny throw the bag full of stolen loot out of the window at the racetrack, the time is not given and there is no voice-over. Still, it should be clear from the preceding sequences (the time of the start of the seventh race is announced, as is the time of the two diversions) that the approximate time of the robbery is between 4:00 and 4:30 P.M.

At times, the ambiguity is more pronounced as in unit 10, when Johnny meets Nikki (Timothy Carey), who is to shoot the horse at the racetrack in one of two planned diversions. In unit 11, when Johnny rents a cabin, the audience has no way of knowing on which day these events occur, let alone the exact time. All we can ascertain is that they occur during the week before Saturday, the day of the robbery, since the fictional time of the film comprises one week (Saturday to the following Saturday).

An important issue involving the use of voice-over in *The Killing* is the extent to which viewers consider the voice reliable. There are two instances in the film's temporal sequencing that lead one to believe that the voice-over has made an "error," which somewhat undercuts its generally reliable use in the film. One error occurs at units 14 and 15. The commentary announces that "at 7:00 a.m. that morning, Johnny began what might be the last day of his life." A scene takes place between Johnny and Marv in which Marv's feelings for Johnny are made relatively clear. In a typical 1950s display of machismo, Johnny treats Marv's show of affection as something of a good-natured joke. Johnny's rebuff leads directly to Marv's drunken condition later at the robbery. Although Marv's role in the heist is not crucial, his drunkenness signals that all will not go well with the robbery.

The scene between Johnny and Marv is followed by a scene showing Johnny arriving at the airport as the narrator announces, "it was exactly 7:00 a.m. when he got to the airport." Either there is an error in the film's temporal sequencing or the voice-over (and, by implication, the film's over-all narration) does not account for the scene between Johnny and Marv that takes place before Johnny reaches the airport. The second explanation does not seem probable. If the audience accepts the first explanation, that there is an error in the film's time structure, is there any way to determine if the error is intentional or merely an oversight?

The second "error" occurs at units 30 through 32. George Peatty announces the time as 7:15 P.M., and he declares that Johnny is fifteen minutes late. If George is to be believed (and generally characters do not openly lie in films such as this, unless motivated by their character or a circumstance within the fiction), viewers must assume that Johnny's original arrival time was 7:00 P.M. In unit 31, the voice-over announces that Johnny arrived at the meeting place at 7:29 P.M. and that made him "still fifteen minutes late." If viewers take this narrative moment to be of some significance, either George is mistaken about Johnny's projected arrival time or the voice-over has made an error. If this is a simple oversight/error in the film's narration, then neither "character" is wrong. But, as in the previous example, this seems the least satisfactory explanation, since elaborating the precise time of almost every sequence has been a critical strategy of the film.

These two temporal errors indicate that a discrepancy exists between the action (or what a character says) and the "voice of God" commentary. There seem to be two conceivable explanations for this discrepancy. Either these two instances in the film's temporal structuring are so minor as to be of no consequence—and the fact that I am even pointing them out is an act of "overreading"—or they have some meaning. If they have meaning, what is the nature of that meaning?

I believe that both errors are meaningful and that perhaps Kubrick is making an authorial comment through them. Both sequences present viewers with something of a dilemma. There is conflicting narrative information, in each instance, but no way of knowing which is the more truthful presentation. Whom are viewers to believe? If they assume that within the fictional world of *The Killing* the omniscient voice-over and the fictional characters have equal status (that is, there is no reason to believe that one has more of a claim to the truth than the other), then there is no clear way to resolve the dilemma. The audience is given no further narrative cues to help resolve this dilemma, since the discrepancies do not occur in any other part of the film.

In general, the use of an omniscient voice-over commentary is associated with a certain kind of filmic authority. The type of impersonal voice we hear in *The Killing* is reminiscent of *film noir*, certain types of documentary film and documentary-style fiction. This kind of voice-over is generally considered reliable, in the sense that it is not known to lie openly. If the two errors that I have pointed out are indeed deliberate, they may constitute an attempt to undercut the conventional faith in the authority of the voice-over.

A central theme of *The Killing* and of Kubrick's work as a whole is the fallibility of the individual. No matter how precisely an action or event is planned, it is impossible to predict its outcome in every instance since one cannot entirely account for the human element. In his meticulous planning of the heist, Johnny is unaware of the subplot involving Sherry and Val that leads directly to the massacre. Moreover, Johnny has no way of knowing that his rebuff of Marv's show of affection will result in Marv's drunken condition during the heist (since Johnny does not indicate that he is aware of the sexual subtext of Marv's behavior toward him). No matter how predictable or rational the world, there are always unforeseen elements that can potentially disrupt this orderliness. The errors involving the voice-over and the film's time structure may be connected to this Kubrickian theme.

Kubrick's work often invokes the idea that nothing concerning human behavior can ever be entirely predictable. Human fallibility is a key element of our humanity—a point Kubrick explores in greater depth in such films as *2001: A Space Odyssey*, *A Clockwork Orange* and *Barry Lyndon*. The beginnings of this exploration can be seen in *The Killing*.

Returning to the film's time structure, we can see that in units 14 through 18, as the narrative follows Johnny, the time structure is chronological. It is also sequential in units 19 through 22, when the film shifts its attention to Mike O'Reilly's character. It continues in this linear fashion as viewers follow Randy Kennan up to the start of the crucial seventh race and the robbery itself in unit 24. In unit 25 there is a backward shift in time as viewers follow Maurice's actions. The film stays with his character until the start of the seventh race in unit 26. As the film switches to Nikki, there is another backward movement in time. It stays with Nikki until he is gunned down. When the film returns to Johnny in unit 28, it has again shifted back in time. Viewers then follow the robbery completely through for the first and only time in unit 29.

Thus, within the overall, dominant framework of the film's nonlinear time structure, there are sections of chronological presentation. In terms of Hollywood convention, it is entirely appropriate to focus on Johnny's character as he carries out the robbery. He is the film's leading character (and star) as well as the only character to go into the money room to execute the heist, a key dramatic moment. What is unusual is to structure the narrative to follow each character essentially up to the same point in the narrative (the start of the seventh race, which is the moment of the actual robbery) but then to follow the robbery through only once when Johnny is involved. This method of structuring the narrative might have resulted in viewer frustration in the hands of a less capable director. As it is, the film is not difficult to follow even though it has an intricate structure.

The narrative action proceeds swiftly and is made more interesting and complex because of this jigsaw-puzzle structure. Some pieces of the puzzle are left unexplained when we finally see the robbery carried through in unit 29. It is not until unit 30 that all is revealed. It is here that we learn how the money bag was removed from the track and the precise role played by Officer Randy Kennan. The shifting points of view contribute to the effectiveness of the jigsaw narrative structure, and they work in tandem with the nonlinear time structure to create a coherence and complexity the film would otherwise lack.

The complicated, nonlinear time structure is also related to the film's reworking of various genre conventions. Two key elements of the robbery or heist film are the temporal construction and the revelation of the mechanics of planning and executing the crime. Every robbery, usually the central narrative event in such films, depends on precise timing. This aspect is prominent in models of the genre such as *The Asphalt Jungle* (John Huston, 1950), *The Killers* (Robert Siodmak, 1946) and *Rififi* (Jules Dassin, 1954). Often these films present an array of details that implicate the viewer in the planning process of the robbery. Viewers frequently share a character's point of view as the films follow the crime to its conclusion. The genre seems to have peaked in the 1960s with films such as *Ocean's Eleven* (Lewis Milestone, 1960), *Seven Thieves* (Henry Hathaway, 1960), *Topkapi* (Jules Dassin, 1964), and *Robbery* (Peter Yates, 1967).To my knowledge, no film elaborates as complicated a time structure as *The Killing.*

The conventions of the heist genre that stress the precise time element and that foreground the planning and execution of the robbery are starting points from which *The Killing* elaborates its complex time structure and shifting point-of-view strategy. Although *The Killing* may appear to have a rather distanced presentation because of this complicating of narrative convention, the viewer is always involved in the narrative action. The material is compelling to watch, and we never lose interest in the central narrative action. Perhaps our understanding of narrative distance needs revision, for it does not always follow that the viewer is uninvolved in the fiction when distancing devices, such as those found in *The Killing*, are used. We see this strategy at work again in *Barry Lyndon*, a more complex later film that also entails complicated distancing strategies yet contains intensely involving dramatics.

The device of allowing Johnny the most sustained point of view is, of course, not unexpected since Sterling Hayden, who plays the gang leader, is the film's star. The character of Johnny Clay is also interesting because he is the most knowledgeable character in the film. Johnny deliberately conceals details of the robbery from the other gang members, and the audience, at various points in the film. This heightens viewer curiosity about how certain narrative actions will be carried out.

But no character in the film, including the commentator, is privileged with all the information. Sections of the film do not involve the voice-over, and there are elements of the narrative of which Johnny seems unaware. For example, Johnny does not see Nikki shoot Red Lightning. He does not see Randy drive away with the money, nor does he see Sherry and Val in their intimate moments as they discuss details of the heist. Most significantly, Johnny is excluded from the film's climactic massacre, although he does see its partial result as George Peatty, covered in blood, stumbles out of the building. The viewer, by contrast, does see these actions. In fact, it is the viewer who is placed in the most privileged position in terms of the film's narrative action. Viewers see every aspect of the robbery, although it is only over the course of the entire film that we can make sense of all the details. The film's presentation of narrative information may be fragmented, but the audience ultimately possesses more information than any of the characters. We share a kind of complicity with the film's narration (and the makers of the film) that places us in a special position.

The unusual structure of the film contributes to the notion of combining familiar, reassuring elements with unfamiliar ones. Many generic elements would have been familiar to a 1950s audience: the archetypal characters, the omniscient voice-over, the stress on time, the emphasis on the planning and execution of the robbery, and the visual and thematic aspects of *film noir*. But it is the way in which these familiar ingredients are combined and elaborated that makes the film interesting and successful. The story may be familiar, but its discourse is unique. The nonlinear time structure and the shifting point-of-view strategy are ways in which the film plays on familiar genre conventions. The unfamiliar elements of its discourse contribute to the film's distanced presentation and reflexiveness, and partly explain why viewers have little emotional involvement with the characters.

The combining of familiar with unfamiliar narrative elements is an important aspect of the director's work and helps explain why his films often contain dissimilar narrative strategies. Kubrick usually combined familiar genre conventions with less familiar, more challenging elements within a single film. For example, *2001* nominally belongs to the science-fiction genre, but it obviously has grander ambitions. *Barry Lyndon* uses the genre of historical drama to explore many contemporary human themes and aesthetic issues. Kubrick combined elements of classical Hollywood discourse with a more modernist narrative mode in virtually every film he directed. These ideas will be explored in greater depth in later discussions.

NARRATIONAL GAPS: ABSENCE
AND PRESENCE IN *LOLITA*

There are several noteworthy features about the scene construction in *Lolita*, Kubrick's adaptation of Vladimir Nabokov's novel. Though *Lolita* runs almost twice as long as *The Killing*, the scene breakdown (see Appendix) reveals that it contains the same number of narrative units: thirty-five.

Lolita begins with an unusual structuring strategy. The opening sequence sets up the central narrative event which the remainder of the film will attempt to illuminate. Humbert Humbert's (James Mason) subjective voice-over begins after this opening sequence, the only scene in the film not included in the overall framework of the character's story. The fact that the audience is made aware of Humbert's crime, though not the reasons for it or its eventual consequences, makes for a surprising and (retroactively) ironic beginning. The positioning of Clare Quilty's (Peter Sellers) murder here does not dissipate suspense, for it is not the *fact* of Quilty's murder that is important, but how and why Humbert has been driven to such extreme behavior.

Additionally, the opening scene echoes other Kubrick films in several interesting ways. For example, the opening shot of Humbert's car driving through a thick fog suggests an actual dream or dreamlike state, perhaps a fairy tale. Kubrick's fondness for the fairy tale can be found in *Killer's Kiss* and *The Shining*. The opening sequence is also similar to later Kubrick films that begin with rather unexpected or overloaded opening sequences or shots. *A Clockwork Orange* is the key example of this informationally loaded opening.

Quilty's first appearance is typical of how the character will be encountered throughout the film. Humbert explores the mansion without noticing that his nemesis is seated on a chair, hidden under a sheet. Humbert is unaware of Quilty's presence until Quilty stirs himself to life beneath the sheet. The encounter foreshadows the elusive relationship the two characters will have throughout the film. The sequence illustrates their adversarial relationship with such verbal, joking allusions as Quilty's reference to "Spartacus," an obvious reference to Kubrick's previous film. The white sheets draped around Quilty's body visually amplify the references to ancient Rome implied by the remark.

Quilty engages a reluctant Humbert in a game of ping-pong, a game the director often played in real life. The ping-pong match also carries metaphoric connotations of the "game" between Quilty and Humbert for Lolita's (Sue Lyon) affections. Another example of the film's preoccupation with game-playing involves Quilty's impersonations, a sample of which viewers see in this opening scene when he reads Humbert's poem with a Western "twang." The fact that Quilty wants to engage a reluctant opponent in this game foreshadows their relationship throughout the film.

The opening of *Lolita* is structurally and narratively important, but it involves an essentially neutral kind of presentation. There is no evidence that the scene is told from any character's point of view. The voice-over does not begin until the end of the sequence. Specifying the precise nature of Humbert's voice-over commentary becomes important because the narrative device of a written diary is introduced in segment 8. A viewer could be tempted to interpret all the instances of voice-over as diary excerpts. In fact, only one voice-over sequence clearly represents an extract from this journal, and this coincides with a visual of Humbert making the written entry. The other four instances of voice-over give no evidence of being journal extracts. They seem to be occurring simultaneously with their visual presentation. Furthermore, there is no indication that Humbert is telling his story after the fact, perhaps from the prison cell which we are told that he inhabits at the film's conclusion. Of the thirty-five narrative units in the film, only five involve Humbert's voice-over. Apart from the one particular journal extract (unit 8), the other four instances are examples of direct address to the viewer.

Though Humbert supplies the voice-over, the film does not restrict viewer information to this character's range of knowledge. An example of this occurs in unit 11 with a prominent camera movement into a close-up of the framed picture of Quilty on Lolita's bedroom wall. The framing points to an important clue in the relationship between Lolita and Quilty; indeed, the camera movement is highlighted so as to emphasize that Humbert is specifically excluded from this piece of information. One is reminded of a similar moment in *Rear Window* (Alfred Hitchcock, 1954) when the descriptive camera reveals Thorwald (Raymond Burr) leaving his apartment as Jeff (James Stewart) sleeps. In both films, the camera excludes the protagonist from a crucial piece of narrative information meant exclusively for the viewer.

A key structuring component of *Lolita* involves the various ways in which the film makes reference to the character of Quilty. His presence can be detected, either implicitly or overtly, in sixteen of the film's thirty-five narrative units, with significantly more references in the later stages of the film. If the film is divided structurally into two parts, with part one ending with Charlotte's death (unit 12), then there are four references to Quilty in this first part and twelve in part two.

The exact nature of these appearances is an intriguing aspect of the film. Almost all of Quilty's scenes in part two involve impersonations (such as Dr. Zempf, the school psychologist, or a policeman attending a convention at the hotel) or contain mere traces of his presence (the sunglasses, a mysterious phone call to Humbert or the ever-present car that follows Humbert and Lolita after they leave Beardsley, Ohio). The involvement of the viewer in trying to solve the puzzle of Quilty's appearances is one of the great pleasures of the film. It contributes to the game-playing strategy discussed above and involves viewers in testing their knowledge against that of the film's protagonist. It quickly becomes apparent, however, that this game will almost always exclude Humbert, who never seems aware of Quilty's presence. Humbert's murder of Quilty in the opening scene seems rooted in Humbert's inability to accept the "impure" relationship that he perceives existed between Quilty and the young Lolita. The murder is also connected to the fact that Quilty (and the film's narration) has made Humbert appear ridiculous for most of the film by excluding him from any awareness of Quilty's presence.

The pattern of Quilty's appearances also merits some comment. The film proceeds from Quilty's actual physical appearances in early scenes (such as the sequence at the school dance), to impersonations that disguise his identity, to evidence or traces of his existence (the sunglasses). Viewers are then presented with the mysterious, almost uncanny presence of the car that follows Humbert and Lolita for three days of story time. Quilty is never seen in these sequences, but the observant viewer understands that he is there. The "appearance" of Quilty in these car scenes is emblematic of the character's earlier appearances in the film. He is there for the viewer but not there for Humbert. Quilty then becomes a disembodied voice at the end of a phone line, followed by second-hand reports of his existence from hospital staff members when Lolita is checked out by a mysterious "uncle." In unit 34, Lolita sums up and fills in most of the details about Quilty for Humbert, confirming all our suspicions. Everything seems a revelation for Humbert. Finally, Quilty is reduced to the flimsiest of references—he becomes a name on the lips of our protagonist and a memory for the viewer. Humbert alludes to the opening scene when he shouts, "Quilty, Quilty." The film comes full circle, although the shooting scene is not repeated.

The character of Quilty is a major presence in *Lolita*, perhaps *the* presence, and more often than not viewers feel his presence by his absence. That is, they are most aware of the character when he is not there. *Lolita*'s narrative construction depends on the ways in which this presence is alluded to throughout the film, especially the strategy of excluding Humbert from much of the film's narrative information.

An example of this exclusion is the scene of Charlotte Haze's (Shelley Winters) death. This is a crucial sequence in narrative terms, but it is played entirely off-screen. Humbert is unaware of the event until after it has occurred. Likewise, much of the film's narrative takes place off-screen or simply outside the main character's field of vision. Humbert's exclusion from much of the narrative information, particularly in contrast with the viewer's privileged position toward this same information, contributes to another important speculation: that despite the film's subjective voice-over commentary, Humbert does not control the fictional presentation. He does not really tell the film's story. The controlling point of view is more properly supplied by the film's overall narrating function. The voice-over is just one more element in that overall narration.

Another major gap in the film is the absence of any overt sexual component in the representation of Humbert and Lolita's relationship. While it is true that censorship constraints at the time would partially account for the absence of any visual evidence of their sexual relationship, it does not entirely account for its nearly complete exclusion. The dialogue only hints at their illicit relationship, with such cryptic lines as "let's tell mother" or "the neighbors are beginning to talk." Alternatively, we get Quilty's vulgar interpretation of the affair when he calls Humbert in the middle of the night (off-screen) and presumably accuses him of licentious behavior. The lack of overt sexual content is more adequately explained in terms of Humbert's characterization. For Humbert, there is simply no appropriate way to illustrate the pure and ideal relationship he imagines exists with Lolita.

The allusions to their illicit relationship point to another major absence or gap in the film: the discrepancy between how Humbert describes Lolita (in voice-over and in his obsessive behavior) and the film's presentation of her to the viewer. Put simply, Lolita is nothing like what Humbert imagines her to be. On the evidence of her behavior in many scenes, most viewers would rightly view Lolita as a vulgar, spoiled and sexually experienced teenager who manipulates Humbert throughout the film. Certainly audiences in the early 1960s were not used to seeing teenage girls in such manipulating, controlling positions. Although by the end of the film viewers sympathize with Lolita's victimization at the hands of Quilty, there is little in her character itself that is out of the ordinary and little, it seems, that could inspire Humbert's obsessive behavior. Lolita does not seem to merit anywhere near the passion and attention Humbert lavishes on her. Although Humbert is not without his cruel side, especially in his treatment of Charlotte Haze, he is portrayed as the real victim in the film. Of course, obsessive behavior is not rational or logical, and the film's characterization of Lolita as merely banal may be one way of reinforcing this idea.

The difference between how Lolita is presented to the viewer and how Humbert imagines her is an interesting disjunction in the film. It is another example of the way Humbert's view of the world is at odds with the omniscient perspective of the film. The information the viewer receives, particularly about Lolita and Quilty, is tangibly different from Humbert's perception of it. There is a clear difference between how the viewer and Humbert interpret many events depicted in the film, and this difference of interpretation is tied specifically to many of its narrative patterns. Complexities in structure and narrative organization help make *Lolita* one of Kubrick's most accomplished and resonant films.

NARRATIVE REVERSAL, REPETITION AND POINTS OF CONVERGENCE

A Clockwork Orange

Our next example of narrative organization is Kubrick's 1971 adaptation of the Anthony Burgess novel, *A Clockwork Orange*. The scene breakdown of *A Clockwork Orange* (see Appendix) reveals that it too is constructed of thirty-five narrative segments, intimating Kubrick's strong consistency in structuring his narratives. Unlike *Lolita,* the subjective point of view in *A Clockwork Orange* is maintained by a more pervasive character voice-over. In the earlier film, voice-over was discerned in five sequences, while in *A Clockwork Orange* it is present in twenty-two of the film's thirty-five sequences. The voice-over in *The Killing*, though not originating with any character from the fiction, is present in twenty-six of that film's thirty-five narrative units.

The narrative breakdown of *A Clockwork Orange* also illustrates that the film is, in some ways, structured around actions and their reversal. Several sequences in part one, before Alex (Malcolm McDowell) is sent to prison, are repeated with variations in part three, after Alex has undergone the Ludovico treatment. For example, unit 2, in which Alex and his gang viciously (and theatrically) beat up the old derelict, is mirrored in unit 25. Here, in a reversal, Alex is viciously attacked by the same derelict and his "gang." Where the first sequence is shot at night in a concrete tunnel with highly stylized, *film noir* lighting, the later sequence is played in broad daylight with Alex's dislocation emphasized by a fragmented editing style.

Similarly, Alex's attack on the writer and his wife in unit 4 is reversed later in the second HOME sequence (units 27 through 30). The first sequence is notable for the way it emphasizes the performance aspect of both Alex and the writer (Patrick Magee). The sequence theatrically presents the victimization of the writer and his wife at the hands of Alex and his gang of droogs. The second HOME sequence also contains extreme performance styles (especially that of Magee), only this time Alex has become the writer's victim.

Another major reversal can be observed in units 9 and 26. In the earlier sequence, Alex is "inspired" to beat up his gang members in a show of authority along a marina. The sequence is highlighted by a striking use of slow motion endowing the scene with a balletic quality. This is reversed in unit 26, in which two of Alex's former gang members, Dim and Georgie (now police officers), victimize Alex by dunking him in a vat of water and viciously beating him with a billy club. There are similarities and differences between these pairs of sequences, but clearly the idea of reversal is present in the structuring of the narrative action.

Even the relatively minor episode of Alex's sexual escapade with two teenage girls, rendered in fast motion (unit 8), finds something of a reversal in the final episode of the film, which involves Alex in a dream-like sexual episode, this time in slow motion. The two sequences have a "theatrical" relationship to each other. Both include Alex in a fantasy in which he is a star performer and sexual acrobat. The other paired fantasies in the film (units 6 and 15) also involve Alex in rather elaborately staged episodes of sexuality and violence. This time, both sequences are immersed in a kind of pulp-movie imagery as Alex again is placed at the center of his fantasies.

In all three films, a crucial sequence begins at unit 12. *The Killing* begins the crucial day of the robbery and enters the middle phase of its development at sequence 12 with a scene of George and Sherry Peatty at the breakfast table. In *Lolita*, there is the key sequence of Charlotte Haze's death, which moves the film to a different phase of its narrative progression. In *A Clockwork Orange*, unit 12 ends part one of the film as Alex is about to be sent to prison.

Another point of convergence in all three films occurs at units 23 and 24. In *The Killing*, the start of the crucial seventh race (and the robbery) begins at unit 24. In *Lolita*, unit 23 takes Humbert and Lolita to Beardsley, Ohio and marks the beginning of the film's third and final movement. *A Clockwork Orange* also begins its third phase at unit 23 as Alex begins his life after the Ludovico treatment and his release from prison. This would suggest that Kubrick consistently placed a high degree of importance on structural organization.

Finally, all three films have something of a narrative climax or crucial development around units 28 to 30. In *The Killing*, the climactic moments of the heist and the massacre occur at units 29 and 30. *Lolita* includes Quilty's elusive car appearances at units 28 and 29. In *A Clockwork Orange*, Alex is involved in his scenes with the writer and attempts suicide.

These plot convergences add weight to the argument that Kubrick is manipulating the traditional three-act story structure. The three films display a degree of consistency in their narrative construction, especially in the placement of emotional climaxes and other crucial narrative moments. These films appropriate and hyperbolize the three-act dramatic structure of classical filmmaking. This manipulation of traditional rules of construction is an important aspect of the director's gradual transformation of the classical Hollywood model into a more modernist narrative style.

Barry Lyndon

Barry Lyndon, a thematically rich and formally audacious film, represents Kubrick at his most radical and adventurous. It is his great essay in aesthetics, his most revealing film in terms of human relationships and his most extreme foray into the "art" film. *Barry Lyndon* incorporates extensive narrative and formal experimentation on almost every level, including *mise-en-scène*, the use of the zoom, the manipulation of performance styles and the subversion of conventional notions of drama.

Based on William Makepeace Thackeray's 1844 novel *The Luck of Barry Lyndon*, the film is divided into two main sections. Part 1 chronicles Barry's (Ryan O'Neal) more picaresque adventures. Barry is forced to leave home at a youthful age after a duel over the affections of his cousin Nora (Gay Hamilton). Viewers see his life as a soldier, in both the English and Prussian armies, his role as a Prussian spy, and finally his life as a gambler. The impression is that Barry is simply swept along by events and circumstance. He does not actively plan many aspects of his life until the end of Part 1 when he meets Lady Lyndon (Marisa Berenson) and takes on the title and new life of Barry Lyndon.

Part 2 of the film, noticeably darker in tone, is concerned with Barry's newfound station in life and his eventual downfall. This section shows Barry as husband and father, and reveals his obsession with obtaining a peerage. The film as a whole is pessimistic in tone and presents a rather fatalistic vision.

In ways similar to *A Clockwork Orange*, *Barry Lyndon* is also structured around strategies of reversal, repetition and variation of narrative incident. The most obvious paired sequences around which much of the narrative revolves are the two major duels. In Part 1, the young Redmond Barry engages in an elaborately staged duel with Captain John Quin for the hand of Barry's cousin, Nora Brady. Part 2 contains a duel between Barry and his stepson, Lord Bullingdon. The earlier scene shows Barry, the youthful upstart and outsider, taking on Quin, who represents the established order. This sequence mirrors the later scene in Part 2 in which Barry, still the outsider, takes on the young Lord Bullingdon, who represents the aristocratic class that Barry has tried so desperately to penetrate. This second duel provides the narrative with much of its structural coherence, acting as the centerpiece and emotional climax for the film. It resolves many of the film's thematic explorations, resulting in Barry's effective elimination from the narrative.

The two sequences form pivotal narrative segments. Both highlight the tensions surrounding class that are central to the film's critique. Each pits a representative of the Old World, aristocratic, landowning class (Quin, Bullingdon) against Barry, who represents the new, ambitious middle class. The later sequence illustrates that Barry has nominally taken on the values of the old order but without conviction. He views his upward progress only as a way to accumulate wealth, not to perpetuate the belief system of the old order, for Barry neither understands nor entirely shares its values. The two sequences are also constructed around the sexual rivalries of the participants. In the second duel scene, the sexual undertones act more as a subtext, whereas in the earlier sequence the sexual aspect is more on the surface.

The strategic placement of dueling scenes points to an important aspect of the film's general pattern of narrative organization. The opening scene of the film presents the death of Barry's father in a duel. In the gambling scenes with the Chevalier de Balibari (Patrick Magee), Barry is seen engaging in duels as a way to extract unpaid debts. An early scene of Barry engaged in a boxing match in the British army is an instance of dueling in a different form.

There are other examples of pairs of scenes that mirror each other or are constructed around the idea of reversal or variation. The early scene of Barry playing cards (and a lover's game) with his cousin Nora forms a part of one such pair. The scene is notable since it is one of the few instances when viewers see Barry with his youthful, romantic ideals still intact. The two characters are strategically framed in front of a fountain containing a statue of a baby, a symbol of purity and innocence. Later in the film, there is a scene of Barry with a German woman that echoes the earlier scene in several ways and rather prominently includes the woman's baby in the framing. One could also view the scene of Barry and Nora in relation to the scene of Barry's first encounter with Lady Lyndon. Both scenes involve card playing, carefully choreographed movements of human figures and sexual pursuit. The young Redmond, of course, is idealistic and still believes in romantic love whereas the older Redmond is world-weary and pursues Lady Lyndon with opportunistic calculation.

The short-lived happiness that Barry shares with his natural son, little Bryan, which is most prominently on view at the boy's birthday party, finds its dark counterpart in the scene of the boy's funeral. Another repetition shows Barry recounting a colorful, highly embellished bedtime story to the boy on his birthday. In the story, Barry performs fanciful, heroic deeds involving "twenty-three rampaging he-devils, sword and pistol, cut and thrust, pell-mell." The tale of imagined heroics and "he-devils" is narrated one final time later in the film, only now Barry is in tears as his young son lies close to death.

Another pair of scenes shows Barry inflicting corporal punishment on Lord Bullingdon. One scene occurs early in Barry's married life with Lady Lyndon. The insolent boy is little more than ten years old. Barry inflicts the punishment in what he perceives to be merely a test of wills with his stepson. He does not understand the deeper, more serious class rivalry or the psychosexual implications of his entry into the Lyndon home, which are at the root of Lord

Bullingdon's hatred of him. Bullingdon is next whipped when he is about age sixteen. In a tearful outburst, Bullingdon warns Barry that he will stand no more punishment from "Redmond Barry." These two scenes of physical punishment further echo a scene of a soldier in the Prussian army "running the gauntlet" and being struck by his fellow soldiers in Part 1 of the film.

Bullingdon suffers another humiliation from Barry when the lad is viciously beaten at a music recital. After this beating, Lord Bullingdon leaves the Lyndon home. This is a crucial scene of thematic importance for it leads to Barry's final contest, the duel with Lord Bullingdon. It is worth mentioning that this key scene of Barry's attack on Lord Bullingdon is prefigured earlier in the film, in the scene of Barry engaged in a boxing match in the British army. Both scenes employ similar formal strategies of hand-held camera, rapid editing and extreme fragmentation, emphasizing their thematic parallels.

Barry Lyndon is one of Kubrick's least hopeful films. It represents his most biting critique of how social mores restrict individual freedom and are responsible for the loss of youthful energy and ideals. The film's narrative construction helps articulate this point. Additionally, the film represents Kubrick's most elaborate statement on aesthetics. As such, its rich thematics are inextricably bound to formal strategies of framing, *mise-en-scène*, use of zoom, the long take, narrative structure, visual composition and the use of music. Although ostensibly an historical drama set in the eighteenth century, the film's concerns are very much of the present. It is as though the director had taken the last scene of *2001: A Space Odyssey* and illustrated that the species was well on its way to this point in its evolution by the eighteenth century. The film seems to be saying that the development of technology after the Age of Enlightenment did not alter, in any meaningful way, the inexorable movement toward the exhaustion of the human race. *Barry Lyndon*'s structuring of narrative incident around reversals and repetitions, as well as other elements of the film's intricate formal design that will be explored in later discussions, helps the film achieve its lofty ambitions.

Eyes Wide Shut

Eyes Wide Shut, Kubrick's final film, continues the pattern established in the director's previous films of repetition and variation of narrative incident as key structuring devices. Additionally, the film weaves a complex web of thematic relationships through allusion, dream logic and repetition in both dialogue and other aspects of the film's construction.

Eyes Wide Shut spins the compelling tale of Dr. Bill Harford (Tom Cruise) in the throes of a tormented odyssey propelled by jealous rage over the revelations of his wife, Alice (Nicole Kidman). In a confessional scene, she claims to have been so attracted to a naval officer the previous summer in Cape Cod that she was willing to abandon her comfortable existence with her husband and child in pursuit of a sexual attraction. This revelation puts the marriage in such crisis that Bill sets out on a nighttime quest for experience and sexual thrills that leads to an extraordinary admission of love from the daughter of one of his recently deceased patients, a masked orgy involving gorgeous women and the death of a prostitute. He eventually breaks down in his own confession to his wife, and both characters begin to rethink their relationship and their inadequate understanding of love and what it means to share one's life with another human being. By the end of the film, the couple have reached the point at which they might possibly begin to understand aspects of human desire they were previously blind to—preoccupied as they were with living a life of comfort and status. Bill and Alice begin to grasp that human behavior and desire are infinitely more complicated than they could ever have imagined. The film ends on what seems like a hopeful note, although we cannot be sure that they have been truly altered by their experience.

Eyes Wide Shut was inspired by Arthur Schnitzler's 1926 novella *Traumnovelle* (*Dream Story*). Although the novella is clearly responsible for much of the film's plot and the dream-like odyssey of the main character, many of the film's structural elements, as with most other Kubrick adaptations, are inventions not found in the source material. The oneiric, dream-like events are clearly transformed, distorted and heightened through the consciousness (or unconsciousness) of Bill Harford. Structurally, the film depends on the idea of variation, repetition of narrative events, and the reverberation of one scene with another.

The most obvious series of repetitions around which much of the film's narrative trajectory is propelled is the series of subjective shots of Bill imagining Alice and the naval officer having sex. These shots are interspersed five times throughout the film, and these fantasy shots help anchor the film to Bill's point of view.

One example of a pair of scenes that echo each other begins with the crucial sequence in which Alice recounts the story of the previous summer in Cape Cod, which comes at the tail end of the sequence where the couple smoke marijuana and argue about how men and women view sex differently. Alice begins: "you and I made love, and we talked about our future and we talked about Helena [their daughter] and yet at no time was he ever out of my mind. And I thought if he wanted me, even if it was for only one night, I was ready to give up everything."

This devastating monologue sets off Bill's self-absorbed wanderings and a reappraisal of his life with Alice. The scene is followed by the first of the subjective inserts of Alice in the throes of passion with the naval officer. This is immediately followed by the remarkable scene with Marion Nathanson (Marie Richardson), which in some ways echoes the naval officer story. In the middle of the scene, as Bill tries somewhat unfeelingly to console her, the grief-stricken and confused woman declares her love for him in an emotional outburst that jolts the viewer with its suddenness and unpredictability.

Similarly, the scene where Bill meets Domino (Vinessa Shaw), immediately after Marion's *cri de coeur*, also sets up a pair of scenes that echo each other. Of course, the fact that Bill has been picked up by the most wholesome prostitute in the city, who apparently is only working her way through college, emphasizes the fantastic nature of the film. As he is about to make love to Domino, Bill's cell phone rings and interrupts the planned lovemaking in a repeated motif of ringing phones and doorbell chimes. The pattern of placing Bill in compromising situations that are never allowed to resolve themselves metaphorically acts as a kind of *coitus interruptus* to the planned sexual trysts. The sequence is mirrored when Bill returns to Domino's apartment later in the film only to encounter her roommate, Sally (Fay Masterson). Bill learns that he was saved from a potentially life-threatening situation by not sleeping with Domino when it is revealed, in a delayed moment of irony, that she tested HIV positive. The two encounters are portrayed in rather idealized terms, clearly from Bill's point of view. Both women offer themselves to Bill, and the scenes play out as repressed male fantasy.

Other examples of scenes that echo each other abound in the film. For example, Bill "saves" Mandy's (Julienne Davis) life at Victor Ziegler's (Sidney Pollack) Christmas party. Bill revives Mandy from her near overdose, acts sympathetically and encourages her to go into rehabilitation. Later, during the orgy scene, the mysterious woman wearing a feathered headdress (Mandy?) rescues Bill when it is revealed that he has infiltrated the orgy. In a highly theatricalized moment the woman (Abigail Good) shouts from the balcony, "Stop! Let him go. Take me, I am ready to redeem him."

The calm demeanor Bill demonstrates when he sees Mandy, the naked woman sprawled in Ziegler's bathroom who has had a "bad reaction" to heroin and cocaine, is consistent with the cool demeanor Bill displays through most of the film. His coolness, however, is often a mask for the repressed intensity of emotion seething underneath his calm exterior. This scene contributes to the idea that the later narrative is fabricated out of Bill's experiences at the Ziegler party and Alice's confession. Certainly, it is at Ziegler's party that much of the "dream movie" has its germination. Bill encounters two models, Nuala (Stewart Thorndike) and Gayle (Louise Taylor), who offer to take him to "where the rainbow ends." Later in the film, he ends up at Rainbow Fashions in need of a costume to attend the orgy at the Somerton mansion (Summer Town? The site of the orgy itself recalls the Cape Cod locale of the naval officer story). The storefront window at Rainbow Fashions also has a sign that says "under the rainbow" on its basement window.

At the Ziegler party, the room is filled with dozens of individuals amid the cheery, elaborate Christmas decorations and light-filled ornamentation, giving the impression that all is well for these affluent party revelers. This world view becomes inverted, most obviously at the orgy scene. Ziegler, the wealthy party host who natters on about his tennis elbow as he greets the Harfords, is revealed in the bathroom scene to be engaged in a much sleazier lifestyle involving prostitutes and hard drugs. Later he mentions that he was in attendance at the orgy, where the powerful elite live out their fantasies of uninhibited sex. At the Ziegler party, Bill is also first introduced to Nick Nightingale (Todd Field), his medical school friend who plays piano and will later be responsible for providing him with the password ("Fidelio") to the orgy. The opening party scene clearly establishes much of the material that Bill's unconscious will rework into the "dream story" as the film's narrative unfolds. Our later discussions of point of view and filmic subjectivity will clarify and elaborate on this idea.

A further example of paired narrative material includes the two scenes at Rainbow Fashions with Milich (Rade Sherbedgia) and his young daughter (Leelee Sobieski). In the first scene, Bill, who is searching for a costume for the orgy, witnesses Milich's discovery of two Japanese men wearing wigs and in various states of undress. Milich reacts with (mock?) horror at the discovery of his underage daughter in the company of the two disheveled men. As he screams insults at his "whore" daughter she hides behind Bill, and once again he has "saved" a woman. In the later scene when Bill returns his costume after the orgy, Milich greets him with a pleasant veneer of normality as he again introduces his daughter to Bill. The two Japanese men again emerge from the back of the shop, only this time they are well dressed, having obviously been accommodated by Milich and his daughter. Whereas the first scene depended on a farcical, almost absurdist tone, the second scene relies on a realist, matter-of-fact presentation. Milich then proceeds to offer his underage daughter to Bill.

Other scenes of a sexual nature that involve similar narrative strategies include a shot of Bill examining a female patient, breasts exposed, with a nurse in attendance. This scene is echoed in Alice's conversation with Bill in the scene where they smoke marijuana together as she reveals her story about the naval officer. Alice discusses what sexual thoughts might run through Bill's mind when he examines women patients and, conversely, what sexual thoughts might go through his patients' minds about him in such moments:

Alice: Let's say you have some gorgeous woman standing in your office naked and you're feeling her fucking tits . . . what are you really thinking about as you're squeezing them? . . . Now, when she is having her little titties squeezed, do you think she ever has any little fantasies about what handsome Dr. Bill's dickie might be like?

One of the most interesting sets of paired scenes is initiated in the scene with Marion Nathanson where Bill briefly examines the corpse of her father, which lies on the bed in his bedroom. Throughout much of the scene the corpse is in full view within the frame and acts as a silent witness to the unusual outburst of repressed feelings that Marion will display towards Bill. The idea of connecting death to love and sexual longing permeates many other scenes in the film where sex and death co-mingle. We saw it operate in the earlier bathroom scene at Ziegler's, in which Mandy's nude body hovers close to death as she recovers consciousness from her drug overdose. Later, when Bill learns of Mandy's overdose, he goes to the hospital where she was admitted and discovers that she died that afternoon. In an extraordinary scene in the hospital morgue Bill takes the hand of Mandy's dead body and bends down to within an inch of kissing her face in a tender moment containing just a hint of necrophilia.

The orgy scene itself, with its statuesque "hookers" and their slim physiques, echoes both the opening scene with the two models and Mandy in the bathroom, as well as a dream that Alice later recounts to Bill about being in the desert where "everyone was fucking. And I . . . was fucking other men, so many, I . . . I don't know how many I was with." Alice's dream refers both to the orgy scene that has just come before and, in a subtle cinematic reference, echoes the writhing bodies in Antonioni's *Zabriskie Point* (1970).

There are many other kinds of repetitions and variation of narrative incident in the film. These include the unusual strategy of having Bill repeat dialogue that other characters say to him as if he were in a state of continual disbelief. Bill's constant repetition of dialogue is felt in many scenes and emphasizes both the "dream story" and the film's theme of looking. A good example of this is the scene in Ziegler's bathroom when Bill attempts to awaken Mandy from her drugged stupor:

Bill: Mandy. Mandy. Can you hear me? Mandy? Can you hear me? Just move your head for me if you can hear me. Just move your head for me if you can hear me. Mandy. There you go, you can hear me. Can you open your eyes for me? Mandy? Can you do that? Let me see you do that. Let me see you open your eyes. There you go. Come on, come on. Look at me, look at me, look at me, look at me. Look at me. Look at me, Mandy. Good. Good.

There are also several scenes in which Bill attempts to gain entry or a piece of important information. In these scenes, he constantly mentions that he is a doctor and eagerly shows his New York State medical card. These scenes emphasize that Bill's identity is inextricably tied to his social status and feelings of self-importance, as well as foregrounding the unreal, dream-like landscape of the film.

The idea of repetition and paired scenes can also be extended to a deeper notion of doubling that permeates the film and contributes to its dream logic. We see this fairly early during the Ziegler party scene, which introduces the idea of public and private spaces, and in such notions as the pair of models, who wrap themselves around Bill while the suave seducer Sandor Szavost (Sky Dumont) dances with Alice. Other paired figures include Domino, the prostitute who picks Bill up in Greenwich Village, and her roommate Sally, who will have a key scene later with Bill; Sandor, the suave Hungarian, and Milich, the East European who owns Rainbow Fashions; Mandy and Bill's mysterious saviour at the orgy (who may or may not be the same woman); the corpses—one in the scene with Marion Nathanson and the other at the hospital morgue. The idea of doubled figures may also be seen in the many couples at the orgy and possibly the twining of Helena, the pre-sexual daughter of the Harfords, with the more sexualized teenage daughter of Milich. Paired locales include Bill's two visits to Rainbow Fashions; his two visits to the Somerton mansion; and the two visits to the Ziegler house. The most embedded of the references to doubling and repetition may be the double sentences that are repeated in the newspaper story Bill reads at Sharkey's Café when he attempts to escape from the menacing man from Somerton.

On the level of the visual look of the film, many shots echo each other in ways that also emphasize the idea of repetition. The camera movements through space—following characters forward or moving backward as the characters move toward the camera—communicate the idea that much of what we see exists in a space between reality and dream. The use of the Steadicam here is as important a technical device as it was in *The Shining*. The careful, hand-held camera work allows for a superb fluidity in the movements. The exacting lighting and highly artificial decor of the film's *mise en scène* also contribute to the feeling that we are in a world where it is impossible to be sure of anything. The state of uncertainty that permeates the film contributes to the feeling that with *Eyes Wide Shut* Kubrick embarked on an odyssey as fantastic and elusive as any in his entire *oeuvre*.

This discussion illustrates the point that Stanley Kubrick conceives of the narrative progression of each film in very precise and structurally coherent ways. The films operate differently, of course, but they share similarities in their organizing principles. The director is clearly conscious of when to create emotional climaxes and how to structure events that relate to incidents at various points in the narrative. The films are often structured around complex temporal ordering, narrative gaps and repetition of narrative incident. This intricate narrative structuring, like so many other aspects of the films' stylistic operation, is absolutely bound to the films' thematics.

NOTES

1. Tzvetan Todorov, *The Poetics of Prose* (Ithaca, N.Y.: Cornell University Press, 1977), 32.

2. Edward Branigan, *Narrative Comprehension and Film* (London, England: Routledge, 1992), 3.

3. Seymour Chatman, *Story and Discourse: Narrative Structure in Fiction and Film* (Ithaca, N.Y.: Cornell University Press, 1978), 25.

4. Todorov, *The Poetics of Prose*, 110.

5. Kubrick values voice-over commentary very highly. It is used extensively in *Killer's Kiss*, made the previous year. *Paths of Glory* and *Dr. Strangelove* contain minimal uses of it, but it is more crucial in *Lolita*. The most significant uses of voice-over

are to be found in *A Clockwork Orange, Barry Lyndon* and *Full Metal Jacket. 2001* originally contained extensive voice-over in the opening "Dawn of Man" sequence, but it was eventually eliminated in the film's final cut. See Gene D. Phillips, *Stanley Kubrick: A Film Odyssey* (New York: Popular Library, 1975), 149. And, as I discuss later in this book, an early draft of the script for *Eyes Wide Shut* contained an extensive voice-over commentary.

      6. Chatman has defined the terms in this way: "Story is the content of the narrative expression, while the discourse is the form of that expression" (Chatman, *Story and Discourse*, 23).

2

Time and Space: Part 1

Spatial and temporal manipulations are a necessary part of both editing and camera-related strategies. Every shot encloses space and also has a temporal factor in the form of shot length. All editing decisions thus involve duration and spatial considerations. A film editor cuts an image that has specific characteristics. A shot, whatever its visual attributes, always has a temporal aspect. How long shots last, precisely at what point those shots are connected, and aspects of the image itself such as shot size, composition, angle of view and camera movement are factors that contribute to the overall aesthetic of a film. They help viewers understand how narrative films are organized and sustain their logic.

Kubrick's films always involve a skillful organization and blending of editing patterns and camera strategies. Although the films often favor the long-take, deep-focus style of construction, shot-to-shot manipulation is still a necessary part of Kubrick's aesthetic, and any serious analysis of his films must acknowledge the complexity of spatial and temporal manipulations that are at the center of his cinematic achievement. This chapter explores some of those complexities.

THE LONG-TAKE AESTHETIC

The extent to which Kubrick accepts the integrity of the uninterrupted dramatic flow of a shot stylistically connects him to such directors as Jean Renoir, F. W. Murnau, and Orson Welles. Kubrick himself has often acknowledged their influence, and his high estimation for the films of Max Ophuls is well known. The extensive use of long takes (shot length) is one way in which his films are aligned with this tradition.

Kubrick's major films all contain sequences of virtuoso editing, but there is likewise a considerable use of long takes, particularly in dialogue sequences.

Although the films do not avoid shot/reverse-shot pairings in dialogue sequences, they just as often contain an entire conversation within one take.

Kubrick established his fondness for the long-take style early in his career, and this style is particularly evident in *The Killing*. Two of the most striking uses of the long take in this film occur in units 5 and 6 (see Appendix). The first sequence, which shows George Peatty at home with his unfaithful wife Sherry, contains a total of six shots. The sequence begins with a deep-focus long shot of George entering his apartment. He walks in and proceeds to the next room, screen right, with the camera tracking with him in what has become a stylistic signature for Kubrick. George finds Sherry sprawled on a couch, reading a magazine. She barely acknowledges her husband's greeting. The conversation quickly reveals the nature of their sadomasochistic and unhappy relationship. The dialogue is filled with catty humor. The two characters are shown in mid-ground with the entire space in focus. As the conversation continues, George gets up and the camera tracks right with him, then follows him left to his original position. George proceeds to recount a sentimental story about an elderly couple, while Sherry barely conceals her utter lack of interest in George's tale. The shot lasts 105 seconds before a cut (all shot transitions in the scene are straight cuts) to a medium shot of Sherry. The camera follows the two actors and keeps them in frame. George inquires about dinner. Sherry flippantly responds that George can't smell dinner cooking because it is still in the supermarket; the shot lasts 43 seconds.

The third shot has George and Sherry return to their original two-shot composition (same as shot 1). The conversation at this point concerns the lack of love and money in their marriage and the obvious disappointments of their life together. George hints that everything will change after the robbery. Sherry replies with such put-downs as "Did you put the right address on the envelope when you sent it to the North Pole?" George stands and exits, screen right; this shot lasts 71 seconds. Shot four, which is a medium, frontal close-up of George lasts 10 seconds. The fifth shot, is a medium view of Sherry who is still seated. George continues to drop hints about the planned robbery and the gang meeting later that evening. The sixth and final shot of the sequence has Sherry at her make-up table, now in medium shot and facing the camera as the conversation continues. The shot lasts 69 seconds, and the sequence ends on a dissolve.

The sequence is thus made up of six shots and lasts a little over five minutes for an Average Shot Length (ASL) of 51 seconds. The camera fluidly follows the characters' movements, and the rhythms of dialogue and the skill of the performers maintain viewer interest throughout. Each cut is dramatically motivated. There is never a feeling that the shots last too long or that the scene would work better if it were more fragmented. The long takes and the slightly low angle of view contribute to the intimacy of the scene, reinforcing the impression that we are eavesdropping on a private conversation. These lengthy takes emphasize the perverse quality of the couple's relationship. The compelling gaze of the camera seems fascinated with the pair, and there is a sense that any tampering with the dramatic flow of the sequence would break its spell.

The next sequence, which shows Sherry meeting her lover Val (Vince Edwards), continues the pattern established in the previous scene with even fewer shots and a longer ASL. The first shot is a medium close-up, side view of Val embracing Sherry. The conversation initially fills us in on their illicit relationship and provides some character information about Val. Both visually and through the informative dialogue, the contrast between Val and George is sharply etched. The shot also highlights the disparity between the youthful, muscular Val and the older Sherry. The shot contains only a little movement for reframing and lasts 100 seconds. It is accompanied on the soundtrack by a bongo-laced jazz score that adds a rhythmic counterpoint to the dialogue.

At this point, the shot fades to black to indicate a time-lapse, while the bongo music grows louder on the soundtrack. The fade to black is an appropriate shot transition, not merely because it indicates a temporal ellipsis but also because it adds to the sexual tension and sense of illicit discovery in the scene. It contributes to the feeling of narrative obfuscation and withholding of information since the two characters (and the audience) are in the "dark" about much of the information surrounding the planned heist. The music comments metaphorically on the illicit relationship with its implication of unbridled sexuality.

The next shot has the two characters in a tight, frontal two shot as Sherry tells Val what she knows about George's planned caper. Again, the film avoids the use of a shot/reverse-shot editing pattern and maintains the spatial/temporal integrity of the scene. This shot lasts approximately 62 seconds. The third shot begins with Val, framed alone in medium shot. The room is dark, as it has been throughout the sequence, save for the harsh lighting of a single lamp. The shot's framing then changes to a medium two shot. The conversation continues, and the shot lasts 58 seconds. The three shots run a total of three minutes and forty seconds, for an approximate ASL of 73 seconds, even longer than in the preceding scene of George and Sherry.

There is an abrupt cut to the next scene, which is gradually revealed to be the gang meeting later that evening. The temporal and spatial ellipsis is sudden but not unusual in Kubrick's work. His films often contain moments of straight cutting from one space and time to a completely different time and space, with no establishing shot or fade-out to prepare for the transition.

As used in *The Killing*, the long take helps efface the passage of time, in contrast to the constant reminders from the voice-over. Static long takes do not necessarily have to function this way, however. The long take can just as easily force the viewer to attend to the image and the passage of time. In *The Killing*, although viewers are aware of the presence of the camera, they tend not to be mindful of the precise time of the action in the shots where the voice-over does not intrude. Additionally, these scenes, with their slower tempo, act as breathers from the relentless pace and precise temporal ordering of the rest of the film.

The use of long takes contributes to the feeling of stasis in these scenes and helps maintain dramatic integrity in a way that a more classically oriented style of editing, such as shot/reverse-shot, might not. The long take, as used here, invites a process whereby viewers can lose themselves in the narrative flow. The film also contrasts static long takes with slow lateral tracking shots that call attention to themselves.

An interesting aspect of the use of long takes in *The Killing* is the way that they contrast with the nonlinear temporal structure. The slow rhythms and integral wholeness associated with these shots act as a counterpoint to the driving momentum and dislocation engendered by the fragmented narrative structure.

In many ways, these two sequences are typical of the film as a whole. Many other sequences in the film involve the same kinds of strategies: long takes, lateral camera tracking from one space to the next and reframing to keep characters and objects centered within the frame. These tactics are coupled with sharp dialogue and a respectful sensitivity to the rhythms of dialogue and the nuance of performance. Neither sequence is burdened with intrusive editing. The cuts all seem perfectly timed and dramatically motivated. One never has a sense that the sequence would be improved by a quicker editing pace. The long take is certainly not the only important element here, or necessarily the most important, but it is crucial to the narrative organization and effectiveness of both scenes.

At this point in Kubrick's evolution, many elements of the director's style are already in place. The editing and image strategies in *The Killing* are not necessarily radical, but they illustrate a certain dissatisfaction with classical film language early in the director's career and hint at a movement toward a more contemporary narrative discourse.

This preference for long takes is also apparent in *Lolita*. As in *The Killing*, scenes are often allowed to run uninterrupted, with little or no fragmentation. *Lolita* has a running time of 153 minutes with a total of 525 shots, for an ASL of 17.5 seconds. This is much longer than typical films of its period. Barry Salt has noted that the trend in Hollywood films in the late 1950s and early 1960s was toward a shorter ASL:

If one looks at the histograms showing the distribution of Average Shot Lengths for American films made during the six year periods 1958–1963 and 1964–1969, based on a sample of more than a hundred films for each period, and then compares them with those for the earlier six year periods, one can easily see the way the general cutting rate speeded up as the sixties wore on. The mean value of A.S.L. for the sample had already come down from 11 seconds to 9 seconds in 1958–1963, and in the next six years it had fallen even further to 7.5 seconds, its lowest value since the silent period.[1]

The overall pace and rhythms of *Lolita* are greatly affected by the longer ASL contributing to the generally somber tone that pervades the film, despite moments of high humor. The dark mood is intensified even further by the insistent use of fades to black.

There are many examples of long takes in *Lolita*, but a few will suffice to illustrate this discussion. The first part of a scene in which Charlotte Haze tries unsuccessfully to seduce Humbert Humbert contains three shots, for a total running time of just over four minutes and an ASL of 81 seconds. The first shot is a medium-long shot of Humbert in mid-ground, near a dinner table loaded with food in the Haze living room. Charlotte, dressed in a provocative leopard-skin outfit, enters frame right. The attempted seduction begins as the camera moves left to follow the actors' movements, then right as Charlotte plays with Humbert's name—"Ah Humbert, what a *thrillingly* different name." She then playfully pressures a reluctant Humbert to dance the cha-cha with her. The camera dollies backward as the two actors move toward it. Humbert sits on a chair, and the shot ends, lasting 109 seconds. Shot two is a low-angle, waist shot of Charlotte as she continues her conversation; this shot lasts 16 seconds. Shot three resumes the straight-on camera framing found at the end of shot one, as Charlotte entices the awkward Humbert into dancing with her. The camera follows their movements in medium shot before it is interrupted by the arrival of Lolita; the shot lasts two minutes.

Shots of this length are not unusual in the film, and they frequently employ great depth of field with an inventive use of foreground and background. This has become a stylistic signature for Kubrick and has remained constant throughout his career. The situating of Humbert within the deep-focus world of Lolita is often accomplished without Humbert's knowledge of the events around him. He does not see what the viewer sees. Humbert's obliviousness to Quilty throughout the film has already been mentioned. The use of foreground/background is a stylistic means of including Quilty in the viewer's spatial field and excluding him from Humbert's. In the scene in which Humbert and Lolita first check in at the hotel, the two characters are shown in the foreground of the shot while Quilty and Vivian Darkbloom lurk in the background. Humbert is unaware of their presence, but the viewer sees them clearly.

An amusing moment in these same hotel scenes presents Quilty and Vivian Darkbloom seated with their backs to the camera in the foreground of a medium shot. They pretend to read the comics to conceal their presence from Humbert, who is in the background of the shot. Humbert sees only a small fragment of the reality (space) around him. Quilty can hover either behind or in front of him, but somehow he escapes Humbert's field of vision. Humbert seems to direct his attention and spatial awareness exclusively toward Lolita. By emphasizing Humbert's obliviousness to the world around him, most especially to the character of Quilty, the film stresses Humbert's subjective experience within a generally objective presentation. Humbert is in company with other Kubrick characters who experience the world in special ways, such as Bowman in *2001: A Space Odyssey*, Alex in *A Clockwork Orange*, and Jack Torrance in *The Shining*.

Dr. Strangelove, adapted from Peter Bryant's novel *Red Alert*, is something of a departure for Kubrick in terms of editing patterns and spatial strategies, though it unmistakably bears the Kubrickian stamp in many significant ways. The fictional or represented time of the film more or less corresponds to the film's running time. This direct correspondence between fictional and real time adds to the sense of temporal compression induced by the film's insistent editing patterns. Although *Dr. Strangelove* employs many long takes, it contains perhaps the shortest ASL of any of the director's films. The film is made up of 700 shots and runs 94 minutes for an ASL of approximately 8 seconds. Despite this rather short ASL, *Dr. Strangelove* still resorts to crucial long takes to slow down the rapid momentum of the unfolding narrative.

An interesting example of a long take occurs in a scene of General Turgidson (George C. Scott) and his secretary in a hotel room engaged in a phone conversation about General Ripper's (Sterling Hayden) mad actions. It is the only sequence that does not occur in one of the film's five major spaces: inside Burpelson Air Force Base, exterior shots of the base being attacked by American troops, inside the B-52 bomber, exterior aerial shots of the bomber, and inside the Pentagon War Room.

As the shot begins, the woman is in the foreground wearing a provocative bikini and lying on a bed under a sun lamp. The phone rings and she jumps up to answer it. The decor is spatially interesting due to the number of mirrors that surround the bed. These will allow the audience to see Turgidson at moments when he is meant to be off-screen. The woman answers the phone and talks to one of the other generals about the crisis. She calls out to Turgidson, who is off-screen in an adjoining bathroom. Turgidson enters the frame and takes the receiver from the woman on the bed. The camera holds this medium shot for most of the remainder of the scene/shot.

Turgidson continues his rather amusing phone conversation ("What's cooking on the Threat Board? Nothing! Nothing at all?"). The scene is punctuated by the physicality of Scott's performance, with such gestures as slapping his bare stomach and inflecting his voice in various ways. He then hangs up and exits frame right, but is still visible in the background mirror. As the camera tracks in and tilts down, he enters right and climbs across a bed to the woman lying on the other bed ("Tell you what you do. You just start your countdown and old Bucky will be back here before you can say Blast off"). The camera stays on the two performers in a medium shot.

The entire sequence is handled in one shot lasting approximately three minutes. The sequence is humorous in its playful use of sexual and military language metaphors. The spatial rigidity and the activation of off-screen space (through the use of mirrors and characters speaking off-screen) hint at the spatial enclosure engendered by the film's other interiors.

The space in this scene is a fantasy room that expresses the macho, sexual swagger of the American military. Turgidson plays out his sexual fantasies in a hotel room, just as Ripper plays out his military fantasies in his sealed office and the Pentagon generals play at nuclear war with their big board in the War Room.

Another excellent example of Kubrick's use of the long take occurs inside Ripper's office. General Ripper is seated at his desk with his back to the camera. The shot is a medium-long shot with the entire room in focus. Mandrake (Peter Sellers), having located one last transistor radio, enters the office to report his findings to Ripper. In a civilized fashion, Mandrake attempts to convince Ripper that if a Russian attack were really in progress there would be no civilian broadcasts on the radio. Ripper walks to the door at the back of his office and locks it. He then moves forward to sit in the foreground behind the desk with his back to the camera. Mandrake continues his futile attempt to reason with the general. Ripper lights a cigar. Mandrake salutes, turns and walks to the door in the background, only to find it locked. He steps left to another door and finds it locked as well. He turns to face Ripper. The camera holds on Mandrake in a medium-long shot. Mandrake moves forward to face Ripper and resumes his earlier position. All this time, Mandrake has attempted to extract the recall code from Ripper without success. Mandrake then claims that he must issue the recall code and attempts to abrogate Ripper's authority. The shot lasts about three minutes with the entire space in focus.

The shot is effective partly because of the attendant feelings of enclosure and claustrophobia within the space. Ripper's distorted world is his personal nightmare. The delayed cut to the next shot, a big close-up at an extreme low angle showing Ripper puffing on his cigar surrounded by swirls of smoke, accentuates the madness of his character and the phallocentric subtext of the scene. The sequence emphasizes shot length and varies shot distance to heighten viewer awareness of the stasis in the scene. The film announces here that it is avoiding the use of rapid montage or a more conventional shot/reverse-shot pairing to employ an unconventional, long-take editing style. Because the cut is preceded by a shot held for three minutes, the scene allows us to experience the confined world of General Ripper more vividly and intensely.

The deep-focus strategy, which operates in all the director's films, is a distinctive and necessary element in Kubrick's aesthetics. In *Dr. Strangelove*, it complements the high level of realism apparent in many aspects of the film, such as the decor. This decision might seem to conflict with the heightened absurdity and surrealism of the narrative events, but, in fact, it makes the satire more effective. The details of presentation, especially aboard the B-52, are impeccable. The sense of reality is convincing, even though the characterizations operate largely at the level of caricature. If viewers did not believe that someone like General Ripper could possibly exist in the military establishment (on whichever side), then the film would not have the kind of resonance it continues to have in our own post-Watergate, post-Reagan era. The lunacy and farce in the film are effective precisely because of the reality of presentation, which includes the skillful manipulation of time, space, details of decor and psychological verisimilitude.

The feelings of confinement, limitation, borders and enclosure are apparent in all the film's interior spaces. The Pentagon War Room seems engulfed by the big board. The cramped space of the B-52 can barely accommodate the crew members. The sense of stagnation and immobility engendered by static long takes and deep-focus photography offer a contrast to the driving momentum and quick cutting that pervade most of the B-52 sequences.

Even within the same film, Kubrick often contrasts long takes with shot/reverse-shot coding and with other strategies of temporal compression or attenuation of narrative. In *2001*, there is a contrast between the editing style of the scenes of space maneuvers, seen in various sections of the film, and the temporal ambiguity and quicker editing patterns of the later Star-Gate sequence. Where the time frame of the earlier scenes is relatively clear and linear, taking all the time necessary to unfold, the latter sequence is unclear, nonlinear and abstract, plunging the film deeply into temporal and spatial ambiguity.

In many ways, *2001* is Kubrick's aesthetic and philosophical contemplation of both time and space. When Dr. Heywood Floyd (William Sylvester) journeys to the moon base (Clavius) in the early part of the narrative, the film goes to great lengths to illustrate carefully the various movements aboard the spaceship. These sequences are presented in ways that emphasize their temporal element. They involve more long takes, and there is a close correlation between screen time and the amount of time it would presumably take for these events to unfold in reality.

By arguing that sequences with more long takes employ different editing patterns, I do not mean to imply that editing itself is less important in these sequences. Obviously such sequences still involve very careful shot-to-shot editing. Nonetheless, there is a sense in those scenes that the film's different conception of time must incorporate a slightly different editing style. For example, when viewers see a steward carry a food tray and walk in a circular movement, upside down, to get to the captain's quarters aboard the spaceship, it is important to see the entire movement in real time and in full view. The audience must be convinced of the illusion of movement and the reality of the presentation of weightlessness. The accuracy of the film's depiction of space travel is important to its project.

There are some instances in Kubrick's work when camera movement is combined with a long take to produce an additional subtext not readily apparent in a shot. Two such shots occur in *Barry Lyndon* immediately before the decisive second duel between Barry and Lord Bullingdon. One shot uses careful, rhythmical panning, while the other involves an insistent backward dolly movement.

The first shot is an interior, medium-long shot of Reverend Runt (Murray Melvin) and Graham (Philip Stone) in the foreground, seated at a table. Lord Bullingdon (Leon Vitali) is in midground, pacing left to right with the camera panning to follow his movements. Lord Bullingdon decides to confront

Barry about his treatment of Lady Lyndon and the squandering of the Lyndon fortune. The shot is not accompanied by music—although some ambient sound can be heard—and lasts 82 seconds.

The pacing of the character and the panning of the camera emphasize the decisiveness of the moment. The presence of the accountant Graham and of Reverend Runt together reinforces the idea that both money and religion are determining factors in Bullingdon's decision. The theatricality of the moment is further emphasized by the frontal presentation.

This leads directly to the dramatic shot of Bullingdon's challenge to Barry, which sets up the climactic duel scene. The shot is accompanied on the soundtrack by the rhythmic, driving beat of George Frederick Handel's *Sarabande*. The drumming sound acts to regulate both character and camera movement. Lord Bullingdon, followed by two men, walks into the room directly toward the camera. The slow, insistent drumbeat begins at this point. The camera dollies back as Bullingdon approaches and holds him in center frame, facing the camera. It tracks with him and dollies back until Bullingdon discovers Barry slumped in a chair. The shot lasts 70 seconds. The uninterrupted camera movement, accompanied by the drum beat, recalls similar shots in *Paths of Glory*, *A Clockwork Orange* and *Full Metal Jacket*. The spatial/temporal unity is maintained to illustrate the unbroken, determined resolve of Bullingdon. The shot highlights the ritualistic, formal pattern of the character's actions and his need to maintain decorum and civility.

In *Barry Lyndon*, the viewer is always aware of the controlled universe on view. There is a sense in which shot length is so emphasized that it too becomes another controlling device. In a film running 183 minutes and containing a fair number of shot/reverse-shot dialogue exchanges, there are only 780 shots for an ASL of sixteen seconds, unusual for a studio film and more comparable to European art films of the period.

Eyes Wide Shut convincingly illustrates the director's fondness for the long take and his disdain for flashy editing, which continued unabated to the end of his career. *Eyes Wide Shut* runs 158 minutes and contains approximately 560 shots. This gives it an ASL of about 17 seconds, similar to *Barry Lyndon* and *Lolita*. What does this tell us about the director's relationship to the editing process and his conception of cinematic rhythm? Certainly Kubrick's respect for the acting process and the importance he placed on the contributions of his actors had in no way lessened in the twelve years since the release of *Full Metal Jacket*. The internal rhythms of a scene and the actor's speech patterns and nuances of meaning continued to be as important to his aesthetic as plot revelation and narrative momentum. In *Eyes Wide Shut*, the viewer is asked to attend to each shot without the reliance on and overstimulation of the flashy hyperediting that typified many films released in the 1990s. At the end of his career, Kubrick made a film that is unmistakably Kubrickian in virtually all respects, especially in its conception of cinematic time and space. Yet, as one watches the film, there is an overwhelming feeling that *Eyes Wide Shut* exists in its own time, unconnected to the latest fashion-able trends in cinema.

Are we also to conclude that Kubrick's self-imposed exile in Britain for so many years and his reclusive lifestyle somehow isolated him from contempo-rary filmmaking practice? I believe it would be wrong to jump to such a con-clusion. Throughout his career, Kubrick always kept abreast of the work of other filmmakers. The most logical conclusion about the lengthy ASL of *Eyes Wide Shut* is that the director simply did not buy into the "film as sensation" aesthetic that characterizes so many commercial films of the 1990s and is best exemplified by the "Bruckheimer" film aesthetic (*Con Air, Gone in Sixty Seconds, Armageddon*), which valorizes noise and special effects over depth and the contemplative. Kubrick simply continued to work in ways that were true to his aesthetic of how to shoot and edit film. He continued to build his narratives in such a way that the spectator had to work at the meanings of the film. The participation of the viewer has always been central to the Kubrick viewing experience. The long-take style demands viewer participation in a fundamentally different way than films that rely on rapid editing. Why would any viewer even remotely aware of the director's body of work expect a film that moved and engaged the spectator in an essentially different way than his other films? With the making of *Eyes Wide Shut*, it's as if Kubrick wanted to proclaim that the direction cinema had taken was misguided or had somehow lost its way, at least in terms of editing.

The opening scene of *Eyes Wide Shut* (after one exterior shot of a New York City street scene) exemplifies the dominant style of the rest of the film. As in so many other charged opening sequences in Kubrick's work, this sequence subtly prepares the ground for many of the themes, motifs and stylistic ele-ments to be elaborated by the rest of the film. The sequence begins with an elegant dance between Dr. Bill Harford and the camera as he moves through his posh apartment preparing to leave for a Christmas party. His wife Alice is also getting ready for the party. Bill Harford's absent-mindedness and dis-traction are evident in many ways. His physical movement through the space, eyes open but totally disregarding his stunning wife, introduces a major theme of the film. Bill cannot find his wallet and discovers it only after his wife suggests where to look for it. He then gazes at himself in the mirror as his wife asks him how she looks. He replies "perfect" without exchanging a glance in her direction. The character's self-absorption is apparent as the shot continues. His wife asks him if he gave "Roz [the babysitter] the phone and pager numbers," and he responds that he did. Immediately in the next shot he asks, "What's the name of the babysitter?" forgetting that he has just re-sponded to his wife's question about Roz. There is a great deal of movement in the scene, both of the camera and the characters within the frame, as there will be throughout the film. We will presently learn that this movement masks a troubling confusion and crisis within the lives of the characters. The cam-era swirls, glides and penetrates the space, but the characters move unthinkingly with only a superficial sense of purpose, as so many contemporary couples do. They are going to a party without knowing anyone but the hosts, wondering why "Ziegler invites us to these things?" They could just as easily ask why they bother to go to such affairs when they clearly have no interest in attending them. This film will plainly be about deluded, self-absorbed characters who look but do not see. Like an opening movement of a musical composition, the opening scene introduces the theme and key motif that will be developed as the film proceeds.

Everything in the opening scene seems smooth and elegant on the surface. But, as we will discover, underneath this smooth surface lie apprehension, blindness and an avoidance of responsibility. Dualities such as the obvious and the hidden, the public and the private, surface and depth will permeate *Eyes Wide Shut* as they never have before in a Kubrick film. It is a film that will depend for its meaning on oppositions and subtext. The notion of looking and not seeing, so strongly felt in the opening scene, could even be extended to the casual viewing of the film itself. How many viewers have completely missed what the film is about because they have only looked to its surface for meaning that clearly lies beneath?

In a film with such a lengthy ASL, it would be simple to catalog many examples of its long-take style, but a few instances will suffice to illustrate both the significance of the use of this stylistic device and how Kubrick's filmmaking at the end of his career evolved into different areas of concern.

The film's dominant style of elaborate long takes with sweeping camera movement—helped enormously by the use of the Steadicam—continues into the opening party sequence, most noticeably in the shots of Sandor Szavost as he dances with Alice and attempts to seduce her. Their scenes together begin in an appropriately intriguing fashion. A shot of Bill talking to his piano-playing, medical-school friend Nick Nightingale dissolves to a frontal, medium shot of Alice drinking champagne at a nearby table. The hand-held Steadicam camera moves carefully to the right and in a circular motion to the other side of the table to reveal Sandor, who stands screen right talking with another woman. Alice is now frame left, mid-ground and Sandor is frame right as he shifts his attention from the other woman to Alice. Many party guests and an elaborate light display line the background of the shot. Alice places her champagne glass unthinkingly on the table, without looking to see where it will be placed (continuing the theme of "not looking" that was introduced in the film's opening.) Alice has her back to the camera. Sandor notices her place the champagne glass on the table. He then picks it up and after she says "I think that's my glass" he cheekily drinks it, introduces himself and kisses her hand. The shot lasts about 70 seconds. It is a carefully choreographed introduction of the character and the theme of marital infidelity. On a stylistic level, the shot also continues the notion of a dance between the characters and the camera that was initiated in the opening apartment scene. Once again, the continuous time and space is uninterrupted by editing, and

Kubrick's choice of a more complicated method of framing and elaborating his shots indicates that the formal design of the shots and shot length will be as important as any dialogue in articulating the themes and ideas of a scene.

When this shot finally ends, there is a cut to a complete reverse angle with Sandor now standing screen left facing Alice, who stands screen right facing him. This is the first of many such 180-degree cuts in the film, and the use of such a radical element of cinematic style acts as an early indicator that the smoothly flowing movement we encounter in many shots must not be taken to mean that the film's complex meaning will flow effortlessly. The shocking spatial rupture is initially jarring to the viewer. The decision to cross the 180-degree axis and rupture one of the key conventions of classical continuity editing will significantly contribute to the film's oneiric, subjective presentation. We will have further occasion to discuss the use of the 180-degree cut later in this analysis.

As the conversation between Sandor and Alice continues into the next shot, Kubrick once again avoids the more conventional shot/counter-shot editing pattern so central to Hollywood classical film style. Although the film does have scenes edited in this style at crucial junctures—most notably the final scene between Ziegler and Bill—the more conventional editing pattern is generally avoided, as it is in many of these shots at the party.

The next series of shots of Alice and Sandor dancing together and Bill's flirtation with the two models tend to be shot in continuous long takes. The first shot of Bill with the two models lasts about 80 seconds. As Bill and the models wander through the party space, the golden hues of the art direction and lighting generate a light-filled, warm glow to the scene and add a kind of dreaminess to this male fantasy. This is the first of many scenes in the film in which women are made available to Bill. The flirtation ends after Bill asks, "Where exactly is this going?"and they respond, "where the rainbow ends." This will resonate throughout the narrative in such details as the costume shop "Rainbow Fashions" and the film's careful color scheme, which often evokes the colors of the rainbow through the decor and lighting. Bill is then called upstairs to attend to the crisis with Ziegler and Mandy who, we are informed, has taken a drug overdose. The space with Bill and the models is intercut with shots of Sandor dancing with Alice, who is having her own sexual adventure, albeit an innocent one fueled by champagne.

The elegance of these shots and the temporal and spatial continuity illustrate the importance Kubrick places on how to shoot each scene and when precisely to end a shot. Finding the exact moment when the life of a shot ends and must make way for a new composition is one of the key aesthetic challenges for any serious filmmaker. Kubrick's editing and use of the long take almost always give the impression that each scene has found its most perfect realization. The preference for the long take, of course, contributes to the very lengthy—and atypical for late 1990s filmmaking—ASL of *Eyes Wide Shut*. Because the film contains many long takes filled with movement and others that are static, their use in individual scenes depends on factors related to dialogue, performance, narrative and other aspects of style. Although Kubrick's style has evolved in *Eyes Wide Shut*, it is also clearly the work of the same individual who directed *Lolita*, *The Shining* and *2001*.

Another significant shot and our last example for this discussion occurs in the scene between Bill and Sally, Domino's roommate, in the latter part of the film. Domino is the prostitute who almost engaged Bill in sex the previous evening. This example of a long take functions in a unique way and bears some discussion. The scene begins as Bill arrives at Domino's apartment with a present of some pastries. Sally invites him into the apartment after informing him that Domino is not there. Bill enters the apartment and walks toward the kitchen with Sally. The camera, in a hand-held backward moving shot, follows their progress until both characters are framed facing one another, almost in a full shot, in the kitchen. Bill takes his coat off after Sally introduces herself. At this point in the shot an unusual blue flare, a result of the camera's reflected lens, is now prominently visible in the lower left corner of the frame. As Bill lays down his coat on the tub, he makes a long glance at the camera (or the filmmaker behind the camera, or the viewer). When Bill says the line "So do you have any idea when Domino will be back?" he looks directly and unmistakably at the viewer, rupturing the fiction. At this point, Bill begins to playfully flirt with Sally ("hel . . . lo Sally") as they discuss the whereabouts of Domino. He begins to fondle Sally's breasts and as it becomes clear that Sally has important information about Domino to divulge to Bill, they continue their conversation seated at the kitchen table. She eventually reveals that Domino has tested HIV positive.

The shot ultimately lasts about three minutes of screen time and involves a delicate bit of plot information. Apart from the length of this shot, one of its most unusual aspects is the presence of the blue flare so prominently visible in the composition. This is by no means a small blemish or one that is on the screen for only a few seconds. It is a clear intrusion into the fictional world from the real technological world of the film's construction. These kinds of shots are commonplace in the films of a director like John Cassavetes, who searched out the emotional truth of a scene rather than the perfectly composed image. But Kubrick, the perfectionist filmmaker notorious for shooting multiple takes of every scene, has clearly made a decision to use a superficially "flawed" image. This cannot be taken as a casual aesthetic decision. In this scene, Kubrick is clearly more interested in the emotional content of the scene and what the actors are doing with the material than he is with any possible accusation of technical imperfection. I have no doubt that Kubrick deliberated long and hard about using the shot, and was probably well aware of the potential accusations from some of his critics ready to call attention to any potential weakness in the film.

The other crucial element of the shot is when Bill/Tom Cruise looks at the camera as he lays his coat on the bathtub. The flare in the image may not have been planned, but the direction of Cruise to look directly at the camera most probably was. This immediately forces the spectators to become conscious of their roles as viewers. But more than that, the look toward the camera seems to break the fiction in a very special way. Bill performs the gesture as if he were being observed by someone behind the camera or on display, as if there was some kind of complicity with the viewer—that we know and he knows that this is only a movie and that he is really Tom Cruise, not Bill Harford. The movement and look are performed in a sweeping, rather deliberate gesture. The camera then re-frames slightly to a closer medium shot as the two characters continue their conversation. When the characters finally sit at the small table the flare eventually disappears and the composition changes. The shot ends and the pattern of shot/reverse-shot now takes over in the scene. It shifts from a hand-held shot to one that is more stable and at a direct, eye-level angle. Bill is now in center frame and the shot is taken from over Sally's left shoulder. The more stable framing seems to "wake up" the characters from the previous reverie and breaks the sexual mood of the lengthy preceding shot, where the flare is visible for at least two minutes.

One last item of interest in this scene is the way Bill keeps repeating dialogue that he hears as if he were not comprehending the language or the world he finds himself in. There are at least five distinct repetitions in the scene. Here are some examples of repeated dialogue as the two characters discuss Domino's whereabouts:

Sally: No, I have no idea.

Bill: You have no idea?

Sally: No. Well, to be perfectly honest, she . . . she may not be coming back.

Bill: She may not be coming back?

Sally: Well, umm . . . I, erh. . . .

Bill: You, erh. . . .

Sally: Yeah. . . .But I don't know.

Bill: You don't know? . . .

Sally: Oh . . . I don't quite know how to say this.

Bill: You don't quite know how? . . .

Sally: I think it would be only fair to you, to let you know that, umm . . . she got the results of a blood test this morning and, erh . . . it was HIV positive.

Bill: HIV positive?

These repetitions are not in an earlier draft of the script.[2] The scene originally contained two female characters, not one, and functioned in a more informational, direct way with little of the sexual play it now contains. The repetitions that currently exist in the dialogue contribute to the feeling of uncertainty and unreality in the situation. It is impossible to know, of course, why or how the scene's dialogue ended up with such repetitions, how the actors might have contributed to its final shape,[3] or how the scene developed and changed shape between the time the various drafts of the script were written and the film's shooting. One of the other crucial differences between this earlier draft of the script and the finished film is the elimination of a pervasive voice-over by Bill throughout the film. I will comment on this issue later in the analysis when I discuss the question of subjectivity and character point of view, since eliminating one of his favorite narrative devices was obviously a significant decision by the director.

Can other conclusions be drawn from this flared shot, which contains a crucial look at the camera as well as an abnormally high degree of repetition of dialogue? It's a surprising and puzzling scene that on the surface is simple and straightforward. Why should Kubrick allow the world outside the frame to penetrate the fiction with such bold, reflexive gestures? In leaving such a noticeably "flawed" shot in the film, Kubrick once again has surprised his viewers and critics, who claim that they know his work well. But the complexity and startling quality of this shot goes beyond the idea of an artist attempting to confound his critics and perhaps throw them a curve ball. The "flaw" in the image must be viewed in conjunction with the other elements of the shot, including the direct look at the camera and the dialogue repetitions. Taken together and viewed within the context of the film, they indicate that the idea of presenting a film from the point of view of its protagonist can be accomplished in many ways, including a kind of self-consciousness on the part of both the filmmaker and the film's protagonist. This shot suggests that Kubrick wanted his audience to think about what they were viewing and how meaning was being generated. The film asks viewers to question their understanding of what constitutes cinematic fiction and how it is presented through the technology of cinema, including the performances of the actors. What is the acting process exactly? What does it mean to compose a perfect shot? What happens if the actor departs from a fictional role or the shot references itself through a reflexive gesture such as a flare in the lens? What happens to our attention or our relationship to the fiction when we think there is something "wrong" with the shot? What is intriguing about this shot is how enmeshed it is in the overarching strategies of the rest of the film, both formally and thematically. The idea that an artist as established within the studio system as Stanley Kubrick, and in a $65 million star vehicle, could even ask questions more typically found in the European art cinema of the 1960s or the late work of a director such as Jean-Luc Godard indicates that at this late stage in his career, the constant tug between commerce and art shifted in favor of art. *Eyes Wide Shut* is unquestionably an art film. And scenes such as this indicate that the film is engaged in a kind of dialogue with the viewer about the very nature of the film experience, between what we know and what we think we know, between fiction and nonfiction. The slippages between certainty and doubt at the center of *Eyes Wide Shut* make it especially intriguing, and the use of a long-take style is one part of a complicated stylistic system that accounts for much of that intrigue.

INDIVIDUAL FILMS

Paths of Glory

Paths of Glory, Kubrick's adaptation of Humphrey Cobb's novel of the same name, represents a noticeable development in narrative complexity from *The Killing* and *Killer's Kiss*. Like *The Killing*, it is clearly the work of a brilliant young director who displays a virtuoso command of the medium. *Paths of Glory* places Kubrick's interest in the camera and spatial concerns in the forefront. The use of decor and architecture as both environment and metaphor is likewise explored in more complex ways than in any of the director's first three features. Kubrick's grasp of narrative development from *Killer's Kiss* through *The Killing* and *Paths of Glory* displays a remarkable progression and sophistication over the short span of two years. Not only is *Paths of Glory* a technical advance over his first three features; it also includes a more resonant and profound treatment of character.

Paths of Glory contains a thoughtful, deliberate spatial and architectural strategy, contrasting interior spaces of the château with the exterior trench scenes associated with the enlisted men (including Colonel Dax who, though an officer, is closely identified with his men). The first scene between General Broulard (Adolphe Menjou) and General Mireau (George Macready) inside the luxurious château neatly introduces this spatial strategy. The two men stand surrounded by much space. The physical luxury of the château's furniture, marble staircase, books, mirrors and paintings surrounds and engulfs the characters. The sense of abundant space becomes their greatest luxury—their physical safety and their distance from the front lines. The two characters conduct their conversation seated and later walk in circular movements with the camera following them. The extravagance associated with these camera movements seems appropriate to the situation. When the cut to the cramped, airless trenches of the enlisted men comes, the contrast is obvious and pointed.

A scene in which General Mireau inspects the troops in a dugout trench is organized around a backward dolly throughout his march, framing him in the foreground with bombs visibly exploding in the background. The film never resorts to an optical point-of-view (POV) shot to represent Mireau's field of vision during this walk. In fact, Mireau's only POV shot comes later as he views Ant Hill through a pair of binoculars. Hence, it is a mediated shot. The reluctance to associate perceptual point of view with the generals applies to the film as a whole. This aesthetic decision is mirrored in the film's thematics, which associates its sympathies with the enlisted men. Mireau's walk is in marked contrast to Colonel Dax's (Kirk Douglas) same walk through the trenches, which begins with the POV shot moving through the trenches and cuts to a frontal shot of Dax. The sequence alternates backward dolly shots with optical POV shots representing his field of vision throughout. The film's sympathy is clearly with Dax. This strategy becomes even more obvious during the attack on Ant Hill when the camera zooms into Dax throughout the battle. In Mireau's walk through the trenches, the moving camera shot is held for about 90 seconds as he makes his way through the dugout. The shot is punctuated throughout by an insistent drumming on the soundtrack, which contributes to a sense of the character's rigidity and control.

The combination of spatial and camera strategies contributes to the emotional distance viewers associate with the generals. The film employs different strategies for the scenes with the enlisted men. When there is a cut to Colonel Dax's quarters, the cramped spaces and low ceilings immediately associate him with his men. The camera is physically close to him, almost on top of him, and the perceptual views act to bring the viewer emotionally closer to the character as well. When Dax looks through binoculars, there is no cut to his optical point of view because his vision must not be mediated. The film instead offers more direct examples of Dax's experience of the world. This is done primarily through unmediated POV shots, framing and the zoom lens as a way of privileging the character, giving Dax a special status that no one else in the film enjoys. These techniques also make Dax and the prisoners more sympathetic.

Paths of Glory also employs striking deep-focus compositions and long takes (as is by now expected in a Kubrick film). In addition, it uses lateral tracking shots reminiscent of the camera movements in *The Killing*. These regulated movements suggest the rigid, cold universe inhabited by the generals. The seeming spatial chaos of the zoom shots as Dax leads his men in the attack on Ant Hill is more random. It suggests a kind of humanity in the midst of the chaos and irrationality of the attack.

The film subtly explores the duality of a rational/irrational world in the brilliant sequence of the court martial of the three enlisted men. The set design and camera strategies set off this sequence as one of the most interesting in Kubrick's entire *oeuvre*. The feeling communicated is one of rigidity and of the impenetrable code of the military. The three prisoners are framed in a medium-close, slightly wide-angle, deep-focus shot. Each prisoner is questioned in turn, and the distorted visual image emphasizes the subjective view of the proceedings. The distorting wide-angle lens communicates a closer, more personalized view of the prisoners' reactions and metaphorically comments on the lunatic, distorted values of the trial.

The sequence recalls the use of visual distortion and confusion of spatial coordinates in the bizarre trial scene in *The Lady from Shanghai* (Orson Welles, 1948). In that film, the distorted world of Mike O'Hara (Orson Welles) is communicated, in part, through a similar use of wide-angle, deep-focus subjective views and the subversion of classical rules of editing (such as the 180-degree rule and consistent eye-line matches). The trial sequence in

Paths of Glory does not subvert spatial coordinates quite so noticeably, but many angles of view do not seem to make (classical) spatial sense. It is difficult for the viewer to know precisely where the characters are in relation to each other and still maintain a logical sense of the entire space. The wide-angle photography contributes to the distorted view. The three accused men are not only entrapped within this insanity, but they (and the viewer) are also incapable of understanding it.

The space of the court martial is often revealed with the camera positioned behind the backs of the presiding judges, their silhouettes visible in the foreground of the shot. As both Colonel Dax and Major Saint-Aubain (Richard Anderson) address the judges (that is, the camera), the seated prisoners are visible in the background at a slightly low angle. When the camera shifts position to reveal the space from the opposite end of the courtroom, it switches to a high angle. If there is any consistent strategy beyond alternating a more objective view of the space with a more subjective one, it is the feeling of spaciousness in the room. This world is unfamiliar and strange to the enlisted men. They cannot comprehend the events that occur there, nor can they share in the power structure. Additionally, the giant checkered motif in the floor tiling suggests a chess game, with the prisoners as pawns in the game.

Unquestionably, it is the presentation of space, decor and camera (including lighting) that gives the film its stylistic distinction. In the scene in which the cowardly Lieutenant Roget (Wayne Morris) leads a reconnaissance mission, the viewer becomes aware of the diversity of spaces in the film. As the three men crawl over the landscape, the camera hovers over, behind and around them; it also tracks with them. It is as if Kubrick has made a wondrous new discovery—that the camera can actually explore different kinds of space and still serve the film's narrative. The landscape is littered with fragments of airplanes and other instruments of war. The camera's proximity to the soldiers in scenes such as this is an important identification device. It contrasts sharply with the distance, both emotional and physical, the viewer feels from the generals.

As Colonel Dax leads the attack on Ant Hill, the camera again gives multiple views of the event. First it is behind Dax and then it tracks laterally with him. The zooms into and out of the character during the attack become the most intriguing strategy in the sequence. They create a personal, privileged relationship between the camera and the character unlike that of any other in the film. The camera, handled by Kubrick himself, picks Dax out of the nameless crowd of troops and attaches itself to him.

Dax is probably the most noble and admirable character in all of Kubrick's work. Never again did the director draw such a positive portrait of goodness. Dax retains his faith in the decency of humanity, even though the leaders (the generals) are corrupt and without morals. Dax represents a ray of hope in the film. The sentimental ending notwithstanding, the film's liberal sensibilities present Dax as a sympathetic alternative to the insidious and corrupt values of the generals.

The contrast between the world of the generals and that of the enlisted men is made through composition, framing, angle of view, decor and the skillful editing of shots, as well as through camera work itself. In the attack on Ant Hill, the scattering of the troops within the frame communicates their essential powerlessness, their role as raw material for the war machine. This contrasts with the execution scene in which troops of the regiment are arranged in sharply defined diagonal lines while the three prisoners meet their fate. The rigid, formal arrangement here is appropriate to the formality of the proceedings and to the spacious world of the château. The long shots, with much space surrounding the troops, and the camera's distance from the massive structure of the château in the background imply a certain inflexibility and unyielding severity. The enlisted men cannot be human here. Their sense of isolation and alienation from the world around them (space) mirrors their exclusion from the aristocratic world of the generals. The brilliance of the formal strategies amplifies an already embedded thematics, emphasizing the doomed nature of this aristocratic world—a key component of the film's antiwar critique.

Paths of Glory is essentially a bloodless antiwar film. Its power and resonance come from the shocking emotional impact of its narrative events and the emphasis on the class distinctions of war. The film is undeniably compelling in its sense of drama and the way characters play off each other. Equally important are the dynamic camera work and other intriguing stylistic and narrative operations. *Paths of Glory* is a virtuoso display of Kubrick's stunning technique and command of the medium. The film's formal design makes war itself an abstraction.

Dr. Strangelove

Several spatial and temporal procedures are at work in *Dr. Strangelove*. I have already discussed some uses of the long take that contribute an intense, compelling quality to the surreal events of the film. Conversely, the B-52 sequences, often accompanied by the humming, vocalizing or instrumental versions of "When Johnny Comes Marching Home," employ different editing patterns than the rest of the film. These editing patterns reinforce the film's theme of the inevitability of the process set in motion by General Ripper.

The sense of enclosure and of the futility of communication is particularly felt in the film's interiors. Thus, Mandrake cannot extract the recall code from Ripper, the crew members inside the B-52 are cut off from the outside world, and President Muffley (Peter Sellers) has great difficulty in communicating with the Soviet premier. As the film proceeds, the continual cutting between these three impenetrable spaces adds to feelings of isolation and hopelessness.

Through editing, the B-52 sequences display a striking conception of cinematic rhythm. The shots here are generally shorter than in other sections of the film, and they significantly contribute to the film's shorter ASL, despite the film's strategic use of long takes. The rhythmical alternation between interior and exterior shots also contributes to the sense of the impenetrability of space. Although the film shuttles between a limited group of spaces, there is still diversity within those spaces.

The creation of rhythmic momentum and variance is achieved through a combination of cutting, musical accompaniment, different shot sizes and diverse shot lengths. In some ways, the film's editing and spatial strategies are a response to an aesthetic (or narrative) problem: how to keep the material interesting within the spatial limitations the film has imposed on itself. The climactic fragment of the final B-52 sequence (see Appendix) illustrates how *Dr. Strangelove* solves this problem and how the film's editing patterns help create cinematic rhythm. They drive the narrative forward and help the different spaces of the film cohere.

The sequence builds cinematic rhythm in several key ways. It continually alternates groups of interior shots with one exterior shot of the flying aircraft. The entire sequence contains ninety-eight shots and lasts seven minutes, for an ASL of 4 seconds. Thus, the quickened pace and narrative momentum is specifically related to the faster cutting. Additionally, the actual shot content, which builds toward the film's climax as the crew members successfully complete their mission, is inherently suspenseful and exciting material. The crew is working against a deadline as they rapidly lose fuel throughout the scene. Major Kong (Slim Pickens) manages to release the bomb doors precisely when the aircraft is over the designated target. But the crucial element in creating the film's insistent rhythmical movement is undoubtedly the editing and its incessant musical accompaniment. The sequence cuts away eighteen times to exterior shots of the flying plane. Each time it cuts away, the exterior image is slightly different. Either the landscape has changed or the plane's direction has altered. These shots are all relatively short (about 5 seconds each) and help to maintain the driving rhythm of the sequence. They continually remind us of the bomber's mission.

The clusters of interior shots aboard the plane are spatially interesting. Not only are the spaces incredibly cramped and confined, but they are also constantly varied through camera movement, the use of angles and different shot sizes. Coupled with the almost metrical alternations between interior and exterior shots, a very insistent, rhythmical progression is created.

The crew's remarkable display of ingenuity and resourcefulness is also amusing, if something of a caricature. Indeed, the spectacle ultimately contributes to an ambivalent feeling in the viewer. After all, what the crew is attempting to accomplish means setting off a nuclear war. Yet, in a strange way, the viewer roots for them and their determination.

Another important editing tactic involves cutting away before actions are completed or when they are at a particularly significant point. This strategy is apparent throughout the film. A scene will appear to be at a critical point in its development, and suddenly there is a cut away to another space. This results in repeated suspensions or delays of narrative progress and resolution.

When the bomber sequence ends, it seems to have brought the film to a point of resolution. Suddenly, it cuts away from the mushrooming nuclear clouds to a silent, interior shot in the Pentagon War Room. Dr. Strangelove (Peter Sellers) is in the midst of a lunatic treatise on the possible survival of selected groups after a nuclear holocaust ("I would not rule out the chance to preserve a nucleus of human specimens . . . at the bottom of some of our deeper mine shafts"). Viewers are left suspended in the middle of a crucial narrative progression and require some time to get their bearings. An earlier scene contains a similar cut away after General Ripper commits suicide, off screen. There is a cut to an interior of the B-52 bomber immediately after the gun blast as Mandrake attempts to extract the recall code ("Now, now supposing I play a little guessing game with you, Jack boy. I'll try and guess what the code is"). Again, the audience is left hanging.

This repeated cutting away at decisive narrative moments reinforces the isolation of the film's interiors. None of the film's characters has much sense of what is occurring in the other spaces. Communication to alter the course of events is impossible. This surreal absurdity is contrasted with the reality of details of decor such as those of the B-52 interior, an emphasis on real time through static long takes, the documentary-like footage of troops attacking Burpelson Air Force Base and other elements that add to the film's realism.

Dr. Strangelove is so tightly enclosed and controlled—spatially, temporally and narratively—that the spectator can do little but be swept along by the driving momentum. *Dr. Strangelove* remains one of the director's strongest and most successful films, though its rationalism and sense of control do not allow for the playful philosophizing and speculation found in the more open texts of *2001* or *The Shining*. Perhaps the film's thesis is simply too unimpeachable. One assumes (or hopes) that even the most ardent militarist could not possibly defend the mad actions of General Ripper or the lunatic philosophy of a Dr. Strangelove.

2001: A Space Odyssey

2001 employs perhaps the most challenging spatial strategies of any Kubrick film. The film's presentation of weightlessness and space travel attempts to achieve a kind of realism and accuracy of presentation. The film also argues that space and time are necessary conditions for any type of movement. Many sequences contain continuous movement and display a fascination with the mechanics, beauty and grace of that movement. The depiction of movement in real time is achieved through a combination of long-take editing, deep-focus photography, smooth camera movements and impeccable model work, resulting in a seamless illusionism. It is impossible to determine how much of the movement visible within the frame is due to model work and/or the movement of actors and how much is a result of camera movement. Often, the effect is a combination of both.

One result of this careful depiction of movement is spatial ambiguity. This ambiguity can be clearly discerned in the two sequences involving Dr. Floyd, the first in which he travels to Hilton Space Station 5 aboard the *Aries*, the second in which he travels to the Clavius moon base. Spatial ambiguity is also central to various sequences aboard the *Discovery* and, of course, as Bowman (Keir Dullea) hurls "Beyond the Infinite" in the Star-Gate sequence. But whereas the earlier examples of spatial ambiguity are dependent on their real-time presentation, the later Star-Gate sequence obliterates any conception of real time and conventional space.

Many sequences in *2001* offer up a kind of cinematic ballet. At times, the narrative momentum seems secondary. The film goes beyond the idea of verisimilitude for its own sake and almost insists that the viewer admire the beautiful images. Not only would the slowness of the editing patterns be unthinkable if the film were made today, at least in commercial terms, but the conception of the film's narrative is of a different order from such later films as *2010* (Peter Hyams, 1984), *Star Trek: The Motion Picture* (Robert Wise, 1979) or, more recently, *Mission to Mars* (Brian DePalma, 2000), a film that borrows not a little from *2001* without the scope, philosophical weight, narrative experimentation or cinematic impact of Kubrick's film. The climate of late 1960s filmmaking also encouraged this experimentation, of course, and the changes in the film industry in succeeding decades have also had an impact on the kinds of films being made and their less risky approach to style and narrative structure.

The radical nature of Kubrick's achievement stems in part from the idea that spatial and temporal ambiguities and movements in space are fascinating to view on their own, with little narrative purpose. These sequences are always engrossing and contrast sharply with the rather flat presentation of scenes showing actors in conversation.

The sequences with actors in movement aboard the *Discovery* are more absorbing partly because of the spatial ambiguities of these scenes. When Bowman interacts with HAL the computer, the scenes are more dramatic and intense than any of the other acted sequences. Here the film strives for more psychological verisimilitude. In scenes that show little interaction between actors, the film achieves a heightened intimacy of the personal. It reaches its most extreme moments of subjectivity, as in Bowman's final sequences, through a process that emphasizes character introspection. It is here that the film's mythopoeic ambitions are most strongly felt. Those sequences envelop and draw in the viewer in a way that amplifies the personal nature of the experience. All people can take the journey with Bowman and make it their own. The experiential becomes personal. All can share in Bowman's experience.

Kubrick's ambition in *2001* is, in some ways, to return to cinema the notion of film as experience, a notion that has often taken second place to the medium's narrative aspirations. Of course, the film is concerned with presenting and experimenting with narrative. At the same time, it seems equally concerned with creating a visual and aural experience so unique that audiences will feel that they are experiencing film for the first time. Audiences now may not remember the tumultuous, divided reception the film originally received or the special nature of its initial 70mm Cinerama presentation. The film's original release was indeed a momentous, controversial and communal theatrical event that should not be overlooked.

Many characteristics of modernist narrative such as the open text, distanced presentation and de-emphasized psychological character motivation can be found in *2001*. Kubrick's film proved that it was possible to create an art film with a modernist narrative form and still devise a popular entertainment with a strong, emotional impact for audiences.

The philosophical and perceptual explorations of Kubrick's film are crucial to its achievement. Very few narrative films take as their subject matter such abstract notions as space and time, but these are precisely the concerns of this film. Of course, the film's thematics, which revolve around the evolution and rebirth of the species and the possibility of alien life forms, are intriguing. But a major concern of *2001* is movement—what it feels like to move in space and the sense of duration that accompanies that movement. The film is also concerned with seeing, both as a perceptual activity and as a metaphor for enlightenment.

Along with its narrative unity and spatial strategies comes a necessary openness and ambiguity that is most apparent in the two sequences that end the film: the Star-Gate sequence and scenes of Bowman in isolation. These sequences offer variations on conceptions of space and time (and vision) as elaborated in the first three movements of the film. The difference is achieved, in part, by shifting the film's visuals from the representational illusionism of three dimensions to a more abstract two-dimensional presentation.

As I have noted, *2001* is most concerned with presenting movement in space and its duration. The film reflexively explores the necessary coordinates of cinematic creation (space and time) within a modernist conception of narrative. That is, it is less reliant on the word and offers a de-dramatized presentation, visual abstraction, unconventional characters and performance styles, and no narrative closure. Despite the fact that the detailed rendering of weightlessness and space maneuvers is astonishing, viewers are still unprepared for the startling perceptual assault of the fourteen minute Star-Gate sequence.

The sequence begins immediately after Bowman hears the prerecorded taped message of Dr. Floyd, ending with the lines, "Except for a single, very powerful radio emission aimed at Jupiter, the four-million-year-old black monolith has remained completely inert. Its origin and purpose, still a total mystery." The title, "Jupiter and Beyond the Infinite," flashes across the screen. The first part of the sequence begins with the screen in relative darkness, while a slow camera movement reveals, in deep focus, various celestial bodies, the spaceship and the black monolith. The eerie György Ligeti music (*Requiem for Soprano, Mezzo Soprano, Two Mixed Choirs & Orchestra*) contributes to the feeling of strangeness in the scene.

The viewer now feels the blackness and isolation of space as never before. Shots last longer than they have at any other point in the film. After several minutes, the "magical" alignment of Jupiter, its moons, the Earth, the Earth's moon and the black monolith appears vertically in the frame. This signals the next phase of the sequence involving the slit-scan, multicolored abstractions. The sequence from the title to the beginning of the abstractions lasts approximately six minutes.

The slit-scan corridor phase of the sequence begins by alternating close-ups of Bowman in freeze frame with the colors, light and a sensation of hurtling into depth of the on-screen movement. It now becomes obvious that these scenes of Bowman's journey will expand on the film's earlier conception of space and time. The freeze frames act as traces of the contortions that Bowman's body undergoes as he completes his mythical, life-renewing mission. The film alternates four times between fairly quick shots of Bowman and shots of the corridor. This phase of the sequence ends with a big close-up of Bowman's eye.

The next segment involves slower movements, as the unfamiliar abstractions,[4] with swirling gases and colored oils, create abstract patterns within the frame. The shapes bend and shift in slow but constant movement. Again, it is difficult to determine how much of the movement is within the frame and how much is the result of the moving camera. This segment lasts approximately three minutes.

There is a straight cut back to Bowman's eye, but now the eye is a different hue. The images are somewhat less abstract and resemble a planet's surface seen from above its atmosphere. They include infrared or negative images as well as landscape shots with crystal-shaped objects lined up in a horizontal line hovering over the terrain. Bowman's eye reappears, now more orange than blue. Cut back to landscape, only now viewers seem to be flying under the landscape as well as over it or possibly even between landscapes. Again there is spatial disorientation. The colored, solarized landscape images are in constant movement. Cut to Bowman's eye—now more blue again—and, as it blinks, there is a cut to long, slower moving, aerial shots of mountainous, colored landscapes (now predominantly shades of brown and blue). The landscape colors vary from greens and blues to reds and yellows; then comes the image of the eye, now blinking, and, as it blinks, it changes color. This fragment lasts approximately four minutes.

The entire sequence lasts fourteen minutes and, as the sequence comes to a close, the blinking eye turns to gray; finally, there is a shot from inside Bowman's space pod. A new sequence begins, and the audience discovers itself inside a room that vaguely recalls the eighteenth century yet seems modern, in that it is predominantly white and filled with artificial light.

This is obviously not a full description of the Star-Gate sequence. It omits references to the music and to the vaguely sexual images of the pod hurtling through space. Likewise, it does not indicate the full range of color, visual experimentation or excitement generated by the sequence. Nonetheless, it gives an indication of the film's radical visual nature and the importance of its editing.

The Star-Gate sequence is notable for its op-art and pop-art color schemes and its occasional similarities to abstract expressionist art. The reflexive eye imagery emphasizes the act of seeing more prominently than any other sequence in the film. The editing between macrocosmic and microcosmic views of the universe encourages a melding of individual subjectivity with the objective world. The combination of cosmic imagery with views of Bowman's body creates an experience that is at once interiorized and exteriorized.

The sequence is impressive in the way in which it confounds viewers' understanding of space, time and notions of subjectivity and objectivity. The spatial and temporal ambiguities themselves become the subjects of the sequence. Viewers are not meant to interpret the world in clear terms. The pulsing eye becomes the universe. Or is the image of the universe merely the image of an eye? It makes no difference, because, metaphorically, the viewer merges with the images on the screen. The Star-Gate sequence presents an argument for a complex cosmology, yet it does so without words. The cerebral has been transformed into the experiential primarily through the masterful orchestration of shot-to-shot editing and elaborate camera strategies.

Rarely, if ever, has a commercial narrative film offered such ambiguous imagery or such a confounding of accepted perceptual coordinates. *2001* abandons its narrative progression in favor of poetic imagery for extended screen time. The landscape abstractions never entirely lose their representational aspect; likewise, the shots of the eye never entirely stop being shots of Bowman's eye. Except for the slit-scan abstractions and the gaseous/oil visuals, the imagery is always grounded, if ever so tenuously, in the recognizable. Perhaps this thread acts as our lifeline. The film rarely breaks the representational link to the universe. No matter how abstract the images may appear, there is always a connection to the world as we know it.

In the next sequence, which shows Bowman in the isolation room, the film pulls viewers back into the commonly understood spatial and temporal coordinates of the world, including its representational aspects. But the representationalism and logical movement of the final scene prove to be just as confounding of our spatial and temporal coordinates as the Star-Gate sequence. While it retains elements that allow some sense of the familiar, they are just as illusory. I will discuss this final sequence, as it relates to the notion of subjectivity, in a later section.

There is no better illustration in *2001* of the importance of editing and camera-related strategies than the Star-Gate sequence. The momentum and sense of visual exhilaration is propelled by the exotic imagery, visual abstractions and rhythmical editing that depends on cutting on movement, shape, shot size and shot length.[5] It is as totally engrossing and involving a sequence of film as one is likely to find in modern cinema. Its complexity rests on both its construction and its perceptual experimentation. It is also one of Kubrick's most philosophically dense exercises in filmmaking. Perhaps more than any other sequence that I can recall, it illustrates how important camera-related strategies and shot-to-shot editing are to Kubrick's stylistics.

The highly visual nature of *2001* has been much discussed. It is well known that the film's 141-minute running time contains little more than forty minutes of dialogue. This is indeed noteworthy. The film's visual organization, coupled with the imaginative use of musical accompaniment, is crucial to its aesthetic impact. What is less frequently mentioned, however, is the precise nature of that visual/aural organization in communicating a particular idea or in organizing narrative action economically and imaginatively.

One forceful example of how editing is used to communicate an idea or narrative action without dialogue occurs in "The Dawn of Man" sequence, when the man-ape (known as Moonwatcher in the novel) grasps how to use the bone as a tool or weapon. The Moonwatcher sequence begins immediately after the apes' discovery of the black monolith. They circle and touch it in great agitation, to the accompaniment of the Ligeti music heard in all scenes that include the monolith, except for its final appearance at the foot of Bowman's bed in the room sequence that ends the film, which is silent. The music adds a strange, semireligious quality to those moments. An extreme, low-angle shot of the black slab is followed by several virtually silent landscape shots.

Viewers see several apes in a long shot, in which they appear generally uninterested in their environment. Cut to a medium shot of Moonwatcher, who squats down directly facing the camera, surrounded by animal bones. He starts to dig the earth in front of him with both hands, puts something in his mouth and suddenly raises his head, as if an idea has come to him; there is a cut to an extreme, low-angle shot of the monolith. The shots are still relatively silent. Cut back to Moonwatcher as he begins to contemplate something. The associative editing retroactively connects the monolith to the ape, and viewers now assume that the monolith is responsible for his thoughts. As the sound of the music (*Thus Spake Zarathustra* by Richard Strauss) slowly increases in volume, the ape picks up a bone and begins to use it to hit bones from an animal skeleton that lies on the ground. Then he hits the animal skull more violently. This shot is held for almost a full minute before a cut to the second shot of Moonwatcher's arm, as he raises and slowly smashes down the bone. On the movement of the arm there is a cut to shot three, a closer, medium shot of the squatting man-ape. The sequence turns to slow motion as he brings down the weapon and shatters the bones around him. The music, gradually building, accompanies these shots.

There is then a cut (shot four) to a medium close-up of the felling of a wild animal, again in slow motion; then a cut back (shot five) to a close-up of Moonwatcher as he faces the camera. His is now the face of a hunter. His bared teeth, in particular, indicate a ferocity not seen in the earlier shots; the sequence cuts back (shot six) to the framing of shot two and then (shot seven) to a close-up of an animal skull as the hand brings down the weapon. Shot eight is similar to shot six of the right hand. Then comes a series of slow motion shots (shots nine through sixteen) where, in fragments, viewers see the bones and skull smashed in a rapidly edited segment. Shot seventeen is another close-up of the tapir falling to the ground, while the next shot (eighteen) cuts to the low-angle, medium shot framing of Moonwatcher (shot three). There the sequence ends.

The man-ape has finished his ecstatic discovery, and his new display of animal ferocity indicates that the species is moving to a new evolutionary stage. The exact ontological status of the shots of the killing of the animal is unclear. It is obviously not occurring as the audience sees it. Those shots, no doubt, indicate how the weapon will be used. This is confirmed in the next few shots showing the apes eating animal meat.

It is an exhilarating and visually exciting sequence that clearly communicates ideas through associative editing, slow motion, fragmentation and use of music. The editing patterns recall aspects of early Soviet montage. Through the insertion of merely one shot of the monolith, the implication is that the slab is responsible for communicating the idea of using the bone to the man-ape. An inattentive viewer might miss the narrative significance of the single, brief shot. It is an excellent example of how Kubrick relies on editing to communicate an important piece of narrative information.

The sequence is blunt in its cinematic impact, but the editing patterns contain a skillful blending of obvious and less obvious organizational principles. As with so much of Kubrick, the scene operates on several levels at once. First, it must work on an almost primal, cinematic level meant for all viewers. This perceptual level is almost tactile in its effectiveness. The sequence contains other levels of meaning, referring to more cerebral material and other styles of filmmaking, which are clearly not designed to appeal to all filmgoers. The attraction of the sequence and of much else in Kubrick's work is that it holds the interest of both a sophisticated viewer and a more naïve one. One might object here that all really interesting films work this way, but I do not think they do. Not all filmmakers expect their work to appeal to a mass audience and also be sophisticated enough to be taken for serious art. It is this ambition that sets Kubrick's work apart from the more obvious art-film directors such as Antonioni and Godard.

After a sequence in which the man-apes use their new found weapons to battle a neighboring group of apes, Moonwatcher hurls a bone high in the air in slow motion. The film elliptically cuts four million years into the future to a spacecraft transporting Dr. Floyd to the Hilton Space Station. The cut takes place on silence, shape and directionality. The spacecraft continues the downward movement of the bone.

In general, Kubrick employs the straight cut, often a shock cut, as his preferred method of shot transition. This can take the form of cutting between long shots and extreme close-ups at crucial moments in a scene. It can also be a more spectacular kind of shock cut, such as the elliptical cut from a bone to a spaceship, which connects the shots graphically as well as metaphorically and thematically. This is one of the most momentous cuts in the history of cinema, not simply because it moves the narrative forward four million years in story time, but because it comes after a lengthy sequence containing no dialogue or conventional exposition. It is a startling, aesthetically audacious narrative moment and a good example of how Kubrick takes a banal device and gives it major significance.

This spectacular shot transition ends "The Dawn of Man" portion of the film. The associative editing patterns, begun with the bone to spacecraft transition, continue with other smooth cuts of spacecraft, the moon, and Dr. Floyd's floating pen and arm as he sits sleeping through the space ride.

In the preceding sequence, the man-ape was shown to be strongly connected to his environment, but Dr. Floyd represents the numbed intellectual who now sleeps through the beauty of space travel, eats flavorless imitations of real food and communicates banalities through language. The scenes of space travel forcefully illustrate how blasé, uninterested and numb man has become in four million years of evolutionary "progress." He takes no notice of what should be an exciting and awe-inspiring experience. These scenes emphasize the exquisite beauty of space, but it seems lost on the character.

At other points during the space ride, we see a steward watching filmed sumo wrestlers and a banal love story on a screen. These sequences illustrate how routine space travel has become, not much different from an intercontinental flight. The scientists of the near future seem no different from businessmen who traverse the country. Dr. Floyd is more concerned with the zero-gravity toilet than with the grandeur of space. Kubrick's attention to the details of space travel and the beauty of his presentation are in sharp contrast to the mundane quality of the human interchanges in these scenes.

Another excellent example of the masterful editing of narrative action occurs in a later scene aboard the *Discovery*, as HAL the computer commits his antiseptically silent murder of the three hibernating crew members. This is an admirable instance of narrative compression without dialogue. The sequence solves what must have been a difficult narrative problem: how to illustrate a crucial piece of action when the leading player (HAL) cannot communicate in any way with other actors or the audience. HAL, of course, is also immobile. Nonetheless, the action must indicate clearly that HAL is responsible for the deaths of the three crew members and also maintain a high degree of suspense. Thus, the narrative information and movement must be achieved primarily through editing. The narrative problem is solved in only eighteen shots and two minutes of screen time. Here is a breakdown of the sequence; all shot transitions are cuts.

Shot 1   Extreme close-up (ECU) of HAL's red "eye." (This is only a partial representation of HAL's total intelligence, of course, since HAL has many components. In a previous sequence, the red "eye" has served to indicate HAL's optical point of view (POV). The first five shots are relatively silent, except for the background drone of the spaceship.)

Shot 2   HAL's POV; a distorted, interior, wide-angle view that has become familiar to us from earlier sequences.

Shot 3   Long shot of one of the three hibernating crew members in a horizontal life-support chamber.

Shot 4   Closer medium shot of the same life-support chamber.

Shot 5   Close-up (CU) of the electronic monitoring chart showing six life functions on horizontal graphs.

Shot 6   CU of the flashing words "COMPUTER MALFUNCTION." A sharp beeping sound begins here and continues until shot 14, when it becomes even more intense.

Shot 7   Similar to shot 5, showing the chart with two of the six graphs flattening to straight horizontal lines, indicating the termination of those critical readings.

Shot 8   CU of one of the crew members (victims) inside their chamber.

Shot 9   Reverse upside-down CU of another hibernation chamber.

Shot 10   CU (head shot) of another crew member.

Shot 11   Overhead long shot of the three chambers.

Shot 12   ECU of HAL's "eye."

Shot 13   CU of flashing words "COMPUTER MALFUNCTION," similar to shot 6.

Shot 14   CU flashing words "LIFE FUNCTIONS CRITICAL." Faster beeping sound begins with this shot, indicating a more critical stage.

Shot 15   CU of chart again, similar to shot 5, with several more graphs going to straight lines.

Shot 16   CU of flashing words "LIFE FUNCTIONS TERMINATED." Silence on the soundtrack, indicating the death of the crew members.

Shot 17   Overhead long shot of the three chambers containing the now lifeless crew members.

Shot 18   CU of HAL's "eye"; sequence ends.

The sequence presents an antiseptic, emotionless murder, with no contact between the murderer and the victims. The sequence works almost as a mini-narrative. It begins with shots introducing the leading character and his victims, proceeds to shots of the crime, its climax, its consequences and finally HAL's reaction. The effortlessness of the narrative organization and the inventive use of sound and silence mask the brilliance and skill with which this sequence solves its difficult narrative problem—almost a distillation of narrative essence at work. Nothing is wasted. No shots last longer than they should. Everything coheres.

2001 is unquestionably one of the masterworks of contemporary narrative cinema, and it holds a unique position in the Kubrick oeuvre. The director's masterful control of almost every aspect of the film's aesthetics (including the conception of the film's special effects) is a powerful illustration that personal cinema is not the exclusive province of the avant-garde. The film also offers a strong argument that art cinema can be both popular and innovative.

NOTES

1. Barry Salt, *Film Style and Technology: History and Analysis* (London: Starword, 1983), 345.

2. This draft of the script found its way onto the Internet. It is dated August 4, 1996.

3. One speculation is that Sidney Pollack, one of the key actors in the film, may have been involved in helping to create the repeated dialogue. Pollack was a graduate of the Neighborhood Playhouse in New York in the 1950s and was a student of the actor/teacher Sanford Meisner, who was well known, at least in acting circles, for developing a series of exercises known as "repetition exercises." These exercises helped actors work off each other in a scene and be more emotionally "in the moment." Tom Cruise's dialogue in this scene and at many other points in the film recalls these acting exercises. It is entirely possible that Pollack worked with Cruise on his performance or at least discussed the technique with him. There is, of course, no way of corroborating this speculation since details of the shoot were kept to a minimum, and actors are generally secretive about their creative process.

4. This, and the preceding slit-scan sequence, may remind some viewers of the films of American experimental filmmakers such as James and John Whitney, and Jordan Belson.

5. Not the least of the many factors that make this one of Kubrick's most successful sequences is the musical accompaniment. Although the use of music is, unfortunately, outside the scope of this analysis, it remains one of the most important and carefully elaborated aspects of Kubrick's aesthetic.

3

Time and Space:
Part 2

INDIVIDUAL FILMS

A Clockwork Orange

A Clockwork Orange contains one of the most highly determined theatrical spaces in contemporary film. Carole Zucker, in her analysis of Josef von Sternberg's Dietrich films, *The Idea of the Image*, has summarized at least four conventions of theatricality relevant to our discussions: stylization and exaggeration, frontality, choreography of movement, and theatrical space and time.[1] *A Clockwork Orange* features a highly exaggerated, stylized visual presentation framed around the subjectivity of its main character. Editing and camera-related spatial strategies combine to create a theatrical space that highlights the "aestheticization" of violence and allows Alex to perform his "act."

The first few sequences immediately "set the stage" for the film's theatricality, both in spatial terms and in the performances. The first shot is one of the most celebrated openings in film history, as well as one of the most informationally dense and revealing shots in Kubrick's work. It announces in a highly striking way what is to follow.

The shot begins with a big close-up of Alex, complete with bowler hat, false eyelash and frozen stare directed at the camera. The camera pulls back in a combination zoom and backward dolly to reveal the four gang members resting their feet on coffee-table sculptures depicting nude female forms. The camera continues its backward movement, revealing more of the Korova Milkbar as the gang members hold their frozen expressions amidst the striking color scheme and *mise-en-scène*. The scene reveals an unfamiliar, expressionistic world. The gang members wear predominantly white clothes with suspenders and black boots. In the background, the available drug-laced milk options are scrawled in white lettering on a black wall with a "*Caligari*-like" flourish. Alex stares directly into the camera as more of the theatrical space is revealed. Floor sculptures of women with colored wigs, milk dispensers fashioned in the shape of women and neon lights symmetrically line the right and left sides of the frame, while Alex and his gang are in the background. Other customers are seated along both sides of the frame, also immobile and frozen from the drugs. The highly studied arrangement is accompanied by synthesizer music. The camera movement at last reveals the entire space in long shot.

Alex begins his voice-over commentary, immediately framing the film's narration as a subjective presentation by its leading player. He introduces himself ("There was me, that is Alex"), and we are immediately struck by the unfamiliar slang that we later learn is the exclusive province of the youth gangs—none of the adults in the film use it. Alex remains immobile, with his expression frozen throughout the shot, which lasts ninety seconds.

The exaggerated, stylized decor and the presentation of Alex immediately signal a theatrically distanced presentation as articulated in Zucker's analysis. The opening shot also encapsulates and introduces an unusual tension between the dominant, subjective mode of presentation and the distanced, emotionally uninvolving stylistics of the film. The opening shot presents the spectator with an enclosed, alienated world where violence, drugs and misogynistic art are dispensed in equal measure. Characters escape the realities of this world through drugged concoctions made palatable and sanctioned by the state. What could be more innocent than drinking milk?

After this opening, there is a cut to an exterior nighttime shot of a derelict sitting against a concrete wall amid litter and debris. He sings an old folk song ("Molly Malone") as the camera pulls back, again beginning on a detail to reveal a wide view. In long shot, the area becomes recognizable as a pedestrian underpass. The space is a kind of dead end. There is no escaping the claustrophobic, nightmarish shadow world of this not-too-distant future. The architecture and decor offer no comfort for this refugee from an earlier, happier time. The space is harsh and brightly lit. As the derelict continues his song, the elongated, exaggerated shadows of Alex and his gang enter the frame, fragmenting the space into light and dark segments. The direct address continues through Alex's voice-over. Is this how Alex sees himself in his drugged state—in exaggerated shadows and harsh lights? Throughout the film, the presentation of Alex's world benefits from many strategies that emphasize the subjective world of the main character. These include the use of wide-angle lenses, slow motion, extreme angles, camera movement, voice-over and expressive editing. It is the most highly subjective presentation in Kubrick's work.

As the derelict continues his song, there is a cut to a reverse-angle, long shot of the gang. The lighting and use of shadows clearly emphasize the artifice and theatrical expressionism of the image. The idea of theater and of an audience is invoked as the gang mockingly applauds the old man's song. Cut to a close, side view of Alex's face as he hunches over his victim. The gang proceeds to beat the old man viciously with their boots, chains and clubs.

After a cut, the third sequence again begins on a detail, this time of faded floral wallpaper. The camera pans down and zooms back to reveal the wall ornaments and stage where Billy Boy and his gang are abusing a "weepy, young devotchka" (woman). A stage with full proscenium makes the theatrical subtext literal. The stage reveals large *papier-mâché* heads, and the shadows of the gang again invoke a fantastic world. The space of the derelict casino evokes a descent into a netherworld, a common theme in expressionist art and cinema. The screams of the woman pierce the space.

Billy Boy and his gang are dressed sloppily in military fatigues, clearly lacking the style of Alex and his gang. Extreme long shots of the stage alternate with closer views as the gang members brutally strip and toss the woman among them. Alex and his droogs emerge out of the darkness as a reverse-angle shot signals the arrival of the star of the entertainment. He announces his entrance ("ho, ho, ho"), even adding a Brooklyn accent ("Billy Boy in poison") for added flair. The woman quickly exits, stage right. To the quickening strains of Gioacchino Rossini's *Thieving Magpie Overture*, a violent ballet begins. The choreography, quick editing and the crescendo of the music combine to create one of the most physical and viscerally exciting sequences in the film. The rumble is filled with crashing, hurtling bodies as Alex disposes of his adversaries with bravado and flourish. He smashes a face with a bottle, screams, runs and drop-kicks a table against a body. The physicality is exaggerated and stylized to create a modern dance of movement and physical abuse.

The violent, choreographed rumble takes place in a pitlike, ground-level space that evokes images of Roman gladiators, contemporary wrestling and other acrobatic movements or sports. One gang member holds two people in headlocks. Another dives off the stage while other characters are tripped and props are smashed against flesh. The exaggerated, fragmented actions are not only theatrical, but also invoke the idea of fantasy. The sequence has the heightened intensity one might associate with the drug-induced reveries of a teenager raised on movies and comic books. In fact, it resembles a cartoon in its removal from reality, since no one seems to get hurt much. The fight accelerates as the music builds in dramatic intensity. The frenzy of violence ends on a shrill note as police sirens announce their impending arrival, and Alex pierces the air with a shrieking whistle as he and his gang escape.

The violence of the first HOME sequence is rendered with cinematic flair and even more distortion mechanisms than the previous scenes. The handheld camera, with a wide-angle lens (probably handled by Kubrick himself),[2] creates unusual, oblique angles of view. The sequence begins with a straight-on view of Mr. Alexander, the writer (Patrick Magee), typing at his desk. The camera moves in a steady, anticipatory, lateral fashion that has become typical of the director's style. "Who on earth could that be?" asks Mr. Alexander in a matter-of-fact tone, signaling the lateral track to reveal his wife (Adrienne Corri) who is seated in a futuristic, podlike seat. As she gets up to answer the door, her striking, bright red, one-piece jumpsuit metaphorically presages the bloody scene to follow. The intervening space of their apartment is visually distorted through the use of a wide-angle lens, creating an exaggerated sense of depth. The wife emerges into a space encircled with mirrored walls, a black and white tiled floor, and bare wood. This is one of the few sets constructed for the film, and it gives an impression of illusion and expansiveness to the hallway space, further adding to the fantasy element.

I have described these opening sequences in some detail because they lay out most of the film's predominant stylistic strategies. They also give a clear idea of the variety of spaces in the film. According to Judith Anne Switzer: "There are over twenty different settings in the film. These are divided about equally into interiors and exteriors, although most of the action takes place in the interiors. . . . The repeated image of a tunnel, cave, or labyrinth is suggestive of Alex's predatory world."[3]

Switzer has described many exteriors as "sinister" and referred to the film's interiors as "psychological landscapes":

They are dark, shadowy caves lit with neon lights and day-glo paint. The Korova Milkbar dispenses drugged milk from the "breasts" of a machine shaped like a woman. The milk feeds Alex's violent fantasies while the Derelict Casino provides a stage to act them out. The Alexanders' house is white and sterile: mirrors, plastic furniture, and polished floors reflect the glaring light. The room and the furniture are uninviting. Alex's room is another uninviting setting. He keeps a combination lock on his door to protect his stolen loot, his stereo, his snake, and his icons (a bust of Beethoven, a painting of a woman apparently engaged in an autoerotic act, and a sculpture of a line of dancing Jesuses). There are no windows in the room, but a mirror on the wall reflects his bed. Between the stereo speakers above his bed is the painting of the woman with her legs spread. The room is a womb-like cave where Alex can safely indulge his fantasies. It is an externalization of Alex's mind—a narrow little space filled with fetish objects.[4]

Switzer has characterized the institutional interiors of the film (the prison, hospital, police precinct, auditorium, and so on) as "uneasy environments in which the characters seem oppressed."[5] They seem like typical, sterile institutional spaces, not unlike many similar environments in today's urban world.

Alex acts out his fantasies in his room as well. We see him end his "wonderful evening" with "a bit of the old Ludwig Van" in a highly expressive montage sequence involving the dancing Jesus sculpture. This masturbation scene is edited with precise rhythms, with a rapid-fire series of images of the sculpture and the music stimulating Alex both sexually and verbally: "Oh, bliss . . . bliss and heaven. Oh, it was gorgeousness and gorgeosity made flesh. It was like a bird of rarest spun heaven metal, or like silvery wine flowing in a spaceship, gravity all nonsense now." The fragmentation continues as Alex's poetic commentary is accompanied by "lovely pictures" (mental images) inspired by movies. Alex is seen in four shots as a vampire, fangs exposed, with fake blood dripping from the sides of his mouth. These shots alternate with shots of a hanging, explosions, and a phony avalanche from a trashy movie of the prehistoric genre. The rhythmical editing is carefully timed to the music and the B-movie fakery.

The theatrical presentation is also evident in the prison/hospital sequences as Alex undergoes the Ludovico treatment. With his crown of thorns (electrodes, lidlocks on his eyes), he is strapped to a chair and forced to watch violent films in a drugged state to alter his violent urges behaviorally. Once again, the film invokes the idea of theater, spectacle and an audience. Alex's aesthetic sense is tested by the films ("It's funny how the colors of the real world only seem really real when you viddy them on the screen"). In the process, his love of Beethoven's *Ninth Symphony* is also expunged.

After Alex's treatment and "crucifixion," he is presented to an elite prison audience in his new role as victim, rather than aggressor. Alex's presentation here is more stripped down than in earlier examples of the film's theatricality. It features Alex in a plain suit on a bare stage with a single spotlight aimed at him. Few props, fashionable clothes or elaborate aspects of *mise-en-scène* intrude on his "act," although the music and lighting have a significant impact in the scene.

Alex performs in two separate skits. The first involves a humiliating episode with "Lardface," in which Alex is forced to lick the bottom of the other man's shoe (recalling the foot fetishist in the Cat Lady's (Miriam Karlin) paintings—a scene we will discuss in a later section). After this sadistic episode, Lardface takes his bow, politely waves to Alex to accept his bows, as any trouper would, and exits. He is followed by the second performer, a tall, icy, topless blonde wearing only a bikini bottom, who demonstrates that Alex's libido has been expunged along with his proclivity to violence. Incorporating extreme high and low-angle shots to simulate the characters' perspectives, the scene feels like a Korova Milkbar sculpture come to life. Alex attempts to put his hands on the woman's breasts but is stricken with the same physical revulsion he felt in the previous sketch. The actress takes her bows to hearty applause and quickly exits.

Sequences such as these display the numerous thematically charged spaces and camera-related strategies employed in the film. They amplify the connection between the film's thematics and its theatrical, stylized presentation. In some ways, the camera is the star of the film. It turns up in the unlikeliest places, often using extreme angles and focal lengths. Much of the time, the film's conception of visual style is rather blunt, though brilliant in execution. Occasionally, the film is more subtle. In one scene, for example, Alex walks along the Thames Embankment, where his dejected feelings and momentary contemplation of suicide are communicated by two very slow zooms: one into the character, the second into the water. The sequence may be referring to the "kitchen sink" school of British realism of the late 1950s and early 1960s, films such as *Saturday Night and Sunday Morning* (Karel Reisz, 1960) and *Look Back in Anger* (Tony Richardson, 1958). Such quiet moments are rare in the film. Mainly, the camera is more noticeable in its intrusions.

The different spaces of the film and the profusion of details in the subjective presentation (to be further examined in Chapter 4) push the film to the limits of cinematic expressiveness. No Kubrick film before or since has incorporated such a variety of devices, including different film speeds, visual distortions, extreme angles, varied shot sizes and others, to create a theatrical space and communicate character point of view.

Barry Lyndon

The ravishing visuals of *Barry Lyndon* are one of its most impressive accomplishments, but what is one to make of this foray into the "painterly"? In their cinematography and decor, other films have imitated the visual style of painting to achieve a particular look. *Lust for Life* (Vincente Minnelli, 1955), *Edvard Munch* (Peter Watkins, 1975), and *Vincent and Theo* (Robert Altman, 1990) come to mind, but none has been so elaborate as Kubrick's film.

Much of the inspiration for the film's pictorialism came from the work of several eighteenth- and nineteenth-century painters in various genres. Ken Adam, the designer on the film, summarized these painterly sources in an interview with Michel Ciment: "Our inspiration came from painters like Gainsborough, Hogarth, Reynolds, Chardin, Watteau, Zoffany, Stubbs (for the hunting costumes) and, in particular, Chadoweicki, an artist who intrigued both of us, a Pole who worked on the Continent and who was a master of drawing and water-color, with a marvelously simple style and a remarkable gift for composition."[6]

The film's visuals allude to landscape, portraiture, "conversation pieces" and satirical painting, portraying the era as it might appear in a painting. The visual portrait offered in *Barry Lyndon* is of a rich, useless society and how it imagined or idealized itself through its art. The film attempts to present an eighteenth-century aristocratic view of notions of beauty, as filtered first through a nineteenth-century novelist and then through the sensibilities of a late twentieth-century filmmaker.

One consistent and important visual strategy Kubrick uses in the film is a slow zoom into a detail from a long shot or a shot that begins on a detail and slowly zooms back to reveal a wider space. This movement into or out from a small detail of the environment emphasizes the rigidity and formal structures of the aristocratic world on view. The strategy activates the off-screen space in a way that connects the detail to the world outside the frame. The tactic is analogous, in a certain way, to the act of looking at a painting. The eye is often drawn to a detail before the viewer explores the larger canvas, or conversely, the viewer experiences the entire canvas before moving into its details.

The use of the slow zoom also stresses various elements of artifice and reinforces the film's sense of fatalism. The zoom is a very particular cinematic device that gives only the illusion of movement. More precisely, it gives an illusion of the illusion of movement. With genuine camera movement, there is at least an indexical relationship between the view on the screen and the physical movement of a camera through space. The camera movement on screen could not have occurred without the authentic movement in space of a camera. With the zoom, there is no real movement through space. The zoom emphasizes the two-dimensionality and flatness of the image, as much as camera movement with deep focus emphasizes its three dimensionality (even if this too is illusory). The zoom is mechanical and artificial in ways camera movement is not. The zoom flattens both physically and metaphorically. The use of this device in *Barry Lyndon* effortlessly communicates the shallowness of eighteenth-century aristocratic society. In conjunction with the stiff, artificial posing and arrangement of characters within the frame, it creates a portrait of a superficial society more concerned with surface beauty than with substantive ideas and human emotion. Rarely has a narrative film incorporated such highly determined spatial strategies to build character, elaborate its thematics and create a philosophical context for its aesthetic investigations.

Despite the surface beauty of this world, the film reveals characters filled with pettiness and human failings. This world is chaotic and cruel. Although it might prefer to do so, this society cannot escape its worst aspects by retreating into the economic, moral, ritualistic and cultural constructs it has so rigidly created for itself.

The painterly world that Kubrick has created is shallow and ephemeral. The arrangement of figures within the frame and other aspects of its *mise-en-scène* combine with various camera strategies to present a particularly distanced universe. A remarkable elegance and orchestration characterize many of the film's camera movements. For example, the scene in which Barry decides to seek the hand of Lady Lyndon coincides with his first setting eyes on her. The sequence depends for its effect on a precise confluence of information conveyed by the voice-over, the combination of camera movement and zoom, and the orchestration of character movement within the frame. The sequence is introduced by a voice-over narration over several landscape and castle shots:

That their life for all its splendor was not without some danger and difficulty requiring talent and determination for success

[Cut to the next shot]

and one which required them to live a wandering and disconnected life. And if the truth be told, though they were swimming upon the high tide of fortune and prospering with the cards, they had little to show for their labor but some fine clothes and a few trinkets.

There is a cut to an exterior long shot. The scene shows a stately garden. The camera tracks slowly left to right on a balcony. In the foreground sit the chevalier (left) and Barry (right) at an outdoor table. The voice-over continues:

Five years in the army and some considerable experience of the world had by now dispelled any of those romantic notions regarding love with which Barry commenced life. And he began to have it in mind, as so many gentlemen had done before him, to marry a woman of fortune and condition.

At this point in the shot, a very slow zoom begins as the voice-over continues:

And as such things so often happen, these thoughts closely coincided with his setting first sight upon a lady who will henceforth play a considerable part in the drama of his life: the Countess of Lyndon, Viscountess Bullingdon of England, Baroness of Castle Lyndon of the Kingdom of Ireland. A woman of vast wealth and great beauty.

During the commentary, the slow zoom begins its "movement" through the space where the two actors are seated and coincides with Barry's directing his glance toward Lady Lyndon (Marisa Berenson) and her entourage, in the depth of the frame. The zoom ends on Lady Lyndon and her entourage, panning right to follow the group. Cut to a medium close-up of Barry. The voice-over informs us that the woman is the wife of Sir Charles Lyndon. Cut to shot three, a long shot of Lady Lyndon, her husband wheeled by a servant, their son Lord Bullingdon and Reverend Runt as they walk toward the camera, which pans left to keep them centered.

In three shots that total about 90 seconds of screen time, the audience has been introduced to the main players of the second half of the film. The necessary background information has been furnished. But narrative economy is only one result of this compression. The commentary introduces Lady Lyndon at the precise instant that the zoom moves closer to her and the group; Barry also turns his head in her direction at this same moment. He confirms the voice-over description of his loss of innocence and how little the two gamblers have to show for their years of wandering. The moment is revealed to the spectator visually and aurally at the very instant that Barry sees Lady Lyndon.

The slow camera movement and the zoom to Lady Lyndon reinforce the mechanical, thoughtless decision Barry has made. His actions have become automatic and shallow. The flatness and unreality of the situation is intensified by the zoom lens. Barry turns his head to gaze at Lady Lyndon as if he were the camera lens. The distanced presentation merges the different points of view, and the flat, two-dimensional world comes sharply to life. The film concisely and effortlessly combines its thematic investigations with its style of presentation. Nevertheless, the orchestration of camera movement and zoom, character movement, timing of voice-over, subtle editing and use of long takes are obviously *not* effortless. It requires precision and a masterful control of the medium. The timing and control evident in this sequence are typical of the film as a whole.

In Kubrick's work, the hand-held camera is most often employed in moments of violence or in unsettling, anxiety-provoking situations. *Barry Lyndon* is no exception. In both examples that I will discuss, the hand-held camera is used not only to present the material in a more interesting and exciting way but also to communicate metaphorically the idea of freedom. In each instance, the viewer experiences a kind of exhilaration when the restrictions of the frame have been transcended.

The first instance occurs in Part 1 when Barry is taunted by a red-haired bully in the English army. Barry's first response is to fight him. What ensues, however, is a carefully regulated fist-fight in which Barry is forced to box his opponent within a square formed by the rest of the troops. There are still limitations imposed on him, even here ("no kickin', scratchin', the last man to remain standing is the winner"). In contrast to his hulking and unrefined opponent, Barry is lithe, graceful and intelligent, and he easily defeats him.

The sequence is rendered through short shots, a hand-held camera and oblique angles. Barry's response is direct and immediate. He learns that society has rules of behavior that he must accommodate; in this case, it is the army that limits Barry's response. Despite these rules, Barry momentarily breaks free from the order imposed on him by society. He also breaks free of the restrictions imposed by the frame edge. It is crucial that this sequence is organized around rapid montage, close-ups and a hand-held camera, in contrast to the long takes, long shots and slow zooms of much of the rest of the film. Although Barry's victory is minor and partial, the film allows him a sense of freedom through this venting of his emotions. The different style of presentation here is essential to communicate the character's momentary sense of freedom.

The other incident in which the limitations of society (and the frame) are transgressed is more significant. It comes later in the film in the sequence in which Barry violently attacks Lord Bullingdon (Leon Vitali) at a music recital given by Lady Lyndon and Reverend Runt. The most notable aspects of Barry's loss of control here are its intensity and the fact that it is done in full view of his invited guests. This is one of the few times in the second half of the film that Barry expresses a direct emotional response to a situation.

The scene begins with a slow, studied camera movement, from left to right, that reveals a small chamber orchestra playing a concerto. Lady Lyndon is at the piano, while Reverend Runt plays the flute. All seems proper, orderly and civilized as the camera reveals about forty guests. Barry is seated in the front row with his mother at his side. The highly structured music perfectly reflects the ordered state of the aristocratic society. Moreover, a recital is the perfect event for Barry to stage in his quest for a peerage. It shows him to be cultured and the epitome of the "civilized" moneyed class he so desperately wants to

penetrate. But the tranquility of the scene is suddenly interrupted by the arrival of Barry's two sons.

Lord Bullingdon, Barry's antagonist since his marriage to Lady Lyndon,
and little Bryan walk in from the back of the room through the guests to the
area where Lady Lyndon plays the piano. What ensues is a domestic drama
(or melodrama), played out as if on stage to an audience. Lord Bullingdon
kneels down to speak to little Bryan. He insults both Barry and Lady Lyndon. She leaves the room in tears, and Barry begins to beat Lord Bullingdon
uncontrollably. It is the only liberating gesture he can make. He jumps on
his stepson, and the sequence immediately reverts to hand-held camera and
rapid montage. The viewer is plunged into the event by the tactile physicality, rapid editing and shot composition. It is a vicious attack, yet there is an
exhilaration about it.

The immediacy and physicality of this sequence are absent from much of
the rest of the film. Barry abandons the pretense and artifice of his new station in life, losing all sense of decorum and of how to behave in society. He is
no longer the lifeless mannequin of earlier scenes. When he pummels Lord
Bullingdon, he is reacting not only to the immediate provocation but also to
the years of constraints and penalties of this society. He abandons all sense of
order and control. Aesthetically, this is echoed in the violence of the montage,
the hand-held camera and the sound. Barry's rebellion is extreme but authentic. His real crime is not that he has inflicted bodily injury on his stepson,
but that he has transgressed the rules of behavior and decorum of his society.

Barry Lyndon relies on complex spatial strategies of camera movement,
slow zooms, long takes, camera position, long shots, rhythmical editing and
character placement within the frame for much of its impact. The framing devices, the precise use of the zoom and the careful camera movements call attention to the spatial and temporal rigidity and orderliness of this world. The
film's characters are trapped within the two-dimensional space of the image.

Many other sequences similarly emphasize visuals and editing structure.
The scene of Barry's seduction of Lady Lyndon illustrates how the film avoids
the use of dialogue, relying instead on musical accompaniment, glances,
rhythmical editing and long takes for its emotional effect and formal arrangement. The sequence alludes to silent film as it illustrates the importance of
spatial relationships in conveying narrative information to carry the emotional
weight of the story.

The sequence begins with a medium shot of Lady Lyndon and Reverend
Runt seated at the gaming table run by the chevalier with Barry's assistance.
Lady Lyndon places a bet, Reverend Runt shakes his head, the chevalier says,
"*Faites vos jeux.*" Cut to the second shot (same interior, candlelit space), with
Barry and the chevalier facing right, seated at the table. Shot three is a
medium-close (same interior candlelit space), two shot of Lady Lyndon and
Reverend Runt facing the camera. Lady Lyndon looks in Barry's direction,
then down at her coins in slight embarrassment, while Runt looks screen right

at Lady Lyndon. We hear again the chevalier's off-screen voice saying, "*Faites vos jeux.*" Lady Lyndon again makes eye contact in Barry's direction. Cut to shot four, showing the same space, with a medium close-up of Barry facing the camera as he looks in Lady Lyndon's direction. Barry seems lost in thought, but he awakens and goes back to the game, eyes downcast.

Shot five, with the same space and set-up as shot three, is a medium-close, two shot of Runt and Lady Lyndon, with Runt looking right at Lady Lyndon. Barry and Lady Lyndon continue to make eye contact. She looks down in slight embarrassment, and Runt looks at Barry. Shot six, showing the same space and set-up as shot four, is a medium-close shot of Barry. He looks directly ahead in Lady Lyndon's direction. The next shot (seven), with the same space and set-up as shots three and five, is a medium two shot of Lady Lyndon and Reverend Runt, with her looking in Barry's direction. Shot eight resembles shots 2, 4 and 6, with a medium-close shot of Barry. He looks ahead in Lady Lyndon's direction, then down and toward screen right, while the music continues.

Shot nine is a medium close-up of Lady Lyndon, who first has her eyes down but lifts them in Barry's direction. Cut to shot ten, a medium close-up of Barry, facing the camera as he looks directly at Lady Lyndon with the same set-up as shots 2, 4, 6 and 8. The next shot (eleven) is a medium close-up of Lady Lyndon, like shot nine. She looks at Barry, then quickly left at Reverend Runt, then down. She seems lost in thought. Cut to shot twelve, a medium two shot of Reverend Runt and Lady Lyndon, with the same set-up as shots 3, 5 and 7. Lady Lyndon places the coins in front of her; Runt looks at her, screen right. The following bit of dialogue ensues:

Lady Lyndon: Samuel, I'm going outside for a breath of air. [She rises from her chair.]
Runt: Yes, my Lady, of course.

There follows a cut to a medium close-up of Barry (shot thirteen). He looks in Lady Lyndon's direction, then down. Cut to an exterior, nighttime, long shot (shot fourteen) of Lady Lyndon as she walks in a courtyard outside the gaming area. The camera pans with her as she walks and slows down near a huge pillar. Cut to shot fifteen, an exterior, nighttime medium shot of Lady Lyndon still moving, center frame, looking screen right. In the extreme background, Barry's figure is barely visible. Finally, there is a cut to an exterior, nighttime medium shot (shot sixteen) of Barry. The camera tracks with him as he moves slowly in Lady Lyndon's direction and stops in a two shot of Barry and Lady Lyndon. She slowly turns and looks at Barry. He in turn clasps both her hands in his and pulls her toward him. They face each other and slowly, amorously kiss. There the sequence ends.

The scene contains almost no dialogue, yet it is full of communication between the principal players. At the gaming table, the rhythmical editing and eye-line glances connect the images and give narrative coherence to the different spaces. The music (Franz Schubert's *Piano Trio in E Flat, opus 100*, which is a leitmotif for their romantic and melancholy affair) provides much of the emotional effect in the scene. The nonverbal communication and editing patterns make narrative sense of the sequence. The body language, primarily the use of eyes, reveals all it is necessary to know about the characters' intentions.

Viewers have been informed of Barry's intentions by the earlier voice-over. They have also seen the crippled, elderly man with whom Lady Lyndon shares her life. The seduction scene makes Barry's motives abundantly clear. He coldheartedly pursues Lady Lyndon with a view to marriage and amassing a fortune. Lady Lyndon seems more interested in an affair since her atrophied husband can hardly provide the emotional and sexual attention she obviously craves.

The sequence amplifies and visually dramatizes these ideas with admirable economy and a beautiful sense of rhythm. The nuances of feeling of the main players are communicated with great delicacy and sensitivity through a subtle use of shot/reverse-shot editing and the glance. Though viewers understand the motives of the characters, the scene retains its romantic feeling. The lush *mise-en-scène* and exquisite lighting contribute to the scene's effectiveness.

The final three shots of the sequence illustrate the importance to the film's stylistic system of foreground and background, deep-focus composition, long takes, rhythmical editing, and the choreography of camera and figure movement. In fact, the choreographed quality is one of the most prominent aspects of the scene.

Lady Lyndon, her breathing noticeably quicker, occupies the foreground of the shot, as Barry appears in the background behind the glass. He exits from the frame as quickly as he enters and, for an instant, the viewer is suspended in anticipation as to how the scene will be played out. The final shot is a long take in which Barry silently takes hold of Lady Lyndon's hands, bends down and kisses her gently on the lips. The sequence plays like a quintessential male fantasy, dispensing with language. Barry pursues his romantic conquest without the complication and tension normally associated with sexual pursuit and desire. No words are uttered as the two principals act out their fantasies. It is a beautiful moment tinged with sadness, since it also illustrates that Barry's innocence and naïveté have been replaced by a predetermined sexual and financial quest. The sequence depends on the pictorialism of its imagery, its precise formal orchestration and the subtle rhythms of its editing patterns. The music contributes to the total effect, but language has been virtually eliminated. Here Kubrick once again discovers the beauty of the silent cinema, as he did in *2001* and *A Clockwork Orange*, films which also have numerous scenes that depend exclusively on image and music to the exclusion of language.

Apart from the use of eye-line matches, music and camera movement, Kubrick resorts to several other formal operations, including strategic uses of ambient sound, to achieve rhythmical editing. Several scenes prominently incorporate ticking sounds, and this metrical orderliness underscores one of the film's important themes: the oppressiveness of time. The notion that time is one of this society's most abundant commodities (for those of the right class) is effectively communicated by the slow character movement within the frame, by sound, and by the film's use of measured camera movement and slow zooms. The aristocratic class spends much of its time in pursuits of pleasure and material gain or in the appreciation of art and culture. If some have objected to *Barry Lyndon*'s pace and slowness of editing and visual patterns, they are neglecting an essential element of its stylistic system and critique.

One example of how background sound and actors' speech patterns combine with editing patterns to create cinematic rhythm is the scene in which Mrs. Barry (Marie Kean) relieves Reverend Runt of his duties. This comes after the death of little Bryan and Lady Lyndon's suicide attempt. Here is a breakdown of several shots from the sequence with the dialogue intact, since language plays an important role in creating the scene's rhythm. The sequence is accompanied by the very prominent ticking of a clock that provides a rhythmical accompaniment to Mrs. Barry's ever more insistent directives to Reverend Runt. This sound underscores the theme of temporal oppressiveness for the aristocratic class:

Shot 1 Interior. Medium shot of Mrs. Barry, seated in center frame, facing the camera. Her hands are folded (as if in prayer) on the desk in front of her.

Mrs. Barry: [Speaking slowly] Reverend Runt, I need not tell you that the recent tragedies of this family have made the services of a tutor no longer required at Castle Hackton. And as we are in some considerable difficulty about money, I'm afraid I must ask you, with the greatest reluctance, to resign your post.

Shot 2 Interior, daytime. Medium close-up of Reverend Runt, center frame, facing camera, clock ticking in background.

Runt: Madam, I'm sensible [slowly] of your predicament, and you need have no concern about my wages, with which I can willingly do without. But it is out of the question for me to consider leaving her Ladyship in her present state.

Shot 3 Medium shot, same as shot (1) of Mrs. Barry.

Mrs. Barry: I'm very sorry to say this to you but I truly believe *you* are largely responsible for the state of mind she is in, and the sooner you leave, the better she will be.

Shot 4 Medium close-up of Runt, same as shot (2).

Runt: Madam, with the greatest respect, I take my instructions only from her Ladyship.

Shot 5 Medium close-up of Mrs. Barry [closer than shots (1) and (3)], center frame, facing camera, eyes slightly left in Runt's direction.

Mrs. Barry: [taking a firmer tone now] *Reverend Runt,* her Ladyship is in no fit mind to give *instruction* to anyone. My son has charged me with handling the affairs of Castle Hackton until he recovers from his grief and resumes his interest in worldly matters, and while I . . .

Shot 6   Medium close-up of Runt [same as shots (2) and (4)].

Mrs. Barry: . . . am in charge, you will take your instructions from me. My only concern is for Lady Lyndon.

Runt: Madam, your *only* concern is for her Ladyship's signature. You and your son have almost succeeded in destroying a fine family fortune. What little remains for you depends on keeping her Ladyship prisoner in her own house.

Shot 7   Medium close-up of Mrs. Barry, same set-up as shot (5).

Mrs. Barry: [very firmly now] Reverend *Runt,* this matter bears no further discussion. You will pack your bags and leave by tomorrow morning.

[End of sequence]

The editing in this scene is admirably timed to the speech patterns of the actors and is punctuated by the sound of a ticking clock in the background. The performers' skill with language, stressing individual words, is complemented by precise and careful shot-to-shot editing to extract subtle nuances of meaning from the scene. The tension between the two characters is barely concealed below the surface civility. It smolders into a more noticeable battle of wills between a mother's love (and concerned self-interest) and Reverend Runt's platonic love for Lady Lyndon (and his defense of the aristocratic value system). The clergyman resembles Lord Bullingdon in that he clearly resents the class difference between the Barry family and the Lyndons. The portrayal of the clergy and of its considerable part in maintaining the class structure is one of the film's sharpest attacks.

The check-signing scene that ends the film is another superb example of rhythmical editing, this time greatly aided by the exquisite orchestration of the musical accompaniment. Because the scene relies heavily on the precision of its editing, here is a brief description:

Shot 1   Interior, daytime; Castle Hackton. Long shot of Lord Bullingdon, Graham, Lady Lyndon (all three seated) and Reverend Runt, who stands. They are positioned around a table with much space between the actors and the camera. The arrangement is formal and symmetrical. Lord Bullingdon places items for Lady Lyndon's signature. The Schubert selection from the previous scene (*Piano Trio in E Flat, opus 100,* second movement) continues.

Shot 2   Medium shot of Lady Lyndon, Lord Bullingdon, and Graham at the table. Lady Lyndon is signing checks. Lord Bullingdon glances at Lady Lyndon as he places one very special item for her to sign. Music continues.

Shot 3   Close-up of bank draft to pay Barry's annuity. There is a slow zoom-in as Lady Lyndon signs it, "H. Lyndon". At this point, the music slows down, and the low cello notes are attenuated over to the next shot.

Shot 4   Close-up of Lady Lyndon, eyes downcast. She looks up and ahead as she contemplates Barry. The music continues slowly as the piano, violin and cello notes are all distinctly defined and the notes are accentuated.

Shot 5   Close-up of Lord Bullingdon, facing camera. He looks up and right as the cello notes vibrate and the sound of the piano is heard.

Shot 6   Close-up of Lady Lyndon, as in shot (4), eyes ahead, but her stare is vacant. Music continues.

Shot 7   Close-up of Lord Bullingdon, same as shot (5), eyes right at Lady Lyndon. He looks down. The piano notes are very slow.

Shot 8   Close-up of Lady Lyndon, same as shot (6), who is distracted. She lowers her head slightly and signs the draft. The shot holds, as the violin is heard, and Lady Lyndon breathes noticeably.

Shot 9   Long shot of four characters, same as shot (1). Lady Lyndon continues to sign the documents. As the final chords of music are heard, the epilogue title card appears.

[End of Sequence]

The sequence benefits immensely from the musical accompaniment used to create its rhythms of cutting, and from eye-line matches that connect the different spaces. The precise editing rhythm can only be hinted at through a written description. The visual poetry and emotional impact of the scene depend on many factors, including the scene's placement at the end of the film. The sequence effectively closes the narrative and must bear the weight of resolving the many narrative and thematic tensions built up in the preceding three hours of screen time. Because scenes are often discussed out of context, there is a tendency in film analysis to overlook the specific placement of scenes within a film's narrative. Films build their effects in cumulative ways, each sequence adding more information, while creating gaps that may be explained at later points in the narrative. Editing decisions must consider the exact placement of a scene within the whole narrative. Discussions of shot-to-shot editing tend to focus on particular cinematic moments and often neglect this structural consideration.

The scene masterfully uses shot size, music, the glance, shot length, character placement and performance to communicate its subtleties of meaning. It makes reference to the sense of loss felt by Lady Lyndon. No words are spoken in the sequence, yet it is full of emotion and meaning. The exchange of close-ups of Lord Bullingdon and Lady Lyndon accompanied by the precise slowing down of the music contributes to a poeticizing of the narrative. Kubrick heightens and accentuates the moment through meticulous timing and the emotional use of music.

The sequence also illustrates the tedium and mechanics of operating a large estate, at both political and emotional levels. Lady Lyndon seems engulfed by her wealth and the process of administering it. Her role in society is to oversee the careful management of this wealth and to maintain the delicate balance between the classes. Under the watchful eyes of her accountant, Reverend Runt, and her eldest son, Lady Lyndon slowly, almost unthinkingly, signs each check. One can only feel compassion for her apparent imprisonment. There is nothing for her to do but to fulfill her designated role methodically. Her melancholy demeanor is the natural expression not only of a woman who has lost a lover, but also of one who can operate only within the confines of her class. The film ends on a sad, reverberating note that is appropriately wordless and ritualistic.

A final example that merits our attention is the climactic duel scene between Lord Bullingdon and Barry. The sequence is significant because it is both the dramatic high point of the film and because it incorporates a different editing style than that used in most of the film. It also mirrors the earlier duel between young Redmond Barry and Captain John Quin. Now, however, Lord Bullingdon "mirrors" Captain Quin rather than the young Redmond of the earlier scene. Bullingdon is closer to Quin in terms of his position in society and the value system he represents.

This second duel also begins differently than the earlier duel sequence. It starts on a close-up of a pistol being loaded, much like the earlier scene, but this time the film does not zoom back to reveal the pastoral landscape of which the main characters form a part. The cut to a group shot of both the main players and their seconds indicates a more dislocated and fragmented world than that of the earlier scene. In the first duel, the zoom indicated that Barry was still idealistically connected to his environment, a part of its beauty. The eschewing of the device here in favor of more fragmented stylistics indicates that Barry is no longer connected to his environment in precisely the same way. The different editing style formally implicates Barry in a more distanced, less idealistic relationship to the world around him. The fragmentation communicates Barry's disengagement from the world, just as the slow zoom earlier had connected Barry to his environment. Barry no longer inhabits the idealistic landscape of his youth; it has been replaced by a cold and unfeeling landscape that reflects the character's cynicism and world-weariness.

The sequence lasts nine minutes and is composed of forty-one shots, the shortest about 1.5 seconds and the longest lasting 36 seconds. The earlier duel is much shorter and contains only twenty-two shots. The scene is shot inside what seems to be an abandoned grange (a tithe barn) and is accompanied throughout by Handel's *Sarabande* and the ambient sound of the cooing and fluttering pigeons. The sequence is environmentally both inside and outside; light streams in, giving the feeling of the outdoors, though it is really inside a barn. The rustic, naturalistic setting contrasts with the formal, ritualistic situation.

On a thematic level, the sequence reveals Lord Bullingdon to be cowardly (he throws up), inept (he misfires the pistol) and contemptible. His victory over Barry, who fires into the ground in a futile though noble gesture, is mean-spirited. Although the viewer understands the motivation for Bulling-don's behavior, it is Barry who gains sympathy in the scene. The sequence is highlighted by an interesting moment (with a Freudian subtext) when Bullingdon fires on Barry's leg, which later necessitates its amputation. This action implies that it is not so much the "low-born ruffian" that Bullingdon resents, but rather the lover his mother has taken to her bed.

The duel sequence is brilliantly cinematic and dramatically edited to bring out all the hidden resentment that Bullingdon has felt toward Barry through-out the film. It clearly illustrates that *Barry Lyndon* contains perhaps the most sympathetic portrayal of character (Barry) in all of Kubrick's work. There is a depth of feeling for this flawed but noble character that contrasts markedly with the unemotional style of character presentation. It is a remarkable ac-complishment that Kubrick achieves this high degree of sympathy for a char-acter within one of the most stylized and distanced presentations of any of his films. The director's conception of character often involves an unemotional, ironic presentation of characters who are frequently very emotional.

The editing of the duel scene varies shot size, shot length and editing pat-terns for maximum dramatic impact. Like the scene of Barry's attack on Bullingdon at the music recital, the duel sequence has greater impact because it does not play in precisely the same style as the rest of the film. Because the predominant stylistics of the film de-emphasize the dramatic presentation, the very limited use of a more exciting editing style has greater impact. It offers a sharp contrast to the ironic distance of the rest of the film. The viewer's emo-tional involvement is crucial in making it one of the most exciting and assured sequences in Kubrick's work.

Barry Lyndon's view of the eighteenth century, beneath the surface beauty of the image, is ultimately a negative one. The film paints a portrait of a soci-ety that values wealth, position, marriages of convenience, philosophy, art, music, fine clothes, grand architecture and good breeding. But while achiev-ing what many consider an apogee of civilization, this society has lost its en-ergy, passion and intensity. It has been aestheticized into numbness and atrophy. The film seems to argue that it matters little what an era may ac-complish if in the process we lose such essential components of humanity as emotion and free will.

Barry Lyndon represents Kubrick's most profound statement on art and human relationships. It is his most fully rounded work. As much as it is about the eighteenth century, it is also about contemporary society. It offers the di-rector's most sustained analysis of male/female relationships, aesthetics, morality and social institutions. It also represents Kubrick's most focused at-tempt at creating an empathetic character. He will not delve into the com-plexities of male/female relationships with the same depth of feeling until *Eyes Wide Shut. Barry Lyndon*'s complicated and radically distanced stylistics are significant factors in creating one of the director's most emotionally in-volving films. This internal tension indicates what, at first, seems a kind of contradiction between a film's style and its thematics. In fact, this tension declares the film to be the product of a complex and invigorating artist whose work is often structured around polarities of meaning and style.

The Shining

One of the most striking features of Kubrick's screen adaptation of Stephen King's *The Shining* is its visual style. This is achieved in part by the innovative use of the Steadicam, which facilitates the extensive choreography of character and camera movement. The film may be an instance of a particular piece of technology helping to determine the specific look and length of many scenes. The use of the Steadicam does more than contribute to the film's visuals; the kinds of spaces it helps create and the character movement it facilitates are substantially different from what is normally possible with the zoom lens or with traditional camera movement.

The Shining immediately announces that its visual style is of crucial importance. It opens with expansive, aerial photography of a varied landscape and highlights the many colors and textures below. The terrain is a combination of waterways, islands, rock formations, mountains and forests. The photography is first high up, then low to the ground. Landscape images (earth tones, rusts, greens) allude to both autumn and a fecund environment. This landscape is majestic, yet the wide-angle lens creates a disconcerting visual distortion.

The view is all-consuming and completely open. Viewers feel that they are over, under and to the side. The vertiginous, forward-moving aerial shots of the opening sequence set the tone for the film. They foreshadow the emotional and visual rollercoaster ride to which the viewer will be subjected throughout. The slower pacing of the film's early sections effectively sets up the quicker pacing of the second half. As the film proceeds, it will elaborate on many narrative and formal ideas introduced in this opening section, including the exploration of space as metaphor, the idea of duality and various generic references.

The film's slow, lateral tracking with characters and the many low-to-the-ground, sweeping Steadicam movements are variations on the opening camera movements. One of *The Shining*'s most impressive features is the way it carefully sets up comparisons between the interior spaces of the hotel and the exterior maze space. The film activates these interior and exterior spaces in several complex ways. Perhaps the most intriguing interpretation of the film's spatial strategies involves reading the space as a metaphorical landscape for Jack's (Jack Nicholson) deteriorating mind. The final nine-minute sequence of Jack chasing Danny through the maze could be viewed as a metaphor for Jack's frenzied mental condition and blocked creativity.

The film's physical locations, such as the hotel and the maze, function metaphorically as characters through a process of spatialization. The notion of a mental landscape is further emphasized by the numerous dissolves and fades to black in the film. The film carefully sets up the different spaces within and outside the hotel: Jack's writing space, the Torrance living quarters, the corridors of the hotel where Danny wheels his tricycle, the Gold Room where Jack has his encounters with Lloyd the bartender, and the outdoor maze. These spaces seem endowed with specific characteristics. The careful presentation of these different spaces allows the viewer to become familiar with them. Many camera movements depict these spaces from numerous angles, in both distorted and nondistorted views. Kubrick has explored space before but never with such cerebral intent.

Viewers get an early sense of enclosed space in the scene that shows Jack driving up to the hotel in his Volkswagen. The restricted space of the car's interior is closely related to other cramped or enclosed spaces in the film such as the Torrance living quarters, which are decidedly shabby and in stark contrast to the rest of the hotel. Jack's writing area is not cramped, but it still seems to envelop the character. The space of the final maze sequence is most oppressive and invokes claustrophobia. Jack's character is clearly affected by the spaces he inhabits. Alternatively, the different spaces of the film metaphorically reflect the character's state of mind.

Many of the film's other spaces, including several hotel interiors and the opening landscape shots, convey the idea of a more open space. The slow, lateral tracking shots as Jack enters the Gold Room and the movement of character and camera through Jack's writing area are similarly expansive. The different camera movements at times convey the idea of openness and at other times they convey the idea of enclosure. The low-to-the-ground Steadicam shots that follow Danny on his tricycle might also be viewed as contributing to the sense of oppressive space, although they offer remarkably inventive views of the boy's movement. These close shots indicate that Danny is very much under observation and will have difficulty escaping this environment. The contrast between open and closed spaces is an important example of the duality on which the film elaborates. The variety of spaces and how they are shown are one way the film articulates its conception of metaphor and mental landscape.

Full Metal Jacket

Full Metal Jacket, Kubrick's long-awaited follow-up to *The Shining*, is an emotionally distanced, ironic and unsentimental work. As in Kubrick's earlier forays into the combat-film genre, it is concerned with the irrationality of war. Despite the film's attention to accurate details of presentation, it offers a somewhat abstracted view of war. Although *Full Metal Jacket* concentrates specifically on the Vietnam experience, its primary concern is the examination of aspects of human behavior that any war or conflict might generate.

Some points of comparison between *Full Metal Jacket* and the director's other films include its exploration of point of view (first person) and filmic

subjectivity, the use of long takes, deep-focus composition, camera movement, rhythmical editing, narrative structure and hyperbolic stylistics. It also
extends and deepens Kubrick's previous explorations into the nature of
human behavior.

An important aspect of the film is the blending of reality and stylization so
prominent in the director's work. The meticulous presentation of aspects of
reality is framed within a stylized, highly determined and reflexive organization. The concept of distancing, as it operates in Kubrick's work, embraces a
belief in the inherent power of illusionistic cinema.

Full Metal Jacket operates at a level of distance that hyperbolizes many of
the image and sound strategies to the point of abstraction. The film meticulously proclaims that this cannot be anything but a movie about the Vietnam
War. At the same time, the film's visual design features a heightened sense of
unreality and absurdity. Many performance and sound strategies lend the film
a further air of unreality.

The use of deep-focus moving camera is particularly arresting in the film.
In the early scenes at Parris Island, many views contain great depth of field.
The scenes of Drill Instructor Hartman (Lee Ermey) as he surveys his men,
often in a diagonal line, depend on this depth of field. They also rely on the
backward-moving camera to record the character's circular movements and to
communicate the repetitiveness of the men's routine. Coupled with the compositions in depth and long takes, these image strategies powerfully convey
the regimentation and powerlessness of the trainees.

The impact of these early scenes depends on both their truthfulness and
their stylization. These scenes of men in close confinement evoke similar
scenes in *Paths of Glory, Dr. Strangelove*, the first half of *Barry Lyndon* and the
prison sequences in *A Clockwork Orange*.

Much of the film, especially after the scenes at Parris Island, emphasizes the
physical textures of this world. This is a Vietnam of concrete, metal, black
smoke, fire and rubble—an inferno of war. In the final sequences, the abstract
soundscape created by Abigail Mead further contributes to the air of unreality. If there is a single word to describe the film's visuals (and sounds), it is hyperrealism, as opposed to the surrealism of Francis Ford Coppola's *Apocalypse
Now* (1979), the impressionism of Oliver Stone's *Platoon* (1986) or the symbolism of Michael Cimino's *The Deer Hunter* (1978). The deep-focus compositions may reveal details more clearly but they do not make the war any
more comprehensible. The lack of sentimentality offers a clearheadedness that
most combat films lack.

Simply to see more clearly does not necessarily bring greater understanding. The film strongly conveys the irrationality, brutality and insanity of war.
This theme is highlighted in the sniper sequence in the final third of the film,
which is marked by an interesting shift to the sniper's point of view. These
final episodes offer a movement into the heart and soul of the war. It is as
though viewers have been observing from a distance for the rest of the film

but now are plunged directly into its center. These sequences are also the most spectacular in the film. They are characterized by the use of slow-motion photography, increasing the distance further from the natural world. All the sniper sequences take place in shattered, burning buildings with twisted steel girders and chunks of broken concrete prominently in view. This is a modern, industrialized inferno, a hell manufactured by humans. There is no sign of the natural world.

The extensive use of slow motion here makes the discovery of the identity of the sniper (a fifteen-year-old girl) all the more surprising. The impact of these scenes cannot be overstated. The war has been reduced to its most basic elements. There is no attempt to explain the politics of the situation or why this young girl is shooting at the squad. Instead, the film is primarily concerned with the nature of violence and with how human beings react in a deadly situation where survival is the only instinct. The scene in which Joker finishes the sniper off after she has been shot by the squad is at once brutal and merciful. Still, it is a painfully difficult decision for the character to make, and it brings the spectacular sequence and main drama of the film to an uncomfortable conclusion.

The film's anti-illusionism and distanced presentation are critical to its aesthetic and narrative project. Examples of the film's self-conscious anti-illusionism occur when members of the squad talk directly to the camera. In the scene of the death of "Hand Job," the squad members stand over his dead body and carefully look into the camera; each in turn makes a comment about his dead colleague. The formal arrangement and precise ordering of each member's comment highlights the theatricality of presentation.

The scene in which a film crew interviews members of the squad at Hue City for a documentary on the war (recalling a similar scene in *Apocalypse Now*) is an example of how the fiction is shattered through a reflexive gesture. The characters' speech patterns and their self-conscious responses emphasize the supposedly extemporized nature of their comments. Many of the speeches have the repetitions and pauses one associates with improvisation. Here is Cowboy talking to the film crew: "When we're in Hue . . . when we're in Hue City . . . it's like a war. You know like what I thought about a war, what I thought a war was, was supposed to be. There's the enemy . . . kill 'em."[7]

The sequence illustrates the conflicted feelings of the squad about their role in the war. The most ironic and flippant response comes from Joker: "I wanted to see exotic Vietnam, the jewel of Southeast Asia. I wanted to meet interesting and stimulating people of an ancient culture, and . . . kill them. I wanted to be the first kid on my block to get a confirmed kill."[8] This sequence emphasizes the unreality of the war, the similarity between a filmed event and the real thing. This point was not lost on many viewers, whose experience of the war was mainly through television. A sequence with a South Vietnamese Army (ARVN) pimp and hooker takes place outside a wrecked movie theater with rows of broken movie seats in view. The decor evokes the idea of spectacle and unreality.

Much of the effectiveness of *Full Metal Jacket* depends on rhythmical shot-to-shot editing, shot composition and the activation of off-screen sound. The sequence at Parris Island in which members of the corps brutalize Pyle (Vincent D'Onofrio) with bars of soap wrapped in towels provides an example. It is a powerful and disturbing sequence that lasts only two minutes and contains six shots. This is another excellent example of Kubrick's economical narrative organization.

The scene comes after several sequences showing Pyle's humiliation by the drill instructor. The towel sequence begins after a fade to black. It is accompanied by the eerie sound of a celesta (recalling the eerie mood created by the use of this instrument in *The Shining*). In the first shot, a bar of soap is wrapped in a towel and strikes the bed. Silently, the corps moves over to Pyle's bed as a blanket is thrown over him. Each corner of the bed is held down by a recruit, pinning the man to his bed. Cowboy shoves a gag in Pyle's mouth. Everyone inflicts several blows. Joker (Matthew Modine), who has been Pyle's only friend throughout the training, inflicts several forceful blows to Pyle's body. After Joker strikes his blows, we hear Cowboy exclaim: "Remember, it's just a bad dream, fat boy!" An overhead shot reveals Joker in close-up with his hands over his ears, trying to block out Pyle's desperate cries of pain emanating off-screen.

The rhythmical editing contributes to the poetic quality and intensity of this scene. It is a pivotal moment in Pyle's transformation from a slow-witted, ineffectual trainee into an unhinged murderer. The following scene dwells on the nature of several recent assassinations in American history and the involvement of the U.S. Marines in each of them. Aside from the humor of this sequence, it reveals how strongly Pyle has been affected by the beating. This is subtly communicated by one slow zoom into the character's face, which declares that he has become unhinged. It is a formal reminder of the slow zoom into Jack's face in *The Shining*, which also signaled the character's derangement. The shot here has the same deliberation and resonance.

Another example of unusual editing occurs in the first encounter between Pyle and the drill instructor. In this scene, Hartman forces Pyle to choke himself to remove a "stupid grin" from his face. What seems at first glance to be straightforward shot/reverse-shot editing is revealed to be a sequence of shots that continually cross the axis.[9] It is another attempt to lend freshness to a well-worn device and is used effectively in both *The Shining* and *Eyes Wide Shut*.

The first part of the film, set at Parris Island, is noteworthy for many rhythmical montages of the recruits, often silhouetted against the sunset or involved in climbing ropes, nets and ladders. Viewers see the recruits double-timing in formation with Hartman calling cadence. The trainees respond in unison, often with an emphasis on military/sexual metaphors ("I don't want no teenage queen. I just want my M-14"). These scenes feel accurate and realistic. The attention to detail is exceptional. They communicate a strong sense of the repetitive monotony of training. Many scenes in this section are bridged by fades to black, contributing to the effortless, almost dreamy, flow of narrative time. Stylistically, they recall the frequent fades to black in *Lolita*.

Eyes Wide Shut

On a thematic level, *Eyes Wide Shut* is surely Kubrick's most Freudian film, as it explores the psychological terrain that drives both human desire and the death instinct. The intermingling of these investigations, often within the same scene, is apparent from the beginning of the film, when Bill Harford is called to the Ziegler bathroom during the party sequence and discovers a near-dead naked prostitute sprawled lifeless on the toilet. The scene reveals the sordid underbelly of the world the rich and powerful Ziegler represents, which will be in full view during the later orgy scene. It is an unsettling scene since we have just seen the effusive (and phony) Ziegler greet the Harfords and engage in the usual superficial pleasantries as they arrive at the party. The revelation that all is not what it seems in the Ziegler mansion is an early indicator that the film's strategies of surface and depth, public and private, and truth and deception will be crucial to our understanding of the film. Nothing is what it appears in *Eyes Wide Shut*. The film demands that viewers constantly revise what they think they know about the characters, the events and how the narrative operates.

The exploration of the sex-death connection continues in the scene in which Marion Nathanson proclaims her love to Bill in an extraordinary emotional outburst done in full view of her father's lifeless corpse. It is as shocking a moment as any in the film. The exploration culminates in the startling scene of Bill hovering over the dead body of Amanda Curran in the hospital morgue later in the film as he bends down and almost kisses the lifeless body. These are only the most obvious illustrations of ideas that are carefully woven throughout the film. As in every other Kubrick film, from such early work as *Killer's Kiss* through to such masterpieces as *2001* and *Barry Lyndon*, thematic investigations are always carefully articulated through the film's visual style, editing patterns and deliberate use of sound. The complexity of the film's visual and aural stylistics goes far beyond the description of Kubrick as being primarily concerned with creating a deep focus, long-take style of presentation. The specifics of the film's use of camera-related and editing strategies are what make it such a fascinating film to examine. The precise organization and orchestration of each scene is astonishing. Each aspect of the film's construction, from the careful use of color to the many references in the script to sight to the multiple allusions to death, all contribute new information that adds layer upon layer of meaning.

The fluid visual style is announced early in the film by the smoothly elegant hand-held moving camera as Bill and Alice prepare to leave for the Ziegler party. Many scenes benefit from the use of the hand-held, Steadicam camera since it allows Kubrick to expansively film the different spaces that emphasize the splendor and elegance inhabited by this wealthy strata of society. The various spaces such as the luxurious Ziegler home, the Somerton mansion, the Nathanson apartment and the Harford home itself are all penetrated with the views afforded by the hand-held camera. These expansive spaces are contrasted in the film with more cramped ones such as Domino's apartment and Milich's costume store, Rainbow Fashions. Other spaces in the film have the air of fantasy spaces such as the Sonata Café with its over-determined use of blue and red color scheme, or Sharkey's Café, which Bill ducks into as he hides from the man menacingly following him in Soho. Mozart's *Requiem* plays in the space of the café, again emphasizing the death theme so prominent throughout the film.

The ways in which the film's many spaces and narrative events are filmed often contribute to the film's thematics in surprising ways. The circling camera movements as Bill is interrogated by Red Cloak (Leon Vitali) at the orgy, or the sweeping camera that follows Alice as she dances with Sandor in the opening party scene are variations on the fluidity introduced early in the film's opening movement in the Harford apartment. This sense of fluid movement, however, is often contrasted with scenes that communicate a deliberate sense of stasis such as the final Ziegler "explanation" scene, which seems to tie up the film neatly but in reality may be as misleading and ambiguous as much of the rest of the film.

The film is careful to articulate different styles of editing and camera work to highlight the different realities that may be at play in various scenes. There seems to be a deliberate nonclassical, long-take style in scenes that are the most ambiguous, and a more conventional shot/counter-shot style in scenes where the meaning is meant to be clearer. In other words, the kinds of spaces we inhabit and the meanings we derive from them depend to a great extent on how the particular scene is filmed and edited, as well as the specifics of the image content and emotional use of music. There appears to be an interesting dynamic between scenes filled with ambiguities, such as the orgy scene, that incorporates moving camera and those that seem more realistic, such as Ziegler's explanation scene, that are deliberately shot in a more static and conventional way. It's as if the film deliberately wants to create a feeling of uncertainty by maintaining a flow to the action through such devices as the moving camera, and then slow things down to offer a possible explanation for some of those events. But, of course, the explanations we receive, along with this sense of stasis and an overall feeling of deadness, are ultimately unconvincing, and we are still left with ambiguities.

We have previously discussed some of the uses of the long take that are so crucial in creating the sense of enclosure and the sense of unreality that pervade much of the film. The dreamy quality and sense of unreality is also felt in the many dissolves that act as major shot transitions in several key scenes, a strategy used extensively in Kubrick's earlier foray into ambiguous narrative, *The Shining*. The use of dissolves—most strongly felt during Bill's walk through the rooms during the orgy scene as he observes the participants in various forms of sexual acrobatics—helps articulate a more subjective point of view closely tied to Bill's perceptual view. Whereas *A Clockwork Orange* relied on a strong theatrical presentation and sense of artifice to articulate its subjectivity, and *The Shining*'s dominant stylistic device was the use of a moving camera, *Eyes Wide Shut* does not seem to have a dominant stylistics. Instead, it relies on several simultaneous formal operations such as moving camera, non-classical editing, repetitions of visual, verbal and musical motifs, and a highly determined use of color in its ambition to create a subjective reality meant to reflect the feelings of its main character. It also relies heavily on theatricality, stylized decor and the empathetic use of music to create its emotional impact.

After the crucial scene in which Alice confesses to Bill her sexual attraction to the naval officer, the film begins to take on an air of unreality that is associated with Bill Harford's feelings. From this point on, the film is meant to be felt through Bill's consciousness. The first in a series of fantasy shots that periodically punctuate the film of Bill imagining Alice in the throes of sexual passion with the naval officer occurs after this confession scene. During Bill's cab ride to Marion Nathanson's apartment, where he is supposedly going to comfort the woman who has just lost her father, we encounter the first of five such inserts. These fantasy shots are generally hand-held and in slow motion, and they illustrate Alice in an imagined sexual encounter that becomes progressively more intense as Bill's jealous feelings intensify. These shots, which convey a strong emotional power and help drive the narrative forward, are always accompanied by Jocelyn Pook's strongly emotional and exotic musical composition ("Naval Officer").

A different kind of moving camera is used during the orgy scene as Bill is interrogated by Red Cloak and eventually "redeemed" by the mysterious woman wearing the feathered headdress. This scene could easily have been handled more conventionally in a series of shot/reverse-shot pairings since it involves shots of Red Cloak cross-examining Bill and shots of Bill's responses, but Kubrick deliberately avoids that strategy. Instead, he utilizes a moving camera for most of the action, in a nonclassical orchestration of shots that emphasizes the theatricality of the trial, the idea of performance and our role as observer of the action. The fake quality of the trial and the carefully arranged redemption of Bill by the mysterious woman is highlighted not only by the way the scene is filmed but also by the deliberately unconvincing performance of the woman. A closer look at this scene will reveal some important aspects of Kubrick's stylistic choices.

Bill is brought into the space of the trial, a white marble hall where he had witnessed the opening orgy ritual. Red Cloak is seated on a throne in the center of a red carpet and is flanked by a few assistants in purple robes standing on either side of him. They are surrounded by a circle of many people in black cloaks and masks. As Red Cloak begins the questioning, Bill stands in front of him and is immediately encircled by various members of the group, who block any kind of escape. Red Cloak then asks Bill the password. Bill responds "Fidelio." At this point, the camera begins to swirl behind the seated interrogator. The colors in the scene are primarily blue, black and red. The scene, of course, is already imbued with the idea of the theatrical, with the staging of the trial and the attending audience. As Bill responds to the question, there is a cut to a swirling shot from behind Red Cloak. Bill is then asked for the password to the house and there is a cut to a closer shot of Bill. Bill feigns ignorance: "I'm sorry . . . ," and there is a cut to another moving camera shot of Bill and Red Cloak from a different angle. They are more in depth now, with other observers of the trial lining the foreground of the shot. As Bill says "I seem to have forgotten it," a general murmur goes up from the standing observers while the camera continues to circle the proceedings. The Ligeti piano extract (*Musica Ricercata II*) is heard for the first time during this scene, punctuating the action with a menacing, disturbing quality that acts as a leitmotif in several other key sequences. The scene generally avoids perceptual point-of-view shots, and the swirling camera places the viewer in the position of the audience within the film watching the staged action.

As the scene develops, Bill is asked to remove his mask, which he proceeds to do. When Red Cloak asks him to remove his clothes, Bill objects. A series of shots of Red Cloak and Bill from different perspectives are now intercut, but they are all shot with the moving camera. The sequence continues to avoid any conventional over-the-shoulder pairings as it reaches its climax with the intervention of the mysterious woman who offers to redeem Bill. We do get one perceptual point of view shot from Bill's perspective before the quick zoom into the woman in the balcony as she shouts "Stop. Let him go. Take me. I am ready to redeem him." Another gasp goes up from the assembled audience. There is a cut back to a moving camera shot of Bill, and the rest of the scene plays out. Bill wonders what will happen to the woman and is informed by Red Cloak that her fate is sealed. He is then warned about the dire consequences that will befall Bill and his family if he breathes a word about what he has witnessed, or if he makes further inquiries about the fate of the mysterious woman. Only toward the end of the scene is there even a hint of shot/reverse-shot editing. The scene lasts about 5 minutes and 35 seconds and contains 42 shots, most of which involve the circling camera. It is an important scene that confirms the idea that scenes of ambiguous meaning are generally constructed in nonclassical ways in how they are both filmed and edited.

In the later explanation scene between Ziegler and Bill, shot in a much more conventional style, Ziegler informs Bill that the trial scene was staged and fabricated to scare Bill into silence. Although the trial certainly feels staged, its meaning is not at all clear. For example, we never learn the true identity of the mysterious woman. Ziegler states that she was Amanda Curran, the same prostitute Bill found in Ziegler's bathroom in the early part of the film and whom Bill has just viewed in the hospital morgue. However, this claim cannot be confirmed. There is certainly no reason to believe that Ziegler is telling the truth since he is hardly the most reliable of characters. If Bill's trial was a fabrication, why couldn't this explanation scene be another staged event meant to ensure Bill's silence about what he has witnessed? Ziegler claims to have witnessed the events at the orgy, yet there is no evidence to confirm this. There is also no reason to believe that Amanda Curran's death wasn't connected, in some way, to the events of Bill's trial and her redemption of him. Of course, this assumes she was at the orgy and is the same woman as the one in the bathroom scene. Certainly the fact that the mysterious woman in the orgy scene is played by a different actor than the actor who plays Mandy/Amanda only adds to the confusion of an already unclear situation. But why should viewers believe anything Ziegler says to Bill? He may be telling the truth, or he may be acting out of self-interest or in the interests of the wealthy class he represents. Ziegler is clearly involved in sordid activities, as the bathroom scene indicates. Yet he gives the impression of being a normal individual concerned only with Bill's welfare and with maintaining a respectable public persona that obviously hides a secret agenda involving sex and the abuse of power by very wealthy individuals. It is not a coincidence that the scenes with Ziegler are shot in a flatter, decidedly more conventional style. But beyond the idea of stasis, the scene has a quality of deadness about it, an airless quality. By associating a quality of death with Ziegler and all that he represents, it offers a kind of class and material critique. Perhaps the world of Ziegler feels dead because it is only concerned with sex divorced from feeling, sex as a spectator sport, sex that is purchased for amusement from expensive prostitutes rather than sex associated with love and feeling.

In *Eyes Wide Shut* we never know who to believe, and the status of the narrative events remains unclear throughout the film. Truth and fiction, objectivity and subjectivity, the public and the private are intermingled to such an extent that the viewer remains in a state of constant uncertainty. The opening party scene has its public face and its more hidden private machinations in the bathroom scene. Bill and Alice, two impossibly beautiful people, have a seemingly normal, happy existence, the perfect marriage, with wealth, status, and a beautiful child. Yet, during her confession scene, Alice recounts hidden urges that threaten to disrupt the life she has built for herself. In the later dream sequence, Alice reveals a side of herself that she has apparently kept hidden from her husband and perhaps herself, as she recounts events that involve her "fucking other men, so many I don't know how many . . . just fucking all these men." Throughout much of the film, Bill engages in clearly destructive behavior that could presumably lead to his death or at the very least, to the disintegration of his marriage. This handsome doctor, who we see in scenes at his practice attending to the needs of his patients, is seen being picked up by a prostitute and then attending an orgy with beautiful women engaged in a spectacle of sexual activities that certainly puts his orderly life at great risk. He is threatened with such "dire consequences" that he fears for the safety of his family. We cannot take anything at face value in the film precisely because Kubrick is concerned with the hidden state of things, those areas we hide from ourselves as well as others. Alice and Bill engage in behavior that shocks them, perhaps more than it shocks the viewer, precisely because they have lived a life on the surface and have never examined who they are, what kind of life they have, what motivates their desires and, in fact, their very existence.

Other intriguing uses of camera-related strategies involve the striking, delicate use of the zoom lens in several key scenes including the morgue scene, where the camera acts as a silent observer which seems almost embarrassed at what Bill allows himself to feel. The zoom moves in on Bill as he hovers over Amanda's body, with her "eyes wide shut," and holds her lifeless hand as he bends closer to her in an unguarded moment. What thoughts can be racing through Bill's mind? Does he regret what happened to him at the orgy? Is he somehow responsible? Could he have done something to prevent her death? Does he desire her? Can he even allow himself to feel such an emotion? Does she remind him of Alice? Of course, we can only speculate about such questions and what the character may be thinking and feeling. And what of our role as viewers of this disturbing scene? What do we think as we view this character act in such a strange way? The scene is certainly mesmerizing in its cinematic construction. Every element acts to draw us closer to the action and share in some very disturbing, possibly trangressive feelings. The viewer is not completely innocent in this scene. We are implicated in a voyeuristic act that makes us question our own attitudes to sexual desire and its connection to death. The zoom immediately moves back from the closer view when it becomes apparent that Bill cannot allow himself to feel what he is feeling.

Another carefully constructed use of the zoom occurs during the initial ritual that Bill observes at the Somerton mansion. It begins with a low-angle shot as it slowly penetrates the space of the balcony and discovers two masked individuals who both turn their heads in unison towards Bill (and the viewer), acknowledging his arrival at the proceedings. Again, the scene is not necessarily a point-of-view shot since Bill's eyes only move up in the next shot in a delayed reaction. It is our role as spectators that is being invoked by the sequence of shots. The delicate use of the zoom lens is felt again during the brief sequence when Bill arrives at his home and discovers Alice teaching Helena math lessons. In this scene Bill's consciousness is invaded once again by Alice's tale of the naval officer. All these sequences benefit from Kubrick's methodical approach to filming and cutting action in ways that not only surprise the spectator but significantly change a scene's meaning to create greater complexity. There is an effortlessness about the construction of these scenes that recalls the use of the zoom and careful cutting patterns in both *Barry Lyndon* and *The Shining*. They bear the imprint of a filmmaker who had mastered the tools of his art and was always concerned to find the most appropriate shape for his scene construction.

Another example of an editing strategy in *Eyes Wide Shut* that deserves some comment is the unusual use of 180-degree cuts that cross the axis, which are inserted at various points in the film and always involve pairs of actors. If such a formal trope were only used once or twice, it would not merit much attention, but its use several times at key points in the film indicates that Kubrick did not casually decide to use such a nonclassical gesture. It could only be used if carefully planned at both the shooting and the editing stages of the film. It is encountered for the first time during the initial meeting of Sandor and Alice in the opening party scene described earlier. When it happens the first time it is jarring and feels odd because it suddenly breaks the fluidity we have thus far encountered with the elegant moving camera. Our eye is startled by the odd positioning of the two actors, which clearly violates one of the central rules of classical continuity editing. The 180-degree cut is seen again during the first scene with Milich at Rainbow Fashions. One of the more amusing scenes in the film—along with the gay hotel clerk scene later in the film—it prefigures the theatrics, make-up and costume, sexuality, and artifice of the later orgy scene at Somerton, with its playful discovery of two Japanese men (Togo Igawa and Eiji Kusuhara) and Milich's under-age but decidedly sexy daughter (Leelee Sobieski) in various states of undress. The men, seen in their underwear and wearing wigs, claim to have been invited for some kind of tryst, although it is never stated by whom. Milich's discovery of his daughter with the men and his (mock?) horror at the tawdriness of the scene, as well as the implication that Bill "saves" the young girl when she runs from her angry father to hide behind him, indicate that the events may not be taking place, but may be Bill's imaginary projections. The shocking cut may be a subtle way for the film to create a sense that something is askew about the whole charade.

Does the 180-degree cut indicate that we have descended further into Bill's dream world? When Bill returns to Milich's store to return his costume and it is revealed that the mask is missing, a two-shot of both men again includes a 180-degree cut that crosses the axis. We encounter the strategy again during the orgy scene when Bill is walking with the statuesque, mysterious woman wearing the feathered headband. It is, of course, not accidental that all the women in the film look like Alice, very tall, thin and beautiful, since they may all be projections of Bill's unconscious.

There may be other instances of this unusual editing pattern, but these are the most prominent ones. The use of such nonclassical editing makes reference to both the dream logic of the film's construction and acts as a reflexive gesture with respect to the film's theme of looking. The idea is deeply embedded in the use of a gesture that always draws attention to itself and which acts to "wake" the spectator from the general tendency of classical continuity editing—with its reliance on spatial coherence, shot/counter-shot editing and other rules of construction—to lull the spectator with its smooth editing patterns. Continuity is only one strategy in the classical system, which argues that whatever obstacles may be placed in front of characters will inevitably be overcome, that the world is generally understandable, and that narrative closure is almost always a certainty. Spatial coherence is an important aspect of the system, and anything that disrupts that coherence and understandability is generally avoided. But modernist narrative has also created a set of conventions over the past forty years, which argues that the world we inhabit is not always understandable and coherent, and editing patterns need not present the world or the characters who inhabit it in smoothly logical ways. The fake "objectivity" of the classical system has been replaced by a more elusive, but perhaps more realistic, ambiguity.

There are also instances in the film where shot transitions are simply so masterful that they deserve some comment. An excellent example of this occurs immediately after the Ziegler explanation scene, when there is a straight cut to the mask that lies on the bed next to Alice as she sleeps. This cut is so elegantly handled and says so much about Kubrick's mastery of the medium at this point in his career that it could serve as a lesson in a filmmaking class. Shifting from the seemingly straightforward narrative space of the Ziegler scene to the more ambiguous world of the Harford home, the cut beautifully shifts the viewer's awareness and immediately plunges the viewer into a state of confusion and uncertainty. Whereas the viewer has just been privy to the logical, patriarchal world of the wealthy Ziegler and his unsavory world—a world that Bill has momentarily plunged into at the Somerton mansion and has observed its devastating effects at the hospital morgue—we are now back in a world that is not nearly as understandable. The shot of the mask reminds us that we do not have all the answers to the puzzle that Ziegler has tried so neatly to explain. How did the mask get on the bed? Did Alice find it after Bill so carefully placed it in his office cabinet when he returned from his nocturnal perambulations? If she did, what was she doing going through his private belongings? Could it be that Alice herself was a participant at the orgy? That possibility seems remote, yet her "dream," which involves "fucking all those men" certainly reminds the viewer of the Somerton orgy. The film, of course, never resolves these issues. How the mask got onto the bed remains a mystery and is never alluded to again in the film.

Thus, as in all of Kubrick's late work—certainly every film since *Dr. Strangelove* and perhaps earlier—*Eyes Wide Shut* operates in decidedly non-classical ways. Although Kubrick still utilizes elements of the classical system, he must be viewed as an artist more concerned with creating the slippery, elusive narrative that we associate with both modernist and postmodern artists. Nothing in this film can be taken at face value. No final interpretation can ever be given. Kubrick is always engaged in finding a way to create meaning that is not apparent in the script. That is why his scripts can only be viewed as a sketch for the final film. The meticulous construction of his films and his careful formal approach to camera and editing are some of the ways he brings out the subtext of a scene, which is always more important than its surface meaning. My sense is that Kubrick takes so long to shoot his films and does many takes of each shot because he wants to dig for things that are not apparent in the script. That means he must also engage in a process of discovery with his actors since they help him create the meaning that lies below the surface.

Kubrick obviously conceives of the shooting stage and the editing stage as two very separate phases of the filmmaking process. That is why analyzing his spatial and editing strategies is both a fascinating process and a frustrating one. His work may never fully reveal itself precisely because ambiguity is built into it. The notion of shifting meaning, which we will examine further in the next chapter, is never so apparent as in *Eyes Wide Shut*, certainly the most elusive of Kubrick's experiments.

The films examined in this chapter illustrate that camera and editing strategies play crucial roles in Kubrick's aesthetic. They contribute significantly to how meaning is generated in the films. Editing is a determining factor in communicating many formal, thematic and philosophical ideas and is a critical component in the narrative organization of the films. A filmmaker as concerned as Kubrick with questions of time and space could never treat the process of ordering cinematic material with casual indifference.

Above all else, Kubrick unquestionably views film as an image-oriented medium. Language is not unimportant to Kubrick's aesthetic, but his work clearly privileges the image. The excitement and stimulation viewers derive from watching a Kubrick film depend, to a great extent, on the rich and sometimes disturbing images on view. Spatial and temporal operations are at the center of what makes cinema distinct from other art forms. Stanley Kubrick's films are emblematic of that centrality.

NOTES

1. Carole Zucker, *The Idea of the Image* (Cranbury, N.J.: Associated University Presses, 1988), 97–104.

2. John Alcott, Kubrick's frequent cinematographer until his death, stated "He [Kubrick] knows exactly what he wants. If he were not a director, he would probably be the greatest lighting cameraman in the world. On the set, he works at the camera and you can learn a lot from working with him" (p. 213). In response to the question, "Is he actively involved in setting up a shot?" Alcott replied:

Yes, particularly for shots filmed with the hand-held camera, because he can see for himself what there is in the frame. He even discovered a simpler, easier way of holding the Arriflex which made it a kind of Steadicam *avant la lettre*. He's the only person I know who has managed to give it such a degree of stability. That comes yet again from the fact that he is, in his heart of hearts, a photographer, and he likes getting the best possible effects out of a camera.

From Michel Ciment, *Kubrick*, trans. Gilbert Adair (London: Collins, 1983), 214.

3. Judith Switzer, *Stanley Kubrick: The Filmmaker as Satirist* (Ann Arbor: University Microfilms International, 1983), 56–57.

4. Ibid., 58. Switzer says of the Cat Lady that "surrounded by monuments to narcissism, she reveals more than a bit of sexual excitement at being ravished by Alex, the slummy bedbug, with the monstrous phallus." Ibid., 59. The Cat Lady strongly resists Alex and strikes him with a bust of Beethoven. The woman is then violently struck (off-screen) by Alex with the giant phallus sculpture. The montage of images from the woman's paintings at the moment of Alex's blow offers interesting areas for interpretation, which I have attempted above. But to claim that the woman derives sexual excitement from the blow seems to be going too far. Although the Cat Lady is metaphorically connected to her paintings, this is not the same as being sexually excited by Alex's brutal attack.

5. Ibid., 60.

6. Quoted in Ciment, *Kubrick*, 205.

7. Stanley Kubrick, Michael Herr, and Gustav Hasford, *Full Metal Jacket: The Screenplay* (New York: Alfred A. Knopf, 1987), 85.

8. Ibid., 86.

9. David Bordwell describes some of the rules of classical continuity editing:

The reliance upon an axis of action orients the spectator to the space, and the subsequent cutting presents clear paradigmatic choices among different kinds of "matches." That these are weighted probabilistically is shown by the fact that most Hollywood scenes begin with establishing shots, break the space into closer views linked by eyeline matches and/or shot/reverse-shots, and return to more distant views only when character movement or the entry of a new character requires the viewer to be reoriented. An entire scene without an establishing shot is unlikely but permissible (especially if stock or location footage or special effects are employed); mismatched screen direction and inconsistently angled eyelines are less likely; perceptible jump cuts and unmotivated cutaways are flatly forbidden.

From David Bordwell, *Narration in the Fiction Film* (Madison: University of Wisconsin Press, 1985), 163–64.

Stanley Kubrick on the set of *Fear and Desire*. Copyright (1953) Joseph Burstyn. Courtesy of the Museum of Modern Art, Film Stills Archive.

Elisha Cook and Marie Windsor in *The Killing*. Copyright (1956) United Artists/Harris-Kubrick. Courtesy of the Museum of Modern Art Film Stills Archive.

Timothy Carey (*left, seated*), Ralph Meeker (*center, seated*) and Joseph Turkel (*right, seated*) in *Paths of Glory*. Copyright (1957) United Artists/Harris-Kubrick. Courtesy of the Museum of Modern Art, Film Stills Archive.

Peter Sellers and Shelley Winters in *Lolita*. Copyright (1962) Metro-Goldwyn-Mayer/Harris-Kubrick. Courtesy of the Museum of Modern Art, Film Stills Archive.

Sue Lyon and James Mason in *Lolita*. Copyright (1962) Metro-Goldwyn-Mayer/Harris-Kubrick. Courtesy of the Museum of Modern Art, Film Stills Archive.

George C. Scott (*left*) and Peter Sellers (*right*) in *Dr. Strangelove*. Copyright (1963) Columbia Pictures./Hawk Films. Courtesy of the Museum of Modern Art, Film Stills Archive.

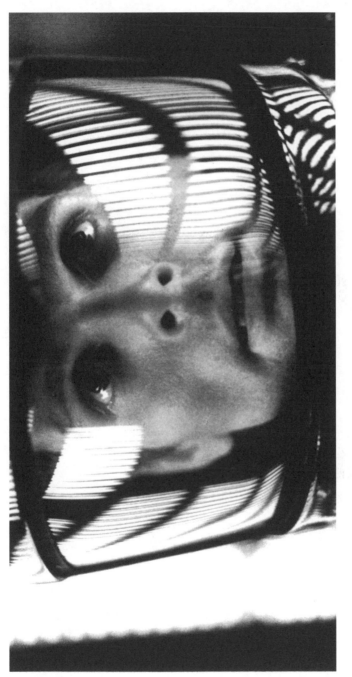

Keir Dullea in *2001: A Space Odyssey.* Copyright (1968) Metro-Goldwyn-Mayer. Courtesy of the Museum of Modern Art, Film Stills Archive.

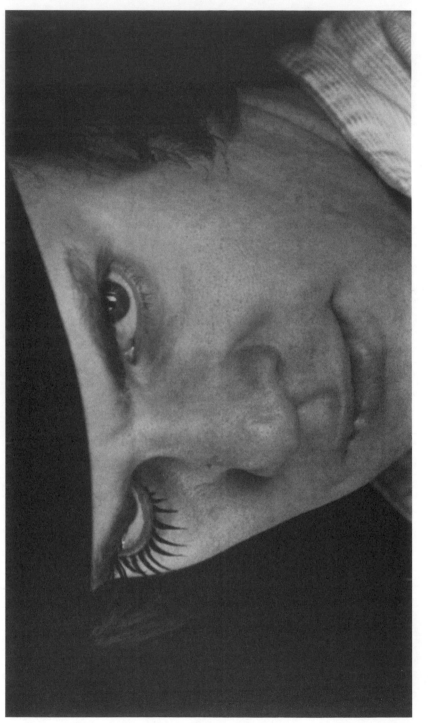

Malcolm McDowell in *A Clockwork Orange*. Copyright (1971) Warner Brothers, Inc. Courtesy of the Museum of Modern Art, Film Stills Archive.

Stanley Kubrick directing Miriam Karlin and Malcolm McDowell in *A Clockwork Orange*. Copyright (1971) Warner Brothers, Inc. Courtesy of the Museum of Modern Art, Film Stills Archive.

Ryan O'Neal in *Barry Lyndon*. Copyright (1975) Warner Brothers, Inc. Courtesy of the Museum of Modern Art, Film Stills Archive.

Ryan O'Neal attacks Leon Vitali in *Barry Lyndon*. Copyright (1975) Warner Brothers, Inc. Courtesy of the Museum of Modern Art, Film Stills Archive.

Jack Nicholson (*left*) and Joseph Turkel (*right*) in *The Shining*. Copyright (1980) Warner Brothers, Inc. Courtesy of the Museum of Modern Art, Film Stills Archive.

Jack Nicholson in *The Shining*. Copyright (1980) Warner Brothers, Inc. Courtesy of the Museum of Modern Art, Film Stills Archive.

Vincent D'Onofrio (*left*), Matthew Modine (*center, standing*) and Lee Ermey (*right*) in *Full Metal Jacket*. Copyright (1987) Warner Brothers, Inc. Courtesy of the Museum of Modern Art, Film Stills Archive.

A scene from *Full Metal Jacket.* Copyright (1987) Warner Brothers, Inc. Courtesy of the Museum of Modern Art, Film Stills Archive.

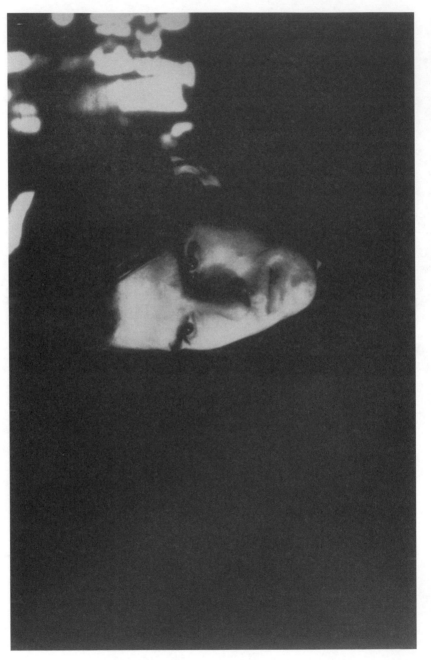

Tom Cruise in *Eyes Wide Shut*. Copyright (1999) Warner Brothers, Inc. Courtesy of the Museum of Modern Art, Film Stills Archive

Tom Cruise and Nicole Kidman in *Eyes Wide Shut*. Copyright (1999) Warner Brothers, Inc. Courtesy of the Museum of Modern Art, Film Stills Archive.

A contemplative Stanley Kubrick on the set of *A Clockwork Orange*. Copyright (1971) Warner Brothers, Inc. Courtesy of the Museum of Modern Art, Film Stills Archive.

4

Filmic Narration: Part 1

VOICE-OVER

First-Person Commentary

One of Kubrick's preferred narrative devices is voice-over commentary. *Killer's Kiss*, his second film as a director, illustrates that the director's fondness for voice-over began early in his development. The voice-over in *Killer's Kiss* begins immediately after the opening credits. The film's protagonist, Davy Gordon (Jamie Smith), stands in a train station lobby in New York City, and a voice begins to narrate what is clearly his story. This voice-over commentary marks the entire film as told through the main character's point of view. In general, the film's use of the device is rather conventional and predictable. Its primary function is to advance the narrative and provide important expository information. It also contributes an appropriate *film noir* tone, particularly in combination with the film's elaborate flashback structure. Although *Killer's Kiss* contains a rather convoluted "story-within-a-story," the flashback structure never overcomplicates the narrative. The film regularly returns to the train station and resituates viewers within the film's narrative.

The key instance in which the film attempts to incorporate a more unconventional use of voice-over involves the film's female protagonist, Gloria (Irene Kane), in an elaborate commentary about her family history. The monologue takes the form of a flashback within a flashback (since this is still Davy's story), as Gloria narrates her tale over the visuals of a ballerina performing a very intense dance sequence.

Her voice-over provides background and motivation for her character; in fact, it virtually amounts to a mini-short story set apart from the rest of the narrative. The most interesting element in the sequence is the disparity between the visuals (a dance) and Gloria's accompanying narrative. Despite the apparent disjunction between film image and voice-over, a metaphorical relationship is created between the intensity of the dance and the dramatic power of her narration, which involves the suicide of her sister and Gloria's subsequent guilt. The ballet sequence is harshly lit and performed on an empty stage with no audience visible. Its major feature is the flashy, lively editing patterns.

Although this material seems extraneous to the main narrative, it is made exciting because of the flamboyant direction. The sequence illustrates that even at this early stage, Kubrick was interested in visual experimentation and questions of narrative organization. Apart from the sheer audacity of incorporating a long monologue over the somewhat abstracted visuals, the commentary itself is not memorable. It compresses too much narrative information to be especially convincing or moving. Nevertheless, one does not expect such an early work to have the dramatic or cinematic strength of the director's more mature work.[1]

Kubrick's next serious use of a first-person, voice-over commentary occurs in *Lolita*. Humbert Humbert's voice-over is associated with five of the film's thirty-five narrative segments. The film does not employ the kind of pervasive, complex voice-over apparent in the commentary supplied by Alex in *A Clockwork Orange*. This voice-over deserves some attention, however, because it relates to a key narrative decision: the disparity between Humbert's view of the world and the spectator's. Although Humbert is the audience's narrator and guide, there are many instances in which the narrative and Kubrick's descriptive camera point to some piece of information of which Humbert is not aware (most particularly in references to Quilty).

Apart from these five instances of voice-over, there is very little evidence that the film represents the subjective presentation of its main character. In fact, the major narrative and visual structures point insistently to an objective presentation. The ironic distance between Humbert's view of the world and the presentation of narrative information is what gives the film much of its resonance and pleasure.

Lolita begins directly with the sequence in which Humbert Humbert confronts and shoots Clare Quilty. If viewers take this unexpected beginning to be the temporal present of the film's narrative, then the temporal movement "four years earlier" immediately after this first scene marks the rest of the narrative as one long flashback. But whose flashback? A final end credit informs the audience that Humbert died in jail awaiting trial for the murder of Quilty, making the film not only one long flashback but apparently the flashback of a dead man. In fact, the beginning and end of the film put into question the conjecture that the film represents a flashback originating with a particular character. Although *Lolita* appears to be narrated from the perspective of its main character, the temporal shift in the film's narrative structure is merely one aspect of its overall narrating function.

Humbert's first commentary is relatively informational and comes over a montage sequence of shots of travel immediately following the initial murder scene. Humbert describes the circumstances of his arrival in America: "Having recently arrived in America, where so many Europeans had found a haven before, I decided to spend a peaceful summer in the attractive resort town of Ramsdale, New Hampshire. Some English translations I had made of French poetry had enjoyed some popularity."

The tone is straightforward, informational, almost cheery—not the kind of writing one would do in a diary. There is no intimacy about the entry, no observation of people or the world, only expository information meant exclusively for the viewer. The extract hints that the film's protagonist is literate and cultured, a view that will be confirmed in the later extracts and the dramatized body of the film. The question of locating the film's "present" in the previous scene is important, because there is no indication that this voice is aware of the event that has just occurred on the screen (four years later in story time) or that it knows its possessor's eventual fate. This first extract is in the nature of a direct address that coincides with the time frame of the visual presentation. This coincidence of the commentary with the visual dramatization is important if one is to argue against the notion of character flashback. This is the audience's first introduction to Humbert's voice-over, and, coming as it does immediately after the previous scene of a distraught murderer, the audience is taken aback and more than a little intrigued by its vocal inflection. From what position does the voice narrate? What is its relationship to the narrated events?

After this initial introduction to Humbert's "voice," the second encounter takes the form of a journal entry. This is apparent not only because viewers see Humbert writing as they hear the words on the soundtrack but because Humbert's language has a literary, intimate quality. Humbert describes his infatuation with Lolita (Sue Lyon) and refers to his role as a secret writer of his thoughts:

What drives me insane is the two-fold nature of this nymphet, of every nymphet perhaps. This mixture in my Lolita of tender, dreamy childishness and a kind of eerie vulgarity. I know it is madness to keep this journal but it gives me a strange thrill to do so. And only a loving wife could decipher my microscopic script.

This extract comes just before Humbert's marriage to Charlotte Haze and ironically predicts her discovery of the diary. It also points to a clarity of thought about his obsession that is not always apparent in Humbert's actions. Humbert's references to madness and insanity interestingly foreshadow the character's mental deterioration in later stages of the film.

Humbert's third voice-over reverts to direct address and is clearly not a journal entry. On the soundtrack, the audience hears Humbert's contemplation of the murder of Charlotte over visuals of him loading bullets into a gun. The sound has a slight echo to it, confirming the idea that this is an attempt to represent Humbert's mental state. This is also the longest voice-over in the film:

No man can bring about the perfect murder. Chance, however, can do it. Just minutes ago she had said it wasn't loaded. What if I had playfully pulled the trigger then. [Now as if rehearsing a speech to the police] "She said it wasn't loaded; it belonged perhaps to the late Mr. Haze. She was having her morning tub. We had just finished talking about our plans for the future. I decided to play a practical joke and pretend I was a burglar. We were newlyweds and still did things like that to each other. Soon, as it happened, I called an ambulance, but it was too late!" Simple, isn't it, the perfect murder.

The commentary comes immediately after a scene in which Humbert and Charlotte have argued and she has stormed out of their bedroom. Throughout the monologue, Humbert loads the gun that he will presumably use on his shrewish wife. As he approaches the bathroom where Charlotte is drawing her bath, he continues:

She splashed in the tub. A trustful, clumsy seal. And all the logic of passion screamed in my ear, "Now is the time." But what do ya' know folks, I just couldn't make myself do it. The scream grew more and more remote. And I realized the melancholy fact that neither tomorrow, nor Friday, nor any other day or night, would I make myself put her to death.

At this point, Humbert discovers Charlotte in the act of reading his journal. Moments later, fate accomplishes what he has been unable to do: Charlotte runs out into the street and is struck by a car. This is the clearest evidence that Humbert's commentary is most often addressed to the audience ("What do ya' know folks"), rather than consisting of diary entries.

The fourth time the audience hears Humbert's voice, it is later in the narrative as he makes his way to Beardsley, Ohio. The tone is again matter-of-fact and contains a curious (and impossible) directive to "forget Ramsdale, and poor Charlotte, and poor Lolita and poor Humbert." The commentary seems to indicate that a new narrative is about to commence, rather than being a continuation of what has gone before. The direct address occurs over another montage sequence of travel images:

You must now forget Ramsdale, and poor Charlotte, and poor Lolita and poor Humbert, and accompany us to Beardsley College where my lectureship in French poetry is in its second semester. Six months have passed and Lolita is attending an excellent school where it is my hope that she will be persuaded to read other things than comic books and movie romances.

Apart from the necessary summarizing function of this commentary, there is a curious tone in Humbert's voice. The commentary gives the illusion of normality in his life with Lolita, but subsequent narrative events reveal that Humbert is unhappy, suspicious and paranoid. None of this is communicated in the voice-over. The naïve view and mystification of reality in Humbert's voice-over is in sharp contrast to the information offered in the visuals. In the voice-over, there is never any hint of the dark, gloomy relationship that engulfs Humbert and Lolita. Humbert's tone is sunny, buoyant and seemingly unaware of the fiction the viewers have been following.

This disjunction is perhaps most evident in the final voice-over. It follows several episodes in Beardsley that effectively dramatize the deteriorating relationship of Humbert and Lolita. Yet, the sunny tone continues:

The brakes were realigned, the water pipes unclogged, the valves ground. We had promised Beardsley School that we would be back as soon as my Hollywood engagement came to an end. Inventive Humbert was to be, I hinted, chief consultant in the production of a film dealing with existentialism, still a hot thing at the time.

The commentary never hints at the real reasons for leaving Beardsley, which revolve around the suspicions their relationship has aroused and Humbert's desire to find a place where he can play out his idyllic fantasy in isolation. The vocal inflection of Humbert's voice-over changes little throughout the film. It remains a generally neutral, if cultured and literary commentary, unaware of the somber events unfolding in the visuals.

In many instances, the film's descriptive camera reveals an important moment relating to Quilty but conceals the information from Humbert. One example occurs after Lolita leaves for Camp Climax, and begins with Humbert sobbing on the girl's bed. After he reads Charlotte's letter his tears turn to cruel laughter, and the camera pans left to a big close-up of a framed picture of Quilty on the bedroom wall. This is clearly a form of emphasis meant for the viewer alone and just as clearly meant to exclude Humbert. Other instances include a scene in which Humbert talks to Quilty at a hotel. Quilty is framed with his back to Humbert, and faces the camera (and hence the audience) in full view. Humbert is unaware of Quilty's identity. The staging of this sequence is emblematic of the ways in which the film's narrative excludes Humbert from most of Quilty's appearances. Quilty's other disguises, such as Dr. Zempf, are obvious to the audience but opaque to Humbert.

A disparity of information occurs not merely because Humbert is oblivious to the appearances of Quilty. It derives from a far more pervasive and all-consuming difference in world views. According to the voice-over commentary, Humbert sees the world in a very particular way that is at odds with the character's dramatized presentation. The character encountered through the commentary is, in many ways, a different person from the protagonist who populates the body of the film. Thus, the dramatization of Humbert's obsession seems to be occurring without the knowledge of the character who supplies the commentary's point of view. This difference between the generally characterless, uninvolved voice that the audience hears and the sympathetic character that it sees provides the film with added ironic distance and a level of complexity it would otherwise not have.

In the commentary, Humbert gives the impression that he is knowledgeable, wise, friendly and in complete control. In the dramatized portions of the film, by contrast, he is most often presented as one whose knowledge is at best fragmentary. He is often shown as foolish, angry and desperate—decidedly not in control.

Though Humbert is ostensibly the first-person narrator, there is clearly another narrating consciousness in the film that organizes and controls its presentation. Seymour Chatman has written: "We must distinguish between the narrator, or speaker, the one currently 'telling' the story, and the author, the ultimate designer of the fable, who also decides for example, whether to have a narrator, and if so, how prominent he should be."[2]

The difference between the film's points of view, as presented in the voice-over commentary and as presented through the overall narrating function as viewed in the narrative action, is one of the film's most interesting and complicating factors. It elevates the seemingly simple and infrequent commentary to a new level of intricacy. Taken alone, the commentary operates on only a few informational and ironic levels. Taken with other narrative strategies, however, it becomes something more. It is through such combinations that *Lolita*'s narrative takes on added complexity and becomes more playful and elusive.

Kubrick's film adaptation (1971) of Anthony Burgess' 1962 novel, *A Clockwork Orange*, represents the director's most complete experiment in presenting cinematic material in a subjective mode. This subjectivity is most apparent in the first-person, voice-over of the film's main character, Alex (Malcolm McDowell), and in the film's insistent use of visual distortion to represent the character's view of the world.

The use of subjective devices within an ironic, distanced mode provides one of the film's most interesting tensions. This tension is connected to the key strategy of using Alex's commentary as the film's narrative guide. The ironic, distanced commentary is not in keeping with the intimate tone that this kind of subjective device ordinarily creates.

The audience's introduction to Alex comes immediately after the credits, in a slow, dolly-back, opening shot. Alex gazes directly into the camera. The direct address accompanying this shot functions in combination with the gaze to set the tone and gradually implicate the spectator in the fiction. A relationship begins to be formed between the viewer and the film's protagonist. The shot calls attention to the audience's role as spectators, both through Alex's stare into the camera and the commentary aimed directly at the audience. The extreme stylization, theatricality and unfamiliar language function as distancing devices as Alex attempts to form an intimate, participatory relationship—even a kind of complicity—with the spectator. As Alex begins to speak, it is clear that the audience is in the presence of an ironic and perhaps unreliable voice, as the following extract reveals: "There was me, that is Alex, and my three droogs, that is Pete, Georgie and Dim and we sat in the Korova Milkbar trying to make up our rassoodocks what to do with the evening."

At first glance, this sounds like a fairly straightforward statement, apart from some unfamiliar terminology. But there is reason to doubt the truthfulness of the statement when the remark is compared to the image on screen. Are there four characters trying to make up their minds about what to do with the evening? There is no visual evidence to suggest that the characters are reflecting or contemplating any action. Their facial expressions suggest a numbed blankness rather than thought. They are posing for the camera. This is the viewer's introduction to the main players in the upcoming entertainment.

Alex calmly introduces the next few sequences as the ironic mode of address continues. His descriptions are humorous and witty. He sets a friendly, intimate tone that is sustained throughout the film. He continually addresses the viewer as his "brother," all the while performing the most despicable acts. There is never any hint in the voice-over that Alex is aware of the extent of the brutality dramatized in the film. Despite the lighthearted, self-consciously ironic tone of the commentary, Alex is not presented as an admirable character, although he is the only character in the film with any degree of charm.

The film goes on to present several episodes as part of the evening's violent entertainment, including an assault on a derelict, a gang fight with Billy Boy and his gang, and a brutal assault on a writer, Mr. Alexander and his wife (Adrienne Corri) in the first HOME sequence. After these sequences, Alex and his droogs return to the Korova Milkbar, and with a sarcastic flourish, Alex proclaims: "We were all feeling a bit shagged and fagged and fashed, it having been an evening of some small energy expenditure, O my brothers." This tone (small energy expenditure, indeed!) is discerned in many other fragments of the commentary, as when Alex states: "It had been a wonderful evening"—surely a perverse assessment.

Nevertheless, Alex's ironic voice-over is an attempt to form a sympathetic relationship with the viewer. Many of his comments illustrate his inventiveness with language. For example, in one scene Alex waxes poetic: "Oh bliss . . . bliss and heaven. Oh, it was gorgeousness and gorgeosity made flesh. It was like a bird of rarest spun heaven metal, or like silvery wine flowing in a space ship, gravity all nonsense now." In other scenes, Alex's role-playing is more evident, as in a scene in which he aggressively asserts his authority over the gang, taking on the role of creative artist: "I viddied that thinking was for the gloopy ones, and that the oomny ones used like inspiration and what Bog sends."

Alex is often aware of his role as narrator, and this self-consciousness contributes to the distanced aesthetics. At one point, near the beginning of the prison section, Alex declares: "This is the real weepy and like tragic part of the story beginning, my brothers and only friends. After a trial with judges and a jury, and some very hard words spoken against your friend and humble narrator, he was sentenced to fourteen years."

Alex's reference to himself in the third person is consistent with his view of himself as a performer. He is aware of his different roles throughout the film. At other points, Alex refers to himself as the "storyteller," the "long-suffering narrator," "your faithful narrator" and "your humble narrator." This irony contributes to the reflexive, theatrical aspect of the film's discourse.

At one point, when Alex undergoes the Ludovico treatment, he assumes the role of a film critic and expounds on the merits of a film that he is shown: "So far, the first film was a very good professional piece of sinny, like it was done in Hollywood. The sounds were real horrorshow. You could slooshy the screams and moans very realistic." His role as a critic takes on philosophical overtones as he proclaims: "It was beautiful. It's funny how the colors of the real world only seem real when you viddy them on the screen."

Another question raised by the voice-over relates to the time frame of the narration. There is only one instance throughout the film that alludes specifically to the time of the narrated events. This one instance suggests that Alex may be speaking from a later point in the narrative. It occurs immediately after his suicide attempt toward the end of the film. He self-consciously states: "I jumped, O my brothers and I fell hard, but I did not snuff it. If I had snuffed it, I would not be here to tell what I have told."

At no other time does Alex's commentary mention the time frame of the narrated events. In general, one is meant to take the commentary as coinciding with its visual presentation. The reference to the later point from which Alex may be narrating is supported by Alex's affable commentary, since he is supposedly "cured" of the Ludovico treatment at the end of the film. The presumption is that he will revert to his earlier violent behavior. The self-conscious revelation is also a dramatic shock that Kubrick has inserted to make the viewer more aware of the narrative construction.

Alex's references to the viewer as his "brother," "friend" and even his "only" friends, and his choice of adjectives to describe his role as narrator such as "humble," "long-suffering" and "faithful" emphasize the playful, ironic quality of the voice-over. They presume a relationship that cannot possibly exist.

It is not difficult to argue that Alex's commentary is ironic. There are many clues in his use of language, tonal inflection, attempts at deception and the disjunction between image and voice-over to indicate that the audience is in the presence of an ironic text. The gap lies between what the audience sees and Alex's description of it.

Apart from its ironic function, the voice-over operates in several other interesting ways. It is a crucial element in setting the film's tone and revealing Alex's character. It also plays an important part in several of the film's complex narrative and aesthetic strategies such as distancing, role-playing, stylization and theatricality. Additionally, the commentary summarizes action at appropriate moments and acts as a narrative guide. The audience's view of most events, based on what is seen in the dramatized portions of the film, is substantially different from Alex's descriptions in the commentary.

Another interesting first-person commentary occurs in *Full Metal Jacket* and is supplied by the film's protagonist, Private Joker. He is the construct for much of the film's analysis and argument. To a certain extent, the audience views events through his eyes, but in other ways, the film's point of view is more objective.

Joker's background is purposely left sketchy. In conventional psychological terms, he and the film's other characters remain vague. As in all of Kubrick's work, character history and empathy are irrelevant to their function within the film. Since Joker supplies the voice-over, the film gradually builds a relationship between him and the viewer. It may not be a particularly empathetic relationship, but the audience does come to know him by the end of the film. Viewers understand him not so much as an individual but as a representation of a certain kind of individual.

Private Joker begins the film as its liberal though cynical voice. He befriends the unstable, slow-witted Private Pyle (Vincent D'Onofrio) in the brilliant opening section of the film set at Parris Island. Despite his good intentions, Joker cannot prevent Pyle's violent, shocking murder of the brutal Senior Drill Instructor, Gunnery Sergeant Hartman, and his subsequent suicide. The first view of Pyle shows him as a typically naïve, slow-witted recruit. Pyle represents everything abhorrent to the military. He is physically, emotionally and intellectually as far from the ideal "killer" as anyone could be. Where the Marines are trained to be hard and quick, Pyle is soft and slow. Instead of the typical emotionless soldier, he wears a "stupid grin." One of Pyle's humiliations is a shot of him with his fatigue pants down around his ankles and his thumb in his mouth. The punishment emphasizes the military's view of him as an infant, far removed from the world of men.

Yet even this improbable misfit can be turned into a killer. Pyle represents the horror of all that is perverted and distorted about the military world. The film argues that, given enough time, training and ideological conditioning, everyone contains the potential for extreme violence, no matter how unsuited or inept. Pyle is transformed into a killer, but at too great a cost. He cracks under the pressure. In the horrific murder/suicide scene that ends the first part of the film, the sorry consequences of extreme military obsession and blindness are made clear.

In the last section of the film, Joker faces an equally problematic situation with the female sniper, in what is simultaneously a brutal yet merciful action. The film's narrative construction is thus circular and symmetrical. The film's ending recalls a key event in the opening section. The two violent situations are not identical, but they echo each other.

The character of Joker provides the film with its moral center, and our knowledge of him is gained partly through the voice-over commentary.

Joker's voice-over is heard on seven occasions. It is not as pervasive as Alex's commentary in *A Clockwork Orange*; it is more akin to the selective commentary of Humbert in *Lolita*. Although Joker's commentary is brief, it does supply an interesting mediation to the proceedings.

His voice-over is partly informational and situates the narrative action. Some extracts reveal that Joker is concerned with observing and commenting on the world around him. He wants to be a writer, and his use of language, though naive, communicates this ambition: "Parris Island, South Carolina. The United States Marine Corps Recruit Depot. An eight-week college for the phony-tough and the crazy-brave."

Some of the later extracts are purely informational and narratively motivated, such as the commentary that introduces the key sequence of Pyle's unhinged action against the drill instructor: "Our last night on the island. I draw fire watch." Brief and succinct, the voice-over tells just enough for the audience to understand the circumstances of Joker's discovery of Pyle in the latrine with the loaded rifle. Other extracts reveal Joker's state of mind and his relationship to the other recruits, whom he describes as: "salty. They are ready to eat their own guts and ask for seconds. The drill instructors are proud to see that we are growing beyond their control. The Marine Corps does not want robots. The Marine Corps wants to build indestructible men. Men without fear."

It is hard to discern if Joker's tone here is simply the naive view of a young recruit just out of high school or whether he realizes that his words sound like a recruiting ad for the military. As the film progresses and Joker sees more action, his language becomes more sophisticated, even poetic: "The dead have been covered with lime. The dead only know one thing. It is better to be alive."

Other extracts reveal the transformation brought on by his participation in the sniper's death. His final commentary reveals a clarity and acceptance of his changed relationship to the conflict:

We have nailed our names in the pages of history. We hump down to the Perfume River. My thoughts drift back to erect nipple wet dreams about Mary Jane rotten crotch and the great homecoming fuck fantasy. I am so happy that I am alive, in one piece. In short, I am in a world of shit, yes, but I am alive. And I am not afraid.

The character that viewers come to know through the voice-over complements their understanding of him from the dramatized portions of the film. The voice-over does not communicate much of the dissenting attitude observable in the character or his doubts about the fighting. Tony Williams, in a perceptive article, has stated that: "Joker's voice-overs are unindividualistic, banal, and uninspired. They anticipate that climactic moment when he will destroy what little is left of his individuality and undergo full integration in the Marine Corps' infantile 'Mickey Mouse' world."[3]

This is not the only way to read the character's commentary. Joker is obviously intelligent and has ambitions to be something other than a grunt (infantry man). He is skeptical about his role as a writer for "The Sea Tiger," the official Marines' newspaper, and understands that the truth can never be located in such a form. His experience as a journalist gives him a privileged, insider's view of the war. He is both in the war and outside of it, simultaneously a participant and an observer. He supports the war but also questions it. He detests the kind of brutality he sees in a character such as Animal Mother (Adam Baldwin) or the Drill Instructor, yet a part of him knows that in warfare these types of individuals are necessary. Joker's ambivalence about the war reflects his role as an authorial device. His function is to ask questions about modern warfare and human nature, thus helping to articulate the film's argument.

In the article cited above, Williams has stated that, "despite Joker's 'Front Page' cynicism about the conflict, the seeds of his boot camp training lie dormant within him. He will never tell the true story of Vietnam but will eventually succumb to a 'world of shit.'"[4] But is this a reasonable expectation for a filmic character? Can any one person be expected to write the true story of Vietnam? Does the "true story" of such a complex event even exist? The film neither condemns Joker for being in the war nor engages in an historical, political analysis of it. The war is a given. It is how humans behave in combat that concerns Kubrick and his coauthors Michael Herr and Gustav Hasford. The transformation of Joker from an innocent youth into a trained killer and his response to the conflict make up the core of the film. At the same time, the film does not shy away from presenting the brutality, racism and misogyny of men in combat.

The sniper sequence, set outside Hue City, effectively dominates the third and final section of the film. It is highlighted by the use of slow-motion perspectives and crucial shifts to the sniper's optical point of view. Up to this point in the narrative, views have been rendered either objectively or through Joker's point of view. In this section of the film, viewers finally get a view from the enemy's perspective, and, not surprisingly, it is a murderous view. The insistent use of slow motion here connects this section stylistically to the Parris Island scenes, which also contain many shots at variable speeds. The use of slow motion tends to poeticize the narrative and pushes it toward greater subjectivity. The slow-motion shots of soldiers receiving gunfire communicate an intensity that the film might otherwise not have. This does not in itself bring the audience any closer to the individuals involved. The same distance and ironic view familiar from other Kubrick films prevails here as well. The film likewise does not bring the viewer closer to the internal psychology of the characters. Instead, these scenes powerfully invoke the horrors of war in a way that emphasizes their spectacular nature.

The first time that the audience becomes aware of the sniper's point of view it is from a concealed position on the second floor of a building. The audience sees an AK-47 raised and aimed at Eightball (Dorian Harewood), a black member of the "Lusthog" Squad. Eightball is shot in the leg, and the view is rendered in slow motion. The second time viewers see the sniper shoot Eightball, he is hit in the arm. Slow motion once again accentuates and attenuates the pain of the character's screams. The sniper continues to fire on Eightball and each time he is hit in a different part of his body his agonized shrieks are emphasized. This slow torture and destruction of a human body become something of a spectacle through the slow-motion views. It recalls the aestheticized violence in *A Clockwork Orange*. The slow-motion shots stress aspects of the discourse and further remove the film from any sort of naturalism. They have great emotional and visceral impact.

The second shift to the sniper's point of view occurs after Doc Jay (John Stafford) attempts to retrieve Eightball's body. He too is fired on and falls next to Eightball's body. The third and final time that the film shifts to the sniper's point of view, viewers see Cowboy (Arliss Howard) shot in slow motion. Cowboy dies in Joker's arms, and this becomes the impetus for Joker's decision to go after the sniper with Animal Mother and Rafterman (Kevyn Major Howard).

It is noteworthy that the sniper is revealed to be both a young girl and Eurasian, clearly implicating the West in a kind of historical corruption. The published screenplay describes her as "a child, no more than fifteen years old, a slender Eurasian angel with dark beautiful eyes."[5] The film contends that the capacity for violent behavior is a human trait, not solely a male one. The eventual discovery of the sniper's identity complicates viewer response. The sniper challenges Joker's and the audience's conception of what constitutes a typical enemy. His cultural conditioning makes it difficult for him to associate a teenage girl with the murderous enemy. *Full Metal Jacket* does not offer a comfortable vision of the typical adversary of war. It is unsettling, but makes for a more complicated film.

Third-Person Commentary

The voice-over in *The Killing* is an impersonal voice that is masculine, deeply resonant and seemingly authoritative. When I discussed the film's commentary in Chapter 1, I focused on its function of ordering the film's complicated time structure and also how the authority of the voice-over was potentially undermined. There seems little reason to doubt the authenticity and veracity of the commentary. The commentary maintains the nonlinear time structure and transmits information related to character motivation and plot. The device serves a natural expository and summarizing function, though the time structure is decidedly unconventional.

The voice in *The Killing* is anonymous and impersonal, yet reassuringly familiar. It adds a note of documentary realism to other details of the film's presentation, such as the use of street locations and the documentary-like shots of the racetrack. It thus contributes to the already high degree of objective presentation in the film.

This level of objectivity serves to distance the viewer further. None of the film's characters is particularly sympathetic. The entire film operates at a slightly cool emotional remove. The device of the voice-over adds a note of reassurance in its familiarity, while the authoritative tone of the commentary guides viewers through the film's complicated, nonlinear structure.

Although the voice in *The Killing* is not prone to making value judgments, there is some question as to its complete neutrality. At the very least, its objectivity appears to be compromised on at least two occasions with respect to the film's time structure. I would argue that in a film of such precise and careful structuring, errors in the voice-over narration must be deliberate, a critique of the very notion of objectivity. This critique is centered on the idea that a single character can possess complete knowledge. Even Johnny Clay, the mastermind of the heist, cannot possibly know or predict that Sherry's relationship to Val will result in the tragic massacre after the heist. Similarly, Johnny cannot predict that in his haste to buy the largest suitcase he can find for the loot, he will inadvertently buy a faulty one, resulting in the films's final bit of irony on the airport runway.

The film likewise argues against the notion of complete infallibility or complete knowledge through its creation of a fallible, third-person commentary. By endowing this narrator with human fallibility, the film acknowledges the limits of human knowledge. Though not with the same force or complexity found in the impersonal commentary of *Barry Lyndon*, *The Killing* represents the beginnings of Kubrick's critique of the notion of objectivity. By endowing (ever so slightly) this most impersonal of narrative devices with personal characteristics, the film argues against the idea of complete neutrality.[6]

The impersonal voice-over narration in *Barry Lyndon* is the most substantive, if problematic, in Kubrick's work. Although this commentator (voice of Michael Hordern) is ostensibly outside the represented fiction, he plays a crucial role in the film, both as a transmitter of information (or misinformation) and in setting the film's tone. The device is problematic because this impersonal narrator is, in fact, fairly individuated and endowed with many character traits. The question of how the commentary functions as an objective device complicates and perhaps undermines the very notion of objectivity.

The importance of the commentary in *Barry Lyndon* goes further than the expository and tone-setting roles already noted. It is through the narrator that many of the audience's views and opinions about the world of the film are formed. The fact that the narration is overtly ironic (while seemingly neutral) complicates the task of deciphering many of the film's complexities of meaning.

A significant difference between the Thackeray novel and Kubrick's finished film is the shift from a first-person, autobiographical mode to a third-person, omniscient narrator. The precise nature of that voice-over and its reliability is an interesting issue in the film. There are several instances when the narrator makes claims that are seemingly unsupported by the image, but Kubrick was dealing with an unwieldy narrative when he came to adapt the novel for the screen. It would be unreasonable to expect every claim in the voice-over to be dramatized. For example, in one scene, Barry receives two *Frederick d'or* (gold coins) for saving the life of Captain Potzdorf (Hardy Kruger). During the ceremony, the colonel tells Barry, "You're a gallant soldier and have evidently come from good stock, but you're idle, dissolute and unprincipled. You have done a great deal of harm to the men, and for all your talents and bravery, I'm sure you will come to no good." There is no corroborating visual evidence for the colonel's opinion of Barry. The remark, however, is supported by the voice-over, which claims:

At the close of the Seven Years War, the army so renowned for its disciplined valor was officered by native Prussians. But it was composed for the most part of men from the lowest levels of humanity, hired or stolen from almost every nation in Europe. Thus Barry fell into the very worst of courses and company and was soon very far advanced in the science of every kind of misconduct.

The narrator seems to share the colonel's poor opinion of Barry, who does not deny the charge and blames "bad company" for his conduct. The question remains, who is to be believed in the absence of any objective visual evidence to corroborate either claim? Perhaps viewers should believe all three—the colonel, the narrator and Barry himself, in the sense that all three probably have reasons for saying what they say. Yet, viewers should remain skeptical that any one view is completely truthful.

Each character in *Barry Lyndon* has his or her particular view of objective reality, which may or may not be an accurate rendering of that reality. In the scene in question, it may be that the colonel is simply an opinionated bigot who hates the British. The narrator has many reasons for supporting the colonel's remarks that relate to his class and his function as an authorial voice. The audience's opinions about Barry's character are formed by many things throughout the film, both visual and verbal. The question of whether one voice (or character) has more of a claim to the truth than any other is one of the film's most intriguing aspects. Even Barry, who has a privileged presentation in the film, is a flawed and opinionated character. Similarly, the voice-over narration has as much or as little claim to veracity as any other character's voice in the film. The off-screen narrator, in fact, should be viewed as a major character in the film, and whatever cues audiences normally use to ascertain a character's truthfulness should be applied to him as well. What is clear about the way the commentary functions is that it is as personal a voice as any other character's. To ascribe to it a particular authority based only on the fact that it is an impersonal narrative device is a naive reading of the film. The narrator is clearly opinionated and often represents a particular eighteenth-century, aristocratic bias. He also functions, on occasion, as the authorial voice in the film and communicates many key thematic ideas.

To my mind, the narrator in *Barry Lyndon* operates in several key ways. The audience is introduced to him in the first shot of the film. In a film composed of 780 shots and running just over three hours, the voice-over figures in 128 shots. Eighty-seven shots in Part 1 of the film, subtitled "By What Means Redmond Barry Acquired the Style and Title of Barry Lyndon," contain voice-over commentary. Part 2, subtitled "Containing an Account of Misfortunes and Disasters Which Befell Barry Lyndon," contains forty-one such shots.

This is not surprising since Part 1 is the more picaresque section of the film, containing accounts of Barry's leaving home at a young age, his life as a soldier and his life as a gambler. This part requires more narrative summary. Part 2 concentrates on the "family drama" involving Barry and Lady Lyndon, Lord Bullingdon and little Bryan; it contains more dramatization.

Although one may not be justified in calling the voice-over in *Barry Lyndon* unreliable, one can still reasonably question its authority. The narration is opinionated, ironic and frequently editorializes the material. It should in no way be treated as neutral, even if it is presented as such.

The first and most obvious level at which the narrator functions is as a device to condense and summarize much of the novel's exposition. Here is an example of the narrator's admirable sense of economy:

It would take a great philosopher and historian to explain the causes of the famous Seven Years War, in which Barry's regiment was now on its way to take part. Let it suffice to say that England and Prussia were allies and at war against the French, the Swedes, the Russians and the Austrians.

Even more impressive is the sequence in which Barry escapes the English army. In Thackeray's novel, it takes an entire chapter to accomplish rather tediously what the film handles in a few shots, with the help of the following voice-over:

Here was the opportunity to escape from the army for which he had been searching. It was only a few miles through the forest to the area occupied by the Prussian allies where this officer's uniform and papers should allow him to travel without suspicion and stay ahead of the news of his desertion, which would be sure to follow.

Equally impressive is the brilliant condensation of narrative information in the scene in which Barry seduces Lady Lyndon, discussed earlier. It takes only a few moments of screen time and virtually no dialogue or voice-over to accomplish what in the novel takes three chapters. The voice-over brackets the actual seduction scene by introducing the main players beforehand and summarizing their courtship in the shots immediately following.

The ironic tone of the commentary is heard in the first extract, when Barry's father is referred to as a "departed saint," and later in references to the "grand and illustrious Frederick" and "those *brilliant* regiments." Other examples of this tone include statements like the following, which refers to a battle: "Though this encounter is not recorded in any history books, it was memorable enough for those who took part." It also appears in this view of war, which surely represents the intrusion of an authorial voice: "Gentlemen may talk of the Age of Chivalry, but remember the ploughmen, poachers and pickpockets whom they lead. It is with these sad instruments that your great warriors and kings have been doing their murderous work in the world."

Viewers are justified in questioning the authority and neutrality of the voice-over. It represents an individuated, privileged point of view. At one point, viewers are informed that the protagonist "could hardly have fallen into worse circumstances than those [in] which . . . [he] found himself. But fate did not intend he should remain long an English soldier." This is typical of the moralizing tone the narrator often takes and the foreshadowing of narrative events to come. The narrator significantly predicts the death of little Bryan and Barry's own end:

Barry had his faults, but no man could say of him that he was not a good and tender father. He loved his son with a blind partiality. He denied him nothing. It is impossible to convey what high hopes he had for the boy; and he indulged in a thousand fond anticipations as to his future success and figure in the world. But fate had determined that he should leave none of his race behind him. And that he should finish his life poor, lonely and childless.

This is not the only time the narrator acts to dissipate the surprise of the ensuing narrative. In an earlier scene, the audience is informed: "But he [Barry] was destined to be a wanderer, and the battle with Quin sent him on his travels at a very early age, as you shall soon see."

Kubrick himself has commented on this aspect of the film. In an interview with Michel Ciment, he stated:

Barry Lyndon is a story which does not depend upon surprise. What is important is not *what* is going to happen next, but how it will happen. Another place in the story where I think this technique works particularly well is where we are told that Barry's young son Bryan is going to die at the same time we watch the two of them together. In this case, I think the commentary creates the same dramatic effect as, for example, the knowledge that the *Titanic* is doomed while you watch carefree scenes of preparation and departure.[7]

In this same interview, the director claimed that the "unreliable" narrator in the novel would not work in the film because of the "objective reality" of the film image. It is interesting that Kubrick himself sees his narrator as reasonably reliable.

Apart from his functions of narrative summary, ironic commentary and foreshadowing of events, *Barry Lyndon*'s narrator acts in what I call an editorializing way. He is very opinionated, and it is perhaps this bias that has led some writers to call him "unreliable." The tender, romantic scene between Barry and the German woman with whom he spends a few nights is undercut by this intrusive voice-over: "A lady who sets her heart upon a lad in uniform must prepare to change lovers pretty quickly. This heart of Lischen's was like many a town and had been stormed and occupied several times before Barry came to invest it."

Another example of the narrator's bias comes after Lady Lyndon's suicide attempt: "Though she succeeded in making herself dangerously ill due to the very small amount which she swallowed, this nevertheless caused an intervention from a certain quarter which was long overdue." The intervention of Bullingdon is long overdue to a narrator who shares the same value system and ideology as Bullingdon. The narrator views the intervention as necessary not because of the illness of Lady Lyndon but because Barry is squandering the Lyndon fortune. The narrator's concern is motivated by class and property. That the narrator has opinions and is very much an aristocratic voice in the film is beyond question. That it is necessarily an unreliable voice is less certain.

Much of the voice-over is informational and reasonably accurate in its descriptions. The gambling sequences with the chevalier, in particular, bear out the narrator's depiction of events. Other sequences, though not contradicting the veracity of the narrator, lend only mild support to his descriptions. Take the following instance:

The Prussian service was considerably worse than the English. The life that a private soldier led was a frightful one. Punishment was incessant and every officer had the right to inflict it. The gauntlet was the most common penalty for minor offenses; the more serious ones were punishable by mutilation or death.

The visual evidence to support this verbal claim is one shot of a Prussian soldier walking through this human gauntlet. It seems to bear out the narrator's claim, if in a kind of visual shorthand. Upon reflection, however, the punishment shown does not seem particularly severe. The narrator's description sounds much worse than the visualization of it. There is no visual corroboration at all of his further claims of "mutilation or death." On the evidence of the visuals alone, the Prussian army seems no worse than the English. What the audience hears, in fact, is an opinion delivered as if it were an incontestable fact. If viewers acknowledge that the narrator often speaks for the aristocratic class in the film, then his motives are more understandable. His chauvinistic claims about the English army are precisely what one would expect from someone of his class. There can be no doubt that he has a particular stance and ideology. Once the narrator's value system is recognized and acknowledged, it is easier to understand how he functions within the film.

This impersonal narrator is, in fact, a very personalized character in the film. His perceptions are colored with the particular bias of the aristocratic society to which Barry aspires. His editorializing, of course, may also stand in for the nineteenth-century views of Thackeray rather than the very twentieth-century views of the director. The narrator, feigning objectivity, disapproves of many of Barry's actions and is often quite moralistic. He exhibits strong opinions about English and European society of the eighteenth century and cannot be taken as neutral. The commentary also may function as a critique of the idea of objectivity. Third-person voice-over has traditionally been viewed as a more objective, less opinionated kind of commentary than first-person. Because he is not part of the fiction, one might assume that the narrator observes events with a kind of incontrovertible wisdom. The device often works well as an authorial voice, not because it necessarily has this wisdom and truthfulness, but because audiences believe it to be a more neutral mode of narration.

Kubrick has taken a device associated with nonfiction film and certain types of fiction film and challenged the popular understanding of it. Michael Hordern's narration is civilized, familiar and comforting to the viewer. On the surface, it represents the same civilized qualities as the people dramatized in the film. But *Barry Lyndon* argues that the superficial values of this society are always present under the guise of an appreciation of beauty and the amassing of wealth. Below this surface lies a flawed, petty society that has lost its humanity to a structured order of behavior and decorum. Similarly, on the surface, the third-person, objective narrator offers the reassuring tone of one who could not possibly be anything but honest and trustworthy. In fact, he is the perfect representative of his class, displaying a similar, flawed world view. The film endows this third-person narrator with character traits and biases, but not to mislead the audience. If anything, the device is meant to sharpen viewers' understanding of how meaning can be generated in this way. The film is an acknowledgment that the "objective" world can be experienced and described only by an individual consciousness, subjectively. No one—not even an omniscient narrator—can exist in the world without bias and an ideological point of view. The functioning of the commentary is another illustration of how complex Kubrick's film is and an interesting critique of the concept of objectivity—a critique not done in isolation but amplified and combined with many complex image and sound strategies.

NOTES

1. On some levels the film is quite accomplished. It is interesting in terms of its overall visual style, the depiction of the boxing and underworld milieus, the metaphorical associations of violence and sexuality, and the effective use of its New York City lo-

cations. There is also a memorable, apocalyptic chase over the urban landscape that culminates in a dynamically edited fight incorporating mannequin parts. Apart from the ballet sequence, however, the voice-over commentary is one of the film's most routine components.

2. Seymour Chatman, *Story and Discourse: Narrative Structure in Fiction and Film* (Ithaca, N.Y.: Cornell University Press, 1978), 33.

3. Tony Williams, "Narrative Patterns and Mythic Trajectories in Mid-1980s Vietnam Movies," in Michael Anderegg, ed., *Inventing Vietnam: The War in Film and Television* (Philadelphia: Temple University Press, 1991), 125.

4. Ibid., 122–23.

5. Stanley Kubrick, Michael Herr and Gustav Hasford, *Full Metal Jacket: The Screenplay* (New York: Alfred A. Knopf, 1987), 113.

6. Once again, this may have its roots in Kubrick's early years as a nonfiction filmmaker and photographer. He, better than most, knew the extremes of manipulation inherent in both these forms.

7. Stanley Kubrick, quoted in Michel Ciment, *Kubrick*, trans. Gilbert Adair (London: Collins, 1983), 170–71.

5

Filmic Narration:
Part 2

FILMIC SUBJECTIVITY

There are many approaches to problems of cinematic point of view, some valuable, others less so. Film theory in this area has been influenced by several lines of inquiry outside the field. Jonathan Culler's summary of the range of critical approaches in literary studies outlines methodologies that have often been appropriated by film studies:

Limiting oneself to the obvious cases, there is the work of the Russian Formalists, particularly Propp and Schlovsky; an American tradition, running from Henry James's prefaces, through Lubbock and Booth, to modern attempts at synthesis such as Seymour Chatman's *Story and Discourse*, has been especially concerned with the problems of point of view. French Structuralism has undertaken the development of narrative grammar (Barthes, Todorov, Bremond, Greimas, Thomas Pavel, Gerald Prince) and description of the relations between story and narrative (Genette). . . . There is considerable variety among the traditions, and of course each theorist has concepts or categories of his own, but if these theorists agree on anything it is this: That the theory of narrative requires a distinction between what I shall call "story"—a sequence of actions or events, conceived as independent—and what I shall call "discourse," the discursive presentation or narration of events.[1]

According to Edward Branigan, "subjectivity in film depends upon linking the framing of space at a given moment to a character as origin."[2] Branigan has gone on to state:

The link may be direct or indirect. In the POV [point-of-view] structure, it is direct because the character is shown and then the camera occupies his or her (approximate!) position, thus framing a spatial field derived from him or her as origin. In character "projection," however . . . there is no coincidence of space, rather space is joined to a character by other logical or metaphorical means. What is important, therefore, in determining subjectivity is to examine the logic which links the framing of space to a character as origin of that space.[3]

Branigan has concluded that three variable and three invariable conditions exist for subjectivity in cinema: "The types of subjective narration depend upon three variables: time, frame, and mind. The remaining three elements of representation—origin, vision, and object—are invariant for all types of subjectivity in the classical film."[4]

Branigan's description is not appropriate for analyzing every kind of filmic subjectivity. One thinks, in particular, of complex examples found in the films of experimental filmmakers such as Stan Brakhage or Maya Deren. Nonetheless, Branigan's categories are helpful in examining contemporary narrative film, even though his analysis is primarily concerned with the classical Hollywood model. At the very least, one can gauge how some contemporary narratives present filmic subjectivity differently from earlier models.

Jean Mitry has also catalogued the different forms that filmic subjectivity may take. Here is Stephen Heath's paraphrase of Mitry:

Subjective images can be many things; Mitry, for example, classifies them into five major categories: the purely mental image (more or less impractical in the cinema); the truly subjective or analytical image (i.e., what is looked at without the person looking), which is practical in small doses; the semi-subjective or associated image (i.e., the person looking and what is looked at, which is in fact looked at from the viewpoint of the person looking), the most generalizable formula; the complete sequence given over to the imaginary which does not raise special problems; and finally the memory image, which is in principle simply a variety of the mental image but, when presented in the form of a flash-back with commentary, allows for a specific filmic treatment which is far more successful than in the case of other mental images.[5]

Kubrick's films use many devices to present character subjectivity, and his work is a good illustration both of Mitry's catalogue of subjective images and Branigan's conditions for subjectivity. One of the most commonly used visual cues to signal the presence of a subjective view, the point-of-view (POV) shot is a key element in Kubrick's cinematic lexicon to help anchor a film to an individual character. The perceptual or optical point-of-view shot is optically positioned or framed to stand in unquestionably for a character's vision. According to Stephen Heath, the optical POV shot is primarily concerned with space:

The point-of-view shot includes "the semi-subjective or associated image" (its general mode) and "the truly subjective or analytical image" (its pure mode, as it were) in that classification but not necessarily any of the other categories (a memory sequence, for instance need not contain any point-of-view shots); what is "subjective" in the point-of-view shot is its spatial positioning (its place), not the image or the camera.[6]

Early in Kubrick's career, as he was defining his style, he experimented with the POV shot in several films. *The Killing* incorporates only one significant perceptual point-of-view shot, but it is so prominent that it deserves some comment. The film reserves its one crucial POV shot for George Peatty. The shot occurs during the final, apocalyptic massacre at the gang's hideout where the gang awaits Johnny's arrival with the loot. Instead, they are violently interrupted by Sherry's lover, Val, and another hood (Joe Turkel). After Val shouts out "Where's the jerk?" there is a cut to George, who responds, "he's right here" while firing his gun at Val. Then Val returns the fire with his shotgun and we cut back to George returning the fire. Cut again to Val falling down and then cut to a frontal shot of George, gun in hand, after he has received Val's gunfire. This is followed by a hand-held, medium POV shot from George's perspective as he walks through the apartment. The moving view hovers over the bullet-riddled bodies until George's hand comes out from behind the camera space to open the door. The shot lasts 23 seconds. It is accompanied by a jazz score and the sound of George's breathing.

Stylistically and thematically, it is a well-motivated shot. It penetrates the space in a qualitatively different way than the smooth tracking shots most often used in the film. As the world erupts into the chaos of the massacre, the film appropriately reverts to a hand-held, individualized POV shot. The shot is not followed by George's reaction shot. There is no particular reason why George's view should be privileged in this way, other than the fact that a relationship exists between him and Val and that George's weakness of character is ostensibly responsible for the massacre. George is also one of the most interesting and sympathetically drawn characters in the film.

In *Paths of Glory*, Kubrick's next film, Kubrick creates filmic subjectivity primarily through the use of perceptual point-of-view shots, most often associated with the character of Colonel Dax (Kirk Douglas). The contrast between Dax's tour of the trenches and General Mireau's (George Macready) tour discussed earlier is an example of how the film uses a stylistic device to create sympathy for a character's belief system. When Mireau inspects the trenches, the film depicts the action in several shots of the character walking toward the camera as it dollies backward. Viewers do not get a shot from the character's point of view to depict his field of vision. The closest the camera comes to sharing the physical view of the generals is when Mireau looks at Ant Hill through a pair of binoculars. The generals' view is thus mediated by a mechanical device and lacks humanity.

In contrast, Dax's tour of the trenches is an extended sequence with slow camera movement that continually cuts between what Dax sees and shots of him walking toward the camera. The first shot in the sequence is a POV moving-camera shot through the trenches (*what* a character sees). It is not until shot two that Dax is revealed to be the origin of the preceding point-of-view shot. But rather than begin with the traditional ordering (first a shot of the character looking, followed by a shot of what the character sees),

Kubrick reverses the two shots. There are eight shots in the sequence. Each of Dax's POV shots is intercut with a frontal shot of him as he walks toward the camera. The sequence ends with Dax, having conducted his tour, looking through a pair of binoculars as Mireau had done, but this view through the optical instrument is withheld. Dax's view is most often associated with his men. Since viewers have shared this view in the preceding eight shots, it needs no mechanical mediation. His is the more human view.

Dax's tour of the trenches has a different status than Mireau's, which indicates that Dax has a different relationship with his men. The use of point of view reflects the film's ideological and emotional sympathies for the enlisted men. Perceptual point of view is used here to share the character's physical view and to make the audience endorse the character's ideas ("views"). The film sympathizes with Dax's politics and his humanism. By privileging Dax's perceptual point of view (none of the generals is ever accorded this privilege), the film also aligns itself with Dax's ideas. Here is an early, sophisticated use of point of view to gain audience sympathy for a character.

We will now turn to a more detailed examination of filmic subjectivity in the four Kubrick films in which this concept is most central: *2001: A Space Odyssey, A Clockwork Orange, The Shining* and *Eyes Wide Shut.*

2001: A Space Odyssey

2001 represents Kubrick's most ambitious presentation of filmic subjectivity, most prominently in the Star-Gate sequence and the final episode of Dave Bowman in an isolation room. These sequences evolve out of a film that for most of its running time has not presented the subjective vision of any one character. In its first two parts, "The Dawn of Man" and "Moon" segments, *2001* offers a largely objective mode of presentation. It moves through a transitional stage in Part 3, aboard the *Discovery*, toward a more subjective rendering. Part 4, "Jupiter and Beyond the Infinite," develops into a full-blown subjectivization of Bowman's journey through the cosmos and his ultimate transformation into the Star-Child.

In stylistic and visual terms, there is also a movement from the more three-dimensional, illusionistic presentation style of the film's first half, to the more abstract, flatter visual style of the Star-Gate sequence. The idea of abstraction continues into the final episode, which relies on a fractured, nonlinear narrative structure and challenges traditional notions of time and space. The abstraction in this final episode relies more on upsetting conventional notions of editing than on the abstract, visual stylistics found in the Star-Gate sequence. The film's movement toward abstraction is thus to be understood both in visual and narrative terms.

Before I discuss the final sections of the film, some comment must be made about the crucial middle section that takes place aboard the *Discovery*. This section is important in that it serves as the transitional stage in shifting the film from its objective trajectory to a more subjective one. The section includes several sequences involving HAL's point of view and the first attempts to associate subjective point of view with Bowman.

One interesting sequence involving HAL shows Dave and Frank having a conversation inside a sound-proof pod about a navigational error that HAL may have made. The sequence contains five shots. It begins with a shot of the two astronauts seated and facing each other inside the pod. Their conversation concerns HAL's "error" in predicting the failure of the Alpha Echo 35 unit and the consequent necessity of disconnecting the computer if it proves to have made such an error. The shot is a static long take lasting almost two minutes. HAL's eye is visible in the center background of the shot outside the space where Dave and Frank are engaged in conversation.

As the two men continue their dialogue, seemingly outside HAL's earshot, there is a cut (shot two) to a closer view of HAL's eye; then a cut back (shot three) to the original framing of shot one. The computer's presence is subtly introduced by the cutaway, although it is still unclear what the significance of the cutaway is; it may be simply a visual reminder of HAL's presence. It is not yet clear that HAL's interaction with the two men will become the crucial dynamic of the sequence. There is a cut to shot four and a big close-up of HAL's eye. The additional background sound here indicates that the perspective is no longer from inside the silent space of the pod. The camera is now physically closer to HAL. Then, in a startlingly beautiful moment, there is a cut to a silent close-up (from HAL's point of view) of Frank's lips, screen right. Then the camera pans left to Dave, back right to Frank, and finally left again to Dave. It should be noted that after this shot, the original film was followed by the title card reading "Intermission," providing a tantalizing end to the first part of the film.

The audience shares the computer's point of view, and it is still a surprise, even though it has been prepared for by the earlier insert of HAL. The shock of recognition and discovery that the audience feels at this point is one of the film's great moments. The precision and subtlety of the sequence, achieved in a mere five shots, is masterful. The sequence ends with a cut on silence to the next shot, which begins in total blackness to reveal an exterior view of the ship. This is one of the first times in the film that the audience shares a character's point of view. Surprisingly, however, it is not an astronaut but the computer HAL that serves as the link to increased character subjectivity.

HAL remains the most sympathetic and rounded character in the film, and the shift to his point of view in such sequences is not totally unexpected. These scenes move the film steadily into a subjective mode and into a view through an individual consciousness, if only momentarily. Scenes such as this are important in that they prepare the audience for the full-blown subjectivity of the final two sequences of the film, in which Bowman's consciousness becomes the film's center.

These sequences individualize and humanize the character of HAL and contribute to the film's ironic tone. In a film that generally operates in a fairly abstract, distanced mode, the audience feels sympathy for HAL when he is finally disconnected. None of the other characters in the film is ever presented with this degree of empathy. Though Bowman becomes the conduit of the film's most sustained and intense subjectivity, the viewer does not enter into an empathetic relationship with him. It is an interesting reversal that the computer is the most human character in the film.

There is also a reversal of expectation in the presentation of Bowman's subjectivity. Although Bowman is the character whose point of view becomes the focus of the Star-Gate sequence, he remains a remote character. The audience learns less about his feelings and inner life than we do about HAL's.

The gradual shift to Bowman's point of view comes in the sequence after the death of Frank, when Bowman is propelled back into *Discovery* from space by opening the hatch door's explosive bolts. The prominent sound of the character's breathing signals the shift to a more personalized point of view. Bowman walks to the interior of HAL's brain (Memory Logic Center), but the camera does not resort precisely to his perceptual point of view. It follows him, is in front of him, beside him, below him, and above him. It is positioned everywhere, in fact, except his precise optical point of view. The proximity of the camera to Bowman and the insistent sound of his breathing effect a closer association with him.

The disconnecting of HAL acts as a bridge to the subjectivity of Part 4, "Jupiter and Beyond the Infinite." Strictly speaking, this is not a subjective sequence. Nonetheless, the audience is intensely involved in the scene, both visually and emotionally. It is with Bowman physically (spatially and aurally) with each turn of the screw as he proceeds to terminate HAL. This sequence accomplishes a movement toward the greater humanization of both HAL and Bowman. There is greater empathy here than at any other point in the film for HAL, through the poignant dialogue and his pathetic little song ("A Bicycle Built for Two"), and Dave Bowman, because he quits his role of intellectual automaton.

Bowman has finally been moved to action. He even displays emotion during this sequence and demonstrates his worthiness to participate in the upcoming, privileged journey of discovery. The blank, subdued nature of his character indicates his suitability for this role. A stronger, more individuated character would not so easily allow the audience to share in the ensuing subjectivity of the final thirty minutes of the film. Bowman's blank personality acts as a kind of *tabula rasa* onto which viewers can project and partake. Through him, they can participate in the character's journey.

The film's final section, "Jupiter and Beyond the Infinite," attempts to involve the viewer in Bowman's experience of cosmic discovery. Though Bowman is the instrument of the film's most intense character subjectivity, he remains generalized and unindividuated. The film is most ambitious in its combining the highest degree of subjectivity with an individual who can somehow stand in for all viewers. This choice presumes a radical conception of film narrative and character. The sequence pushes the film to a new level of involvement, which is filtered through an individual, subjective consciousness. It achieves a mythopoeic level as a journey of discovery and renewal that all viewers can share with the character.[7]

The most critical image in expressing Bowman's point of view in the Star-Gate sequence is that of the eye. Shots of Bowman's eye are repeatedly intercut with images of what Bowman sees or experiences. His visionary journey is not represented through any conventional chain of point-of-view shots. The sequence contains abstracted landscape imagery, freeze frames of Bowman's face, repeated shots of his pulsating, colorized eye and colors and shapes produced by the slit-scan device. These are meant to merge Bowman's journey through the cosmos with his interiorized, subjective experience of that journey. Bowman's journey is illustrated with images that transcend the viewers' experience of landscape and with abstractions that seem to have no origin in the objective world. Bowman is not merely seeing the universe, he is experiencing it. The film attempts to create an involving subjective experience that strains not only the limits of narrative cinema, but the audience's understanding of filmic subjectivity. If this strikes some viewers as more than a narrative film can bear, viewers can at least applaud Kubrick's ambition.

Although music and sound play crucial roles in this sequence (and in the entire film), it is the sense of sight that is most privileged. Above all, *2001* is a visual experience. Bowman's cosmic journey is primarily a visual record of what he experiences, and the film resorts to a perceptual point of view to communicate the character's perspective cinematically. The key structuring device is the repetition of shots of Bowman's eye, which stress even further the visual nature of the sequence. Along with optical point-of-view shots, the film resorts to nonnarrative strategies of abstraction to present the journey.

The sequence strains narrative convention and can be taken as a grand reflexive statement about the cinema since the necessary condition for all cinema is the visual. It is primarily through the camera that the extraordinary nature of the world is revealed. Kubrick's immersion in the film's technical wizardry and his involvement in the conception and design of the film's special effects confirm the view that he regards film as a mechanical art. The film's concerns are primarily perceptual, but in terms of perception as knowledge. We as humans can *know* the world. We can penetrate the mysteries of the universe through a greater awareness of what is around us. If we open up our senses, we can experience the extraordinary. The Star-Gate sequence in *2001* represents Kubrick's most sustained and aesthetically ambitious meditation on knowledge through perception and on the ability of technology and art to reveal that knowledge.

The final sequence shows Bowman and his space pod inside a room decorated in what appears to be eighteenth-century decor yet is enveloped in a kind of clean, sterile modernity. The question of point of view is just as tantalizing and enigmatic here as in the Star-Gate segment. The temporal and spatial shifts are even more difficult to follow, and there is a kind of ambiguity built into this sequence that even the Star-Gate sequence does not contain. Here is a brief description and analysis of the sequence; all shot transitions are cuts. Several shots of Bowman's blinking, colorized eye are followed by:

Shot 1   Long shot of the room from inside the space pod, representing Bowman's perceptual point of view.

Shot 2   Close-up of Bowman's trembling face through the reflecting glass of the space pod window.

Shots 3–5   Three long shots of the room from different positions inside the room, with the space pod in each shot.

These three shots cannot represent Bowman's perceptual point of view. The theory that perhaps Bowman is in a kind of observation room (made more precise in the novelization of the film) gains some weight here as the music and sounds give the impression of electronic "voices." The rapid shots from three different perspectives may possibly represent "alien" points of view. Although the audience never sees anyone else, the idea of a presence is communicated.

Shot 6   Bowman's face once again in the same set-up as shot 2.

Shot 7   Shot from same perspective as shot 1, from inside the pod. This time Bowman is shown full figure, still in his space suit in the space of the room. He is looking at the camera (himself? the pod? the spectator?).

This is an important moment in the sequence because the audience has a shot (presumably) of Bowman inside the pod (at a particular space and time) looking at himself in another space and time. Bowman, outside the pod, is also looking back at the camera. Has the spectator now been substituted for Bowman inside the pod? The sequence begins to suggest that it will be organized around the gaze, off-screen space and elliptical cutting. The audience's understanding of spatial and temporal continuity now begins to be seriously undermined.

Shot 8   A closer view of Bowman (3/4, knees-up shot) inside the room. He still looks at the camera (the pod? his other self? the spectator?).

Shot 9   A close-up of Bowman (same set-up as shot 8). Bowman has already visibly aged.

Shot 10   Long shot of the empty room with Bowman visible in the right side of the frame.

The ambiguity in shot 8 creates a participatory role for the viewer, as in the Star-Gate sequence. At whom is Bowman looking? It is unclear. Shot 10 cannot represent Bowman's point of view from the previous shot since he is in the frame. But the fact that the pod has suddenly disappeared means that the space/time continuum, as it is normally understood, has clearly been ruptured. The viewer's sense of a linear progression of time and space is undermined. During the shot, Bowman continues to walk back to the camera through the space of the room.

The audience clearly cannot rely on its cognizance of traditional point-of-view coding (a shot of a character looking, then a cut to a shot of what the character sees) to navigate through this territory. In the first two shots, the shot/counter-shot sequence is reversed, beginning instead with a shot of the space that the character sees, followed by a shot of the character looking. This is determined retroactively.

Shot 10 continued	Bowman walks through the room. The sound of his breathing becomes prominent. He walks into the depth of the frame. He is still in his suit. The camera does not move. He is in the middle of the empty room, except for a few pieces of furniture and some wall paintings, as the shot ends.
Shot 11	3/4, frontal shot of Bowman. He looks not directly at the camera but slightly off to the right side. He does not seem to be in the middle of the room any longer. There has been a temporal ellipsis from shot 9 to shot 10. He seems to see something and looks off-screen.
Shot 12	A circular panning shot, left to right showing an ornate bathroom. This represents Bowman's perceptual point of view.
Shot 13	Close-up, side view of Bowman moving into the space, right to left.
Shot 14	3/4 shot of Bowman, as he continues his movements and his exploration of the space. His breathing is audible. Suddenly (retroactively) the audience realizes that it is looking at a mirror image as the "real" Bowman walks partially into the right side of the frame.
Shot 15	Close-up of Bowman's head in the mirror, still in his space helmet, and part of the real Bowman extreme right of the frame. He contemplates himself, no doubt surprised at how he has aged.

The self-absorption apparent in these shots adds to the notion of cinematic reflexiveness. As Bowman contemplates himself, the film contemplates itself. Kubrick's radicality is shocking because he incorporates nontraditional cinematic rhetoric within a commercial entertainment.

Shot 15 continued	Bowman hears something off-screen; he glances right and turns his head in that direction.
Shot 16	Short, moving POV shot as Bowman moves in the direction of the bedroom.
Shot 17	Close-up (head and shoulders) frontal shot of Bowman. He walks toward the camera.

Shot 18   Moving POV shot, continuing the perspective of shot 15. The breathing
               continues. The camera movement ends, and Bowman sees someone eat-
               ing at a table with his back to the camera.

Shot 19   Close-up reaction shot of Bowman in space suit, presumably seeing an
               older self (later stage of development). The breathing stops. Bowman's
               mouth is open; he seems amazed.

Shot 20   Same view as shot 17. It is no longer Bowman's point of view (in space
               suit); it has now turned into the spectator's point of view.

This is another manifestation of how the film manipulates point of view, in
what I refer to as dissolving point of view. The sequence sets up a view of
what Bowman sees (shot 18), cuts to Bowman looking (shot 19) and cuts
back to the same view of what Bowman was looking at; now it no longer
represents Bowman's point of view. It has dissolved, disappeared, been transformed into something else. The sequence upsets the audience's understanding of cinematic rhetoric to such an extent that it can no longer trust its
understanding of how to read a series of shots. The concept of how to read a
point-of-view chain of shots has been challenged. It is no longer clear who is
doing the looking, though Bowman is the only visible participant. Even this
belief proves false; there is more than one Bowman in the sequence, since the
character splits into several selves. Viewers are implicated to the extent that
they wonder if Bowman is not reacting to their presence.

When the older Bowman, seated in the room, turns around he senses a
presence. He turns back in his chair and pauses at his meal. Although he has
sensed something, he does not see anything. The viewer's presence has momentarily been activated. The involvement of the viewer continues in this way
throughout the sequence. Still sensing something is there, the elderly Bowman drops his napkin on the table, rises from his chair and walks toward the
camera (which has remained immobile throughout the shot). He wears a luxurious dressing gown. We see that he has aged considerably now. He continues to chew his food. His movements are careful and slow. He stops and looks
around, still facing the camera. He seems puzzled. His doubts reflect the
viewer's state of confusion. He has not discovered any other physical presence. Neither has the viewer, although the audience has become intensely
aware of its own presence watching the film. There is thus a sense in which
the audience becomes the object of Bowman's visual gaze.

Shot 21   High-angle, reverse, long-shot view of the room as Bowman walks back to
               the table and chair. He positions himself in his chair and unfolds his napkin.

Shot 22   Closer, medium shot of Bowman seated at the table, from the same
               angle. He places the napkin on his lap, picks up a glass and drinks from it.
               He puts the glass back on the table, picks up his fork and continues to eat
               his food. He then looks for something else on the table and knocks over
               a glass with his right hand, screen left.

Shot 23   Close-up of the glass shattering on the floor.

Shot 24   Medium, side view of Bowman pushing his chair back as he stares down at the shattered glass. He suddenly hears breathing (as the audience does). He looks up.

Shot 25   Medium shot of Bowman as a very old man, lying on the bed, while the other Bowman is still partially visible, frame right.

Thus, this shot cannot be Bowman's perceptual point of view, since both Bowmans are in the frame. Again, shot 23 has set up a shot/counter-shot pairing that never materializes; shot 24 never completes the sequence, offering instead a new view with both Bowmans in the frame.

Shot 26   Side view, medium close-up shot of the very old Bowman on the bed. His breathing is audible. Again he *sees* something off-screen. The breathing stops. What has happened to the elderly but younger Bowman of the earlier shot? He has dissolved, disappeared. This very old figure on the bed raises his arm and points off-screen, frame right. He rises slightly from the bed.

Shot 27   Medium-long shot from behind the bed. The black monolith cuts a vertical figure in the shot, mid-ground, center frame. Bowman is on the bed at the bottom of the frame with the bed creating a horizontal shape. Statues and chairs symmetrically line both sides of the frame in the background space, with the monolith in the center. Breathing is still heard as Bowman continues to raise his arm.

Shot 28   Long shot of Bowman in bed, screen left (horizontal), with the monolith, screen right (vertical). Bowman's breathing is audible. He continues to rise slightly.

Shot 29   Medium frontal shot of the monolith. (Is this Bowman's point of view?)

Shot 30   Medium close-up of the bed with the fetus on it now instead of the ancient, atrophied figure. The music begins to fade in this shot.

Once again, the character point of view has been dissolved. It is unclear whether shot 29 represents Bowman's point of view. Shot 30 does not complete the sequence by confirming that shot 29 was a view of the space from Bowman's point of view. Again the spectator's point of view has been substituted for the character's.

Shot 31   Close-up side view of the fetus as the Richard Strauss music (*Also Spracht Zarathustra*) begins.

Shot 32   Close-up of the monolith. The camera moves into the monolith until the screen is totally black.

We are now in space. The shot begins with the moon in center frame and pans down to reveal the Earth frame right, the fetus screen left. The Star-Child turns (or the camera turns) in a circular movement. The eyes of the fetus stare at the camera (the spectator) ending the film by acknowledging the audience's position off-screen as spectators. The sequence contains no dialogue and lasts approximately nine minutes.

The radical nature of the sequence comes from reworking one of the oldest conventions of the classical cinema: the shot/counter-shot pairing. This final segment shifts to a more cerebral mode of discourse. The abstraction of the Star-Gate sequence depends largely on the colors, special effects, editing patterns and sound to involve the viewer. That abstraction can be experienced in a relatively nonintellectual way and still be exciting. In other words, a viewer can miss many filmic and art historical allusions in the sequence and still be intensely involved. But, in this final sequence, comprehension of Kubrick's intentions depends on a sophisticated understanding of film language.

As I have tried to illustrate, the sequence is predicated on classical, perceptual point-of-view shots (the character looking, followed by space seen from the character's position), and on upsetting those conventions. It is built on retroactively altering the viewer's understanding of how one shot works with another, how the space within a shot relates to the space off-screen and how the time of one shot relates to the time of another. Even more than the Star-Gate sequence, the final sequence upsets an understanding of continuous space and linear time. Unquestionably, it represents Kubrick's most radical narrative experiment. By setting up and dissolving character point of view, by invoking the participation of the spectator off-screen and by meditating on itself as a work of fiction, this sequence is Kubrick's most extreme attempt at stretching the boundaries of narrative film. It also alludes to psychoanalytic categories as it invokes the splitting of the self through its fragmented, shifting points of view.

Both the Star-Gate sequence and the final scenes of Bowman in isolation represent Kubrick's most extreme experiments in creating filmic subjectivity. In the Star-Gate sequence a personal, individuated point of view dominates, but the sequence also can be read metaphorically. Bowman's journey beyond Jupiter operates within a logic that in some ways cannot be represented, both because space and time are presented differently and because Bowman's momentous journey of renewal cannot be taken literally. Bowman becomes the personification of the film's allegorical mode of operation. He can be viewed as a symbol of a dying species, and his spiritual journey of self-renewal may be a warning of the dangers of our technological age. He symbolizes the exhaustion of the human race.

The subjective mode of operation of the final room sequence is equally complicated and difficult to read. The notion of character as the origin of subjectivity seems to break down here. The ambiguous point of view complicates the notion of individual point of view itself. Again, a metaphorical reading is illuminating, since the audience's understanding of the space/time continuum and the codified rhetoric of traditional narrative cinema is unable to reveal the full meaning.

Perhaps what both sequences make clear is that conventional notions of filmic subjectivity are insufficient to deal with the complex ways in which this film operates. In some ways, the Star-Gate sequence is designed to contrast with the illusionistic, three-dimensional (objectified) rendering of the earlier space travel and docking sequences. Where those earlier scenes were rendered in precise detail in the darkness and void of space, with the slow movement of objects emphasized, the audience is now bombarded with opaque abstractions and intense colors. Viewers experience the speed of movement with Bowman. In the earlier scenes, there was a dark, colorless world with detailed objects and precise movement set to the accompaniment of a Strauss waltz. Now there are intense colors and varied landscapes accompanied by the modern sounds of Ligeti compositions. The space is disconnected. The images—at times gaseous, at times liquid—are characterized by their imprecise details and unbounded indefinability.

The film attempts to represent an interiorized journey as well as movement into space. But how does a narrative film do justice to the idea of representing interior experience? The solution to the problem of how to represent the "unrepresentable" is to include a metaphorical level on which to read the film. This metaphorical reading argues that to view Bowman's journey in purely literal terms is indeed to miss the complexity of the film's operation and to misjudge the filmmaker's ambition. The visual journey becomes a metaphor for a spiritual or cosmic journey. The sequence is about subjectivity and how cinematic representation of individuated character point of view can never fully represent human experience. Each viewer can absorb and interact with Bowman's personal, allegorical experience.

The freeze frames of Bowman indicate he (and by extension the viewer) is traversing a limitless universe, unbounded by human laws of time or space. The film needs the anchor of an individuated point of view if its mythopoeic ambitions are to be realized. The shift to a personal subjectivity (Bowman's) allows the spectator to be more involved and helps make the leap to a metaphorical reading.

The "arrival" of Bowman in the room after the Star-Gate sequence is signaled first by Bowman's sight, then by his breathing. The perceived objectivity here is again confounded as the sequence begins to upset notions of spatial and temporal continuity. The ambiguous play with point of view emphasizes that viewers are still in the realm of the subjective but not necessarily in the realm of an individual consciousness.

The shift from the Star-Gate to the final room sequence also can be viewed as a shift from a high modernist discourse to a more postmodern one. Individual consciousness gives way to a fractured, disengaged point of view, with no individual character as origin. The audience's role as observer and participant is invoked as the film plays not only with our sense of logic but with the very concept of subjectivity.

These final two sequences are constructed around the idea of individual experience, which is, of course, predicated on the idea that each person experiences the world differently. The film's challenge is how to create an experience that is at once individuated and universal. How can each viewer share Bowman's experience? The film's solution is to incorporate visual abstraction and fractured point of view in the hope that each viewer will create his or her own meaning out of the sequences.

Another important strategy in both sequences is the elimination of all dialogue. *2001* argues that a different form of communication may be needed, both by the human species as it moves to exhaustion and by the medium of film as it endeavors to create a nonliteral, metaphorical level of meaning. The film attempts to engage the viewer in a form of communication that does not depend on language. Consequently, it puts little emphasis on verbal language as a means of communication. At several points in the film, language becomes a way to mask or obfuscate the reality of a situation (Dr. Floyd), a conduit for the transmission of banalities (Frank and Dave) or the pathetic plea for an impossible humanity (HAL). For a truer understanding of the mysteries of the universe, the film seems to argue, language is a hindrance and perhaps unnecessary. Thus, Bowman's individual subjective experience in the final sequences cannot contain language. The experience must remain as open and undefined as possible. The more open the experience, the more viewers can relate to it. The built-in ambiguities of both sequences are one of the film's great accomplishments. *2001* does not claim to reveal the mysteries of the universe or what the future may hold. How could it? But it does argue that perhaps a different process of inquiry is needed to move the species to another level of development.

2001 represents Kubrick at his most ambitious and curious. The film constitutes the director's greatest meditation on the self and what it means to experience the world through individual consciousness. A careful analysis of the final sequences is a necessary prelude to understanding the film's complexity. The experiments with point of view and filmic subjectivity are at the center of that understanding.

A Clockwork Orange

Perceptual point-of-view shots in *A Clockwork Orange* are one of the key strategies in the film's depiction of Alex's view of the world. They are often characterized by the use of a wide-angle lens or other distorting device. When such shots occur, the spatial field is always connected to the character's field of vision. Perhaps the most surprising example of a perceptual POV shot appears in the sequence in which Alex attempts suicide. The shot takes place as he jumps out of a second-story window in the second HOME sequence. Alex's failed suicide attempt is recorded by a hurtling camera that simulates the character's field of vision.

There are other instances of perceptual point of view in the police interrogation scene when Alex spits into the face of his post-corrective adviser. The camera is positioned from Alex's field of vision on the floor. In a later scene, when Alex, now cured after undergoing the Ludovico treatment, is "presented" to his prison audience, there are two theatrically staged performances that utilize Alex's perceptual point of view. The first involves "Lardface," and Alex's humiliation includes licking the bottom of the other performer's shoe. The second sketch involves a topless female "performer" who humiliates Alex by demonstrating that the Ludovico treatment has eradicated his libido as well as his violent urges. We see Alex on his knees from an extremely high-angle view (the woman's perspective). There follows a cut to Alex's perceptual point of view from an extreme low angle as he reaches for the woman's breasts with both hands. Alex is unable to touch the woman and sinks to the floor in physical revulsion. Again, both sequences involve distorted views created by the use of a wide-angle lens, with the camera positioned precisely in Alex's sight line.

Extensive uses of perceptual point of view can also be found during the Ludovico treatment scenes, when, in a drugged state, Alex is subjected to a steady barrage of violent films. These sequences generally involve simple pairings of shots, showing first the character looking and then cinematic material from the films he is viewing. The scenes are presented in close-up with the sound pushed to extreme levels. These sequences are intensely involving and operate in a heightened, hyperbolic way. Many of the film's distorted views are designed to indicate Alex's subjective view of the world. As such, they are meant to present the generally heightened awareness and sensory overload that the character experiences as a result of his constant use of mind-altering drugs.

Not all uses of the perceptual point-of-view shot involve such hyperbolic stylistics. A very subtle use of point of view occurs in a sequence that shows Alex walking along the Thames Embankment. Through the device of the slow zoom, the simple pairing of shots first into Alex's face and then into the water effectively communicates his depressed state. The slowness of the zoom and the relative calm of these two shots is in marked contrast to the succeeding barrage of close-ups of old derelicts as Alex now becomes the victim of those he had earlier attacked. The big close-ups represent his perceptual point of view as he crouches to the ground and lifts his arms to his face in an effort to protect himself from his attackers. Still on his knees, he is saved from the group by two former members of his gang, Dim and Georgie, who are now police. Once again, the audience shares Alex's low-angle view as his victimization continues at the hands of his former mates.

The use of perceptual point of view in many of these scenes creates an involvement with Alex that complicates the viewer's relationship with him. It contributes to the interesting tension between the subjective presentation of events through Alex's consciousness and the distanced, ironic tone of the film.

A Clockwork Orange represents the most consistent depiction of character subjectivity through visual distortion in Kubrick's work. The film's wide array of scenes that incorporate some kind of visual distortion creates a visual correlative to Alex's distorted, drug-induced perceptions. The techniques include slow motion, fast motion, lighting effects, wide-angle lenses, angles of view, shot size and montage to create character subjectivity. The visual distortions amplify the subjective presentation created by Alex's voice-over and the extensive use of point-of-view shots.

Slow motion is used in the sequence where Alex asserts his authority over the other gang members along the Flatblock Marina. The sequence is set up through Alex's commentary: "I was calm on the outside but thinking all the time. But, suddenly, I viddied that thinking was for the gloopy ones, and that the oomny ones used like inspiration and what Bog sends."

The moment of creative inspiration and Alex's violent ballet emerge out of the calmness of the image. The slow motion heightens the violent moment and extends it temporally. Alex's cutting into Dim's wrist is not the vicious act of a young punk but rather the creative act of an artist. The brutality of Alex's actions is overwhelmed by the balletic, aestheticized presentation. Although the slow motion contributes to the subjective presentation, the sequence avoids the use of perceptual point-of-view shots. It contains a total of sixteen shots but not a single point-of-view chain.

A similar use of slow motion to heighten the moment occurs after Alex has terrorized and brutally murdered the Cat Lady. Alex leaves the woman's house only to find his three gang members outside. Dim violently smashes a milk bottle over Alex's face, and the action is rendered in slow motion. Coming as it does after the murder of the Cat Lady with a giant sculpture of a penis, the shot vividly renders the metaphorical relationship between violence and sexuality. The slow-motion shot of the milk bottle as it smashes against Alex's face heightens and extends the narrative moment.

The viciousness of the attack extends the notion of pain and pleasure introduced in the preceding sequence. The slow-motion eruption of the milk bottle becomes the hyperbolically exaggerated "ejaculation" from the giant "penis" in the previous scene. The sequence becomes a supremely heightened moment of violence against the "narrator." The memory of this event is filtered through Alex's consciousness and presented as Alex might remember it in his drugged state.

The Cat Lady sequence itself is another instance of using visual distortion to create a heightened subjective presentation. Much of the sequence is photographed with a hand-held camera and wide-angle lens. The camera shoots from extreme angles, and the sequence includes perceptual point-of-view shots to communicate the intensity of the attack. The sequence illustrates the sexual and aesthetic subtext of the attack by integrating samples of the woman's autoerotic wall paintings through rapid montage. Alex's selective memory does not allow for an illustration of the moment of impact, except as a kind of painting come to life.

In the commentary, Alex seems unaware of the brutality of his attack. He recalls the murder as another of his artistic creations rather than the vicious act it undoubtedly was. The attack is rendered in a flurry of shots that temporally compress the event. This contrasts with the next sequence in which Alex is struck by his gang members. This attack is not simply shown. It is attenuated through slow motion, and the moment of impact is hyperbolized and exaggerated to an extreme degree.

These are not the only instances in which the film resorts to visual distortion to render subjective experience. My intention is not to catalogue every occurrence. Still, mention should be made of the use of the wide-angle lens during the first attack against the Alexanders (first HOME sequence), Alex's brutal interrogation at Police Headquarters and the extreme exaggeration in low-angle of Mr. Alexander's face during the second HOME sequence. Most of these sequences incorporate visual distortion to stand in metaphorically for Alex's twisted view and selective memory of events.

The question of character subjectivity and its rendering through visual distortion is apparent in many other sequences. Alex's "masturbation" fantasy begins with a montage of a dancing Jesus sculpture set to Beethoven's *Ninth Symphony*. It ends with several violent mental images that look very much like Alex has become the star of his own trashy Hollywood movie. The sequence presents violent images of explosions, hangings, Alex as a vampire, and a patently "movie" image of an avalanche crashing down on several prehistoric characters. The images have the artificial look of the movies, and they all involve violence.

Alex sees his acts of violence as his "creative act." He has removed himself from the reality of his actions so completely that violence is now a piece of theater, a performance. Alex's life has become a movie or play, and he is the star performer. There is little difference between Alex's fantasy life and his day-to-day reality. His drug-induced reality is mediated and filtered to the point that his violent actions become theatricalized and aestheticized. This aestheticization carries over into his imaginative life to the point where a simple act of masturbation becomes a poeticized series of trashy movie images ("it was gorgeousness and gorgeosity made flesh. It was like a bird of rarest spun heaven metal").

How do we demarcate where Alex's reality ends and his fantasy life begins? What is the difference between the fantasies in his mind and the fantastic reality of his life? I would argue that there is very little difference. Alex's reality and his imaginary life both contain strong elements of fantasy. Put another way, there is as strong an element of imagination in his real life as there is to his fantasy life. In fact, Alex's "reality" is distorted to such an extent that it is more interesting and more fantastic than the mental images in his fantasies, which pale by comparison. Even the biblical frescos that illustrate Alex's imaginings as he reads the Bible in prison have a kitschy, comic-book look to them. Not surprisingly, Alex's view of the Bible involves him as a centurion slitting a throat or lolling on a bed with buxom handmaidens. Again, the images that originate in Alex's mind stress the artifice of the situation and are not nearly so exciting or dynamic as the movie that his life has become.

Two interesting sequences incorporating visual distortion to render Alex's experience of the world are revealing of his character. One, a high-speed orgy with two teenage girls he has picked up at a record store, suggests the mechanical nature of Alex's sexual performance. The scene is humorous, but it illustrates that sex for Alex involves no human contact or emotion. It is merely another way for him to place himself at the center of his actions. This performance aspect is also seen in the final shot of the film, a mental image rendered in slow motion. The shot involves Alex rolling around with a naked woman on a bed of feathers, applauded by an audience of men and women dressed in fine clothes. Presumably the effects of the Ludovico treatment have worn off ("I was cured all right"), and Alex can regress to his previous behavior. He can revert to being the star performer in both his fantasies and his real life. Both examples illustrate how Alex has removed himself from his fantasies. They are presented to us for our enjoyment, and he views them with us. The "sexual acrobat" is simply another persona to display. Alex has presented so many different characters that the real Alex is hard to discern. Just as Alex's reality is difficult to separate from his fantasies, Alex's view of himself, rendered through the devices we have catalogued, is pure fabrication. All is distorted.

Is it possible to say with certainty that all the narrative events are filtered through Alex's consciousness? The generally heightened, stylized presentation of events in the first part of the film clearly stands in for Alex's distorted view of events as they might be filtered through a drugged consciousness. During the prison sequences and after the Ludovico treatment, the film's ironic tone diminishes, and other characters (the prison chaplain, Mr. Alexander, the government minister, the psychologist) emerge to comment on and qualify Alex's view of himself.

On its surface, the film seems a cautionary tale about the future with a clear, unambiguous argument. On closer examination, the film's meaning proves almost as elusive as the director's most ambiguous narratives. *A Clockwork Orange* is a complex essay on the manipulating, distorting capability of human consciousness and on the power of film to reveal this aspect of human capability.

The Shining

The Shining raises some of the most intriguing questions of character subjectivity in Kubrick's work. The film's plot revolves around the following situation: writer Jack Torrance (Jack Nicholson) has been contracted to be the winter caretaker at the Overlook, a magnificent rustic hotel located in the mountains of Colorado. Jack takes along his wife and son to the hotel. The film is made up of a series of terrifying and funny episodes in which Jack becomes emotionally unhinged and tries (unsuccessfully) to murder his family. It is a complex and very effective ghost story that incorporates several generic conventions, only to undermine them as the film progresses.

The character of Jack Torrance is ostensibly the center of the film's narrative, and, because of his deteriorating mental condition, he becomes the conduit for many ghostly encounters. Jack's son, Danny (Danny Lloyd), is also granted several significant instances of subjectivity, as are Halloran (Overlook's black cook, played by Scatman Crothers), and Jack's wife, Wendy (Shelley Duvall).

What is of particular interest in the film is the relatively objective way many subjective encounters are presented. The line between objective reality and the subjective, interior life of the characters becomes blurred. Mental imagery, such as the "elevator of blood" shots, is given the same ontological status as the presentation of ghosts such as Lloyd or Grady. Danny and Halloran's visions take on the status of events that may be occurring, perhaps now or at some future or past time. The relationship between such mental imagery, reality and the ghosts is one of the film's most intriguing aspects. The complexity resides in the myriad possible interpretations of the film's view of the fantastic.

The notion of character subjectivity and individual points of view are invoked during the film's opening credits. The spectacular aerial shots that begin the film (incorporating wide-angle views) conjure up the idea that someone or something is observing Jack's Volkswagen as it makes its way up the mountain to the Overlook Hotel. If these are point-of-view shots they remain unresolved since they are not connected to any individual character. As the film progresses and in particular during the low-to-the-ground, Steadicam camera movements following Danny as he rides his tricycle, the idea that someone or something is observing the proceedings is given added weight. This impression is never proven, but the unusual views (from above and below) suggest a ghostly point of view. The idea of both objective reality and a reality below the surface (or on a different plane) pervades the film.

The first indication of a character's interior life occurs during Danny's first blackout. The sequence begins with Danny conversing with his imaginary friend Tony in front of a bathroom mirror. A slow zoom into Danny's mirror image initiates a series of shots that the audience interprets as the first of Danny's visions. This series of shots includes a shot of the two Grady girls (not twins, although they have that appearance), shots of Danny with his mouth wide open and several slow-motion "elevator of blood" shots. The sequence indicates that these images originate in Danny's mind. The segment ends on a fade to black, with Danny awakening to the words of a doctor (Anne Jackson) who is examining him.

Danny is granted a second "vision," this time only of the Grady sisters. This vision is signalled by a fast zoom into Danny's face as he plays darts, followed by a point-of-view shot of what he sees. The chain of shots continues until the sisters walk out of the room. This sequence contrasts with the earlier vision, for now Danny is presented with what seems to be a corporeal presence occupying space. This is an important shift from the earlier subjective presentation of images originating in the mind to a materialization of that subjectivity.

The zoom also figures into the next exchange of character subjectivity, this time between Halloran and Danny. It occurs as Halloran gives Wendy and Danny a tour of the kitchen and storage rooms. A slow zoom into Danny's face is followed by a slow zoom into Halloran's face, while Halloran continues his conversation with Wendy. Halloran's voice-over, at a different sound level, accompanies visual cues that signal Halloran's subjective communication directed at Danny ("How'd you like some ice-cream, Doc?"). The shot of Halloran is followed by a reaction shot of the dumbfounded little boy.

The "ghostly" point of view is one of the film's most fascinating constructions. The grandiose opening credit sequence immediately suggests such a possibility. As Jack snakes his way up the curving road to the Overlook Hotel, with aerial photography observing the car's movements, one wonders whose view this is. Perhaps the view belongs to Jack himself, the ghostly Jack who has always been the hotel's caretaker. Alternatively, it may represent the views of other ghostly inhabitants of the hotel. It also may be interpreted as a kind of "authorial" view, with only a suggestion of a ghostly perspective to add ambiguity to what is surely one of the most ambiguous narrative films yet made.

The first time the audience seems to share Jack's subjective view, he is standing over a model of the outdoor maze. This is followed by what we initially take to be a POV shot from Jack's perspective over the maze model that suggests Jack can view the real maze outside by hovering over the model. What is unusual however, is that this is not actually a perceptual point-of-view shot, at least not one linked to Jack. If we take Branigan's definition (quoted earlier) about positioning the camera to stand in for an individual's optical view, then this cannot be Jack's spatial position hovering over the maze model. Even allowing that this could be an approximate view would not account for the spatial inconsistency that Jack is positioned at the end of the rectangle and the POV shot is from the middle of the rectangle. More importantly, it cannot account for the fact that the maze looks very different in the POV shot. It is much more artificial looking and far more detailed than the model Jack stands beside. As the shot slowly zooms down, the audience sees not his POV of the model he stands near, nor does he view the real maze outside, but a bird's-eye view of an entirely different model. The shot operates more like a fantasy space, a mental landscape perhaps representing the ghostly point of view of the Overlook. In the very center of the model, the real maze has been optically inserted within the special matte painting representing the rest of the maze. We now can see the minuscule figures of Danny and Wendy walking in the center of the maze. There is a kind of impossibility about the physical perspective of this overhead maze shot. If Jack actually originated the point of view, it would contribute to the idea that Jack believes himself to be part of a grand game, involving the murder of his family, that must play itself out endlessly, as the final shot of the film implies. But if the hotel actually is responsible for such ghostly views, then Jack is a mere pawn in the game. Kubrick has made things more complicated than at first glance, and the sequence confirms that an understanding of the film relies on what the viewer can see and what is hidden from view, what we think we know and what we can only speculate on, what is possible and what seems impossible. Nothing is ever as it seems in Kubrick's world.

The ghostly perspective may also account for the many low-to-the-ground views of Danny as he rides through the hotel on his tricycle. Danny's first ride is followed by a low Steadicam view only inches above the floor. If viewers take this surprising perspective to be a point-of-view shot, it cannot be followed by a shot of the character who originates the point of view, if my theory is correct that this perspective belongs to a ghostly presence (or to the hotel itself). Similarly, shots following Danny and Wendy inside the maze may have a similar status (that is, they belong to no one the audience can see). Of course, shots such as these do not have to originate with any character, visible or invisible, if viewers take them to relate to an authorial narrating function. The film does not necessarily insist that the audience choose between these possibilities, and the built-in ambiguity creates a fascinating set of potential interpretations.

The second time the camera follows Danny as he rides the tricycle, he stops in front of room 237. As the child attempts to open the locked door of the room, an insert from Danny's point of view of the Grady sisters is flashed on the screen. Again, the film has reverted to an image originating in the boy's mind, similar to his first blackout. Danny's third ride down the corridor combines this subjective imagery with an objectification of the ghosts. The scene begins with low-to-the-ground shots following Danny (from whose point of view?) and develops into a physical encounter with the Grady girls. This is intercut with shots (visions) of the hacked-up bodies of the girls in a Hitchcock-like montage of ever closer shots. The sequence combines Danny's interiority with the physical presence of the girls. The scene is resolved when Danny puts his hands to his face in an effort to blot out the violent images. The visions stop, and the girls disappear. Has Danny really blocked them out, or have they simply removed themselves from the space? It is impossible to determine.

Occasionally, the film will set up a point-of-view chain but leave it unresolved, contributing to its deliberate strategy of ambiguity. One such shot begins as a very slow zoom into Jack's face. It seems from the shot that Jack's mental condition has reached a critical point. But the shot into Jack's face is deliberately not followed by a shot of Jack's interiority or subjectivity. The elusiveness of the shot lies precisely in the fact that it wants to suggest something but leaves it to the viewer to determine the precise nature of Jack's mental state. The slow zoom into Jack's face, in fact, serves to distance the character even further, although a slow zoom is traditionally used in films to create a closer emotional relationship to a character.

Jack's interior life remains closed to the spectator. Viewers know him only through his actions and words, not through the traditional point-of-view chain. It is through the process of externalization (movement, gesture, voice and action) that his character is known. This is why Jack's encounter with the bodily presences of the ghosts takes on such importance and why Nicholson's very physical performance is so critical. When Jack has his nightmare, he is not afforded any subjective point-of-view shots to illustrate what he has dreamed. The audience hears him scream and sees him huddle on the floor like a wounded animal as he recounts the dream to Wendy, but his interior visions are not represented cinematically as Danny's were.

Jack's first visit to the Gold room and his first physical encounter with a ghostly presence are precipitated by Wendy's accusation that he is responsible for an attack against Danny. Jack walks into the empty room and sits at a bar emptied of its liquor stock. As Jack ironically invokes the Faust legend ("God, I'd give anything for a drink. I'd give my goddam soul for just a glass of beer"), there is a cut to a shot of him rubbing his face and eyes, recalling Danny's gesture as the boy tried to blot out his visions. Jack acknowledges another presence ("Hi Lloyd, a little slow tonight, isn't it"). This is followed by a reverse angle (not Jack's perceptual point of view) that reveals Lloyd the bartender and the shelves of now well-stocked liquor bottles.

What is particularly noteworthy about this sequence, apart from the objectification of the ghost as if he were simply another character, is the casual, matter-of-fact tone of the entire sequence. Jack registers absolutely no surprise at the appearance of Lloyd. He is friendly and familiar, even joking with him. The sequence is played out in essentially shot/counter-shot pairings, with no evidence that Jack's subjective state is responsible for manifesting the personification of the ghost, save for Jack's rubbing of his eyes, which might have conjured the presence out of his mind. The audience often sees both characters in the same frame, however, contributing to the idea that Lloyd is conceived and presented in objective terms.

The sequence begins as if it will be a subjective encounter, but it is presented in an objective way. Wendy suddenly enters in an agitated state and reports that Danny has been attacked by a woman in Room 237. Lloyd is now gone, and the bar has reverted to its earlier state. The only evidence of the previous scene is Jack's wobbly, liquor-soaked responses to Wendy's assertions. This scene strongly suggests that Jack operates on different levels of experience, and the film continually shifts back and forth between these different levels.

Jack's second encounter with Lloyd is predicted both visually and aurally when Jack hears the music and song emanating from the Gold Room and sees evidence of a party in the corridor leading to the room. This time, the room is filled with hundreds of revelers. Again, Jack is casual in his responses. He registers no surprise and acts as if the party with hundreds of guests dressed in the fashion of the 1920s was a common occurrence. As Jack attempts to pay for his drink, Lloyd mentions that there is no charge ("orders from the house"). Lloyd's remark takes on added meaning since viewers have already suspected that the Overlook is a main player in the film's unfolding narrative. This scene leads directly to Jack's encounter with Grady, which is played out primarily in a strikingly decorated red and white bathroom. Again, if Jack has conjured the party out of his imagination, the film does not present the ghosts as his subjective vision, but as objective, solid masses occupying space. There is nothing particularly "ghostly" about their presentation.

In Jack's encounter with Grady, viewers discover (if they are to believe Grady, and there is no particular reason to believe or disbelieve him) that Jack has always been the caretaker. This is the first introduction of the theme of reincarnation and the idea that Jack is a perpetual tenant of the Overlook involved in a never-ending cycle of murder and mayhem. This theme gains added resonance in the final image of the film, which shows Jack in a group photograph with other revelers, dated July 4, 1921.

An unusual aspect of Jack's scene with Grady is the use of several 180-degree cuts during their conversation that continually cross the axis. We discussed this strategy earlier when we analyzed the use of this rupturing of classical continuity in *Eyes Wide Shut* to help communicate Bill's subjectivity. It operates in a similar fashion here and emphasizes the fact that the events in the film are not objective views conforming to our own understanding of time and space. The world of *The Shining* can only exist on film. It operates by its own rules. The delicate play between subjectivity and objectivity is crucial to its operation. It should also be mentioned that Kubrick used the trope again in *Full Metal Jacket*, primarily to communicate Pyle's descent into madness. Each time we see such cuts in Kubrick's work they remind us of how strong a hold classical continuity editing still has on contemporary film practice. They seem strange and jarring precisely because they are so rarely used. When an artist of Kubrick's caliber uses them, we are reminded how much power a single cut can have in helping to communicate the ideas of a film.

An interesting example of character subjectivity with delayed point of view occurs in a remarkable sequence involving Danny, Halloran and Jack in different spaces. The sequence begins with a slow zoom into Halloran's face as he lies on his bed in Miami. The soundtrack features the prominent sound of a beating heart that metaphorically comments on the intensity and terror of the ensuing scene. Halloran registers stark terror as the camera zooms into a big close-up of his face. This is followed by shots of Room 237 and Danny on his bed in the middle of an apparent seizure. Then there is a cut to a shot of someone's point of view moving through the space of Room 237 and into its bathroom; the slight wavering of the camera as it moves through the space indicates it is someone's view. The origin of this point-of-view shot is not known until the next shot, when it is revealed to be Jack's. The strategy of beginning the point-of-view chain with the character view, rather than a shot of the character who originates the view, is another example of the kind of delayed or discovered points of view encountered in other Kubrick films, such as *Paths of Glory* and *2001: A Space Odyssey*. It is also a familiar device from horror films of the 1960s and 1970s such as the works of Mario Bava, Dario Argento and John Carpenter.

The context of the terror that both Halloran and Danny experience at this particular moment is still unclear. Jack wanders toward the bathroom as he notices a naked woman in the bath. The scene begins as Jack's perceptual point of view and then turns into an objective presentation, as both actors are presented within the same frame occupying physical space. Jack embraces the woman but notices her transformation into an old hag as he glances into a mirror behind her. Jack is in complete shock, as is the audience, since the sight of a badly scarred, blotchy, naked old woman is a surprising reversal of generic convention. The horrific scene is intercut with shots of Danny, who presumably sees what the audience does.

Until the scene plays itself out, it is not clear what Halloran and Danny are seeing to cause them such anguished reactions. Again, there is a delayed revelation of the point of view, as all three spaces and characters are connected by the scene in Room 237. The film sets up the delayed point of view by showing Halloran and Danny in reaction before the scene is acted out by Jack. The viewer's horror coincides with Jack's but is foreshadowed by Halloran and Danny. The three points of view are connected and originate with the same vision. Halloran "shines" with Danny, and it is Danny's point of view that accounts for both their reactions. Through delay, and the connecting of the different spaces and points of view, the sequence has more tension and complexity. The resolution is withheld until the end of the sequence, and, in a retroactive process, the audience can make sense of the action in the different spaces.

The interconnecting and delay of point of view continue in the scene in which Wendy discovers Jack's "manuscript." As the scene between Jack and Wendy plays out, shots of Danny are intercut; again he is having a vision. These shots are overlaid with Jack's dialogue ("Maybe it was about Danny"), but it is not clear, at this point, what the exact relationship between the two spaces is. It appears that Danny may be reacting to the scene with Wendy and Jack, yet the crosscutting does not confirm this speculation.

Once again, Danny's subjective views (shinings) are cued by a slow zoom into the child. Danny is not reacting to the confrontation between Wendy and Jack but to earlier "elevator of blood" shots. A shot of Danny is followed by floating furniture, in what is now a "sea of blood" in the lobby space in front of the elevator doors. This is interspersed with shots of the wording ("*REDRUM*") scrawled on a door. The audience has encountered this lettering earlier in another of Danny's visions in a series of shots intercut with images of the "elevator of blood." That earlier sequence was a fairly straight-forward subjectivization of Danny's vision, again cued by a slow zoom into the child.

Danny's subjective vision is accompanied by Jack's distorted voice-over from the other space. The origin of the point of view is clear (Danny), but the inclusion of Jack's voice adds a level of ambiguity. Why is Jack's presence invoked here? Other than the build-up of terror and the foreshadowing of what Jack might intend for Danny, it is not narratively motivated. Metaphorically, however, it has its own resonance. The blood can be viewed as a metaphor for all the blood that's been spilt at the Overlook over the years. Jack is also implicated by the voice-over. The distorted vocals contribute to the idea that the evil presence of the hotel is working through Jack. This sequence continues back on the stairs with the shot/counter-shot chain of Jack threatening Wendy. The intense sequence culminates with Wendy bashing Jack twice with a baseball bat to the precise accompaniment of the Béla Bartók music.

This sequence leads directly to Jack's second encounter with Grady, while Jack is locked in the storage cooler. Grady's presence in this scene remains aural, since the character stays off-screen. The presence of Grady could conceivably be the result of Jack's subjectivity, except that Jack is literally freed from the locked cooler by the "ghost." Again, the ghost is presented in human, objectified form though he remains off-screen throughout the scene. The sequence consists of only two shots and lasts over three minutes. The first shot begins with Grady's knock outside the cooler. A slow zoom back from Jack lying on the floor is followed by a tracking shot of Jack as he goes to see who is at the door; this shot lasts 75 seconds. The second shot is a medium, side view of Jack as he looks off-screen to the right. There is no camera movement throughout his conversation with Grady, but the audience clearly hears both characters. There can be no doubt that Grady is physically present off-screen. The shot lasts a full two minutes and results in Jack's release from the cooler. The audience assumes Grady is responsible.

As Jack roams the hotel with axe in hand, the brutal murder of Halloran is possibly "seen" by Danny. This is intercut with three shots of Danny screaming in terror at the death of his only link to the outside world. Although Danny is in a different space, his screams and the piercing music punctuate Halloran's death scene.

As the film progresses, Wendy's mental state becomes part of the scenario as she begins to see ghosts. Perceptual point of view is invoked in one shot by a quick zoom into a male couple that suggests they are engaged in fellatio, with one partner dressed in a bear suit. When Wendy discovers Halloran's body, another quick zoom into the body is associated with her point of view. When she is startled by another ghost ("Great party isn't it?") holding a drink up to her, a quick zoom into the ghost again cues Wendy's point of view.

The film culminates in Jack's spectacular chase of Danny through the snow covered maze, intensified by the use of the Steadicam. The sequence continually shifts between shots of Danny and Jack. It also crosscuts with shots of Wendy inside the hotel. The final sequence is loaded with shifting points of view, and the status of many of these shots is not clear. Some shots of footsteps in the snow are unquestionably Jack's point of view. Other shots, which are low to the ground, closely following and almost straddling Danny, cannot be Jack's perceptual point of view. The sequence continually shifts or intermingles individual character points of view with objective presentation, continuing the pattern established throughout the film. Because the sequence is climactic and cinematically intense, determining the exact status of each shot is unnecessary. The sequence jumbles together the points of view of Jack, Danny, Wendy and that of something indeterminate, as well as an objective presentation. There is a kind of built-in ambiguity that cannot be entirely resolved, which is a necessary part of the sequence and the film.

The film continually cuts between the outdoor maze sequence and views of Wendy inside the hotel, as she now encounters ghostly presences. As with Jack and Danny, her subjective experience is presented in an objectified way as existing in reality and occupying space. The confusion of her mental state about the exact status of what she sees is complicated and made more ambiguous when she sees the "elevator of blood." Wendy's view is not presented as a mental image, like Danny's, but as a physical, objective event. It is presented as Wendy's perceptual point of view, and her stunned reaction indicates that for her, at least, it is indeed occurring.

The Shining puts into question the very idea of actuality. If, as the film posits, there are different planes or levels of experience, what difference is there between objective reality as it is usually understood and the subjective experience and visions of individual characters? The ontological status of these different levels of experience is virtually identical. It is this convergence of the subjective and the objective that accounts for much of the film's complexity and originality.

Eyes Wide Shut

Kubrick's final film admirably illustrates that questions revolving around filmic subjectivity were of central importance to the director at the end of his career. The uncertainty in both the tone and status of narrative events in *Eyes Wide Shut* is felt throughout the viewing experience. The film's ambiguities are so deeply embedded that a definitive interpretation of this elusive film is virtually impossible. Are the events we see really happening? If they are happening, is it in the precise way they are presented? Why does the world of the film seem so unreal in virtually every scene? The film's highly original and complicated conception of subjectivity and the idea of poetically evoking the character's interior state are undoubtedly key to understanding its ambitions.

The conception and articulation of Bill's subjective universe is often expressed through a deliberate use of perceptual point-of-view shots to create an emotional, as well as spatial, relationship to his world. Overtly subjective imagery, such as Bill's walk through the Somerton mansion as he observes the sexual activities in various rooms or Bill's imaginings of his wife's supposed infidelity, helps connect the spaces of the film to Bill's consciousness. Bill's walk through the rooms of Somerton mansion is an especially illuminating scene in terms of the use of POV shots. These shots not only contain the sexual activities that Bill views, but they are filmed in such a way that the ornate, excessive details of the mansion and its extravagant decor are highlighted. The golden hues of the color scheme and lighting and Jocelyn Pook's exotic musical composition ("Migrations") with its heavily Middle Eastern rhythms also add enormously to the exotic atmosphere of the shots. The sequence begins on a dissolve of Bill after the mysterious woman with feathered headdress, who has been walking with Bill, is led away by a masked man. Here is a quick breakdown of the shots:

Shot 1   Moving perceptual POV shot through the space of the mansion. We see a naked woman and black-cloaked man in the center of the frame with their backs to the camera, as well as many other observers both seated and standing on various levels of the room, some in balconies, observing the proceedings. The camera moves through a doorway.

Shot 2   Frontal medium shot of Bill, masked and in a black cloak, as he walks toward the moving camera.

Shot 3   Moving POV shot of sexual activities, which are being observed mostly by couples—sometimes naked women, other times women and cloaked men. The precise details of the copulating couples are partially obscured. All these POV shots are from Bill's perspective; dissolve to

Shot 4   Moving POV shot of observers, some standing, many seated around a red table, which contains several figures involved in more sexual acrobatics.

Shot 5   Frontal moving shot of Bill observing the activities.

Shot 6   Moving POV shot, a little closer to the table with three naked, masked women seated on chairs fondling each other while another naked man and woman are on the table top performing sex. It is important to mention that all the cloaked and masked figures, both standing and seated, are virtually motionless throughout the entire scene.

Shot 7   Moving frontal shot of Bill. He and the camera are the only ones moving, apart from the carefully choreographed motion of the women on the table; dissolve to

Shot 8   Moving POV shot of a man having sex with a woman, with observers, both naked and clothed.

Shot 9   Moving frontal view of Bill who now stops his movement.

Shot 10   Full shot from behind of Bill observing a couple having sex.

Shot 11   Shot of naked masked woman on the arm of a masked, cloaked man who walk into the room.

Shot 12   Shot of Bill and the couple behind him all facing the camera. There is no camera movement now. The man signals to the woman to approach Bill. She moves closer to Bill as the masked man exits the space.

Shot 13   Slightly different framing of Bill and the woman, who now addresses Bill.

This involving sequence feels exotic and surreal, and is greatly aided by the use of extensive hand-held camera with wide-angle lens. The POV shots allow us to share the character's field of vision. The viewer may be mesmerized by the images, but these are not necessarily highly charged partly because the observers within the spaces seem quite dazed, exhibiting no reaction to the proceedings. They are frozen in disinterested poses.

It should also be mentioned that this scene has now become infamous in North America as much for its "censored" views as for how it functions within the fiction of the film. It contains the computer-generated imagery inserted to obtain an R-rating for the film's initial North American release. In several shots, computer-generated, black-cloaked figures obscure a full, unobstructed view of the explicitly sexual imagery. Although smoothly integrated, these inserted figures now act to underscore the unreal, artificial quality of a scene already heightened by the theatricality and choreography of movement (both camera and figures). All the observers are detached from what they see and are as much on display with their posing as the sexual athletes they observe. No one has any visible reaction, of course, because the scene operates outside the realm of what we take to be real. It's doubtful that, even without the censoring, the scene would feel any more real. There would simply be more of it on view.

Another sequence that creates an interiorized moment of filmic subjectivity through the POV shot, as well as the remarkable orchestration of zoom lens, subtle editing patterns and sound, occurs when Bill arrives home to find Alice helping Helena with her math at the kitchen table. Bill walks into the space of the kitchen, takes a beer from the refrigerator, and there is a cut to a POV shot from his perspective of Alice and Helena at the table. A close-up follows of Alice smiling at her husband. When we cut back to Bill and zoom closer to him, Alice's voice-over from her confession about the naval officer invades his consciousness and completely alters the meaning of the sequence.

Although sequences such as these are undoubtedly important, they do not in themselves reveal the full scope and radicality of the film's conception of filmic subjectivity. To gain a fuller sense of how subjectivity functions we must look to such formal elements as the film's highly determined visual design, the striking color scheme and lighting, the repetitive use of camera movement, the static long take and repeated motifs in both image and sound.

If we take the film's opening narrative sequences, including Ziegler's party and Alice's subsequent confession to her husband, as being set in some kind of recognizable reality, much of what follows can be viewed as filtered through Bill's consciousness or, at least, a poetic rendering of his interiority. Kubrick's decision to eliminate an extensive first-person voice-over from an earlier draft of the script suggests that he was deeply concerned with precisely how to translate Schnitzler's novella to the screen, and the issue of subjective point of view in particular. The idea of using a first-person voice-over would certainly have been consistent with Kubrick's successful use of the device in other films. The elimination of it for the final version of *Eyes Wide Shut* argues that the director was searching for a different form in which to render Bill's subjective feelings—one that would still retain the poeticism of the events but imbue his characters with more psychological complexity; and also, one that relied less on language for its effect.

The first scene in the film that attempts to get closer to the interior life of a character is the mirror scene that begins immediately after the party sequence. The shot begins by framing Alice, naked in front of a mirror, as she prepares for bed. The half shot of Alice begins with a slow zoom into the character as her naked husband enters the frame. The couple is now visible in both the mirror image and the nonmirror composition within the shot. As they passionately embrace, there is a cut to a closer mirror shot of the couple that focuses primarily on Alice, who begins to observe herself in the mirror. She seems to be thinking about something and is detached from the physical act of lovemaking. She does not appear to be "in the moment" although she apparently goes through the motions. The ironic use of Chris Isaac's song "Baby Did a Bad Bad Thing" helps make the scene intensely involving, but it is imbued with more complexity by its self-consciousness. The film's theme of looking and not seeing, having "eyes wide shut," is again made literal, but beyond that it is an elusive shot. Who is this character, and what does she feel? What are her thoughts? Alice may be contemplating the evening's events such as the attempted seduction by Sandor, and this may be triggering memories of the previous summer with the naval officer. The act of looking is obviously invoked, as is our role as film viewers. Is Alice looking at us as well as herself? It is a reflexive moment that also invokes the real world of the viewer contemplating a filmed image. Reality seeps into the fiction in a way similar to Bill's direct look at the camera in the scene with Sally. It is a privileged moment that again highlights Kubrick's dissatisfaction with the classical model of illusionist cinema. The use of the mirror shot recalls similar shots in *The Shining*, another film that self-consciously invoked different levels of reality and notions of surface and more deeply embedded meaning.

This scene is followed by a few shots of supposed "normality" the following day, which describe the life of the couple: Bill arriving at his posh office, Alice spending time with Helena, Bill again with his patients. These shots convey the public face of the couple and their social roles: Bill the handsome and status-conscious professional, the bread-winner of the family, and Alice the caring (and somewhat dissatisfied) young mother. This surface reality, of course, will soon be ruptured by the subsequent events of the film.

Bill's restlessness and confused feelings of jealousy and betrayal are first felt during Alice's confession of her sexual attraction to the naval officer. After this scene, during Bill's cab ride to Marion Nathanson's house, the first of the overtly subjective, slow-motion inserts of Alice in the throes of sexual passion with the naval officer is seen, a fantasy image that acts as a kind of leitmotif to signal Bill's further descent into a confused, anxious interior state. These inserts occur five times throughout the film, and each time they are visually altered to be more sexually explicit and aggressive as Bill's feelings intensify.

After the extraordinary scene in which Marion Nathanson suddenly declares her love to Bill, we follow Bill as he walks the streets of downtown Manhattan in an emotionally confused state. He is first pushed to the ground by some gay-bashing youths and then (conveniently) picked up by a woman who seems like the "nicest," most attractive prostitute in town. It is never tawdry sex that Bill is offered, but sex from the most beautiful women (and some of the most attractive men and girls). From Milich's daughter at Rainbow Fashions to the impossibly beautiful, statuesque "hookers" at the orgy to prostitutes like Domino, Bill clearly views himself as the central, privileged character in his dream world. These encounters with women (and sometimes men, as in the case of the gay hotel desk clerk) are portrayed in fantastic, unbelievable terms.

The scene with Marion Nathanson is a revealing example of this kind of encounter. When asked by Bill how she is holding up, she responds, "it's so unreal," cuing the viewer to the possibility that these events might not really be happening. Marion's improbable outburst of love played out in full view of her father's dead body also hints at the unreality of the situation. The sequence is unusual because it keeps shifting in tone and is completely unpredictable in its trajectory. It ends with Marion offering to abandon her planned, conformist life with Carl (Thomas Gibson), her dull fiancé, to be near Bill. The scene, of course, comes immediately after Alice's confession and her willingness to throw away her own life of privilege and stability if the naval officer had asked her to spend just one night with him. The scene with Marion echoes, and in a way is an acting out of, the naval officer story. In the middle of the scene, as Bill tries somewhat unfeelingly to console the grief-stricken and confused woman, she declares her love for him:

Marion: I . . . oh! No, my God! No! I . . . I love you. I love you. I love you. I love you. [Marion kisses Bill passionately on the lips]

Bill: Marion.

Marion: I love you. I don't want to go away with Carl.

Bill: Marion, I don't think you realize . . .

Marion: I do, even if I'm never to see you again. I want at least to live near you.

Marion's excessive outburst of emotion is contrasted with Bill's cool reserve, which he maintains throughout most of the film until he finally breaks down in a flood of tears in his own confession scene with Alice later in the film. The scene with Marion continues and is (conveniently) interrupted by the chimes of the doorbell as Carl arrives. The scene is genuinely shocking. What could possess this woman to express such an outburst of emotion and feeling to Bill? The overwhelming sense of grief and confusion that comes from the death of her father may, on the surface, provide a rationale. However, the scene is as much about Bill's repressed feelings as it is about Marion's fragile state of mind.

The first real hint—apart from the obviously subjective shots that Bill imagines of the naval officer and Alice—that the filmed events may not be happening precisely as we perceive them occurs in this scene. Alice's feelings seem to have been transferred to Bill, who is presented with a situation mirroring Alice's fantastic and hurtful story. The sequence with Marion puts into relief for the first time that Bill's subjectivity guides and distorts the world around him. This is how he *feels* the events. Whether these events are actually happening is never resolved, but there is mounting evidence that the film is a poetic rendering of his state of mind.

Carl's interruption at the door continues a pattern we have already encountered during Alice's story when the phone rings during her confession. It will be repeated with variation at crucial junctures in the film whenever Bill is at a delicate point in a scene and *needs* to be interrupted, such as the ringing of his mobile phone during the scene with Domino when they are on the verge of making love or during the orgy when the mysterious woman intervenes, saving Bill from the humiliation of having to remove his clothes.

The removing of clothes will be alluded to obliquely in the scene in which Alice recounts her dream, another revealing sequence in terms of character subjectivity. It immediately follows the orgy, and seems to recount, in a different form, the events of the orgy and Bill's humiliation; it also predicts Bill's wanderings through the deserted streets of Soho. It begins as Bill arrives home late in the evening and discovers Alice murmuring in her sleep. He sits on the side of the bed, and Alice's murmuring turns to laughter. She is awakened by Bill, and her reaction is initially disturbed and almost hysterical. After she calms down a little, Bill asks her to recount her dream, which she proceeds to do, asking Bill to first lie down beside her. She then recounts her dream, accompanied by another remarkable Jocelyn Pook composition ("The Dream") that underscores the intensity and dreaminess of the scene:

Bill: What were you dreaming?

Alice: It's just a . . . just weird things.

Bill: What was it?

Alice: Oh . . . so weird.

Bill: Tell me.

Alice: We . . . we were . . . we were in a deserted city and . . . and our clothes were gone. We were naked, and . . . and I was terrified, and I . . . I felt ashamed. Oh, God! And . . . and I was angry . . . because I felt it was your fault. You . . . you rushed away to try and find our clothes for us. As soon as you were gone it was completely different. I . . . I felt wonderful. Then I was lying in a . . . in a beautiful garden, stretched out naked in the sunlight, and a man walked out of the woods, he was . . . he was the man from the hotel, the one I told you about . . . the naval officer. He . . . he stared at me and then he just laughed at me.

Bill: That's not the end of it, is it?

Alice: No.

Bill: Why don't you tell me the rest of it.

Alice: It's . . . it's too awful.

Bill: It's only a dream.

Alice: He . . . he was kissing me, and then . . . then we were making love. Then there were all these other people around us . . . hundreds of them, everywhere. Everyone was fucking, and then I . . . I was fucking other men, so many . . . I don't know how many I was with. And I knew you could see me in the arms of all these men, just fucking all these men, and I . . . I wanted to make fun of you, to laugh in your face. And so I laughed as loud as I could. And that must have been when you woke me up.

Alice's dream reflects Bill's experience at the Somerton orgy in several key respects. The similarities include not only the references to naked men and women fucking, but the idea of humiliation, the removal of the couple's clothes, and the reference to the woods since the mansion itself is situated in a heavily wooded area outside the city. The allusion to the deserted city prefigures Bill's wanderings through the streets of Soho as he is stalked by the mysterious man trailing him. What is also odd about the scene is that Alice is laughing before Bill awakens her, seemingly not experiencing a nightmare, but something much more pleasurable. If the events at Somerton are taken as constructed out of Bill's feelings of guilt, repressed desire and his fear that his marriage is collapsing, the dream could possibly reflect Alice's own feelings of guilt or sexual repression. Perhaps Alice's dream is a way for Bill to justify his behavior to himself, to transfer his own feelings of repression and guilt onto his wife. It raises the possibility that Alice was a participant at the orgy, which could explain the mask lying by her side after the Ziegler explanation scene. Although this seems unlikely, the scene illustrates the point that the interior life of the characters is crucial to any interpretation of the film. Moreover, the scene's inconclusive quality is in keeping with the tentativeness of the entire film.

The film's highly determined color scheme, recurring elements of costume and decor, and repeated musical motifs are other ways that the film articulates narrative meaning and the idea of a poetically inflected, subjective universe. The warm, golden hues that dominate the opening apartment scene are carried over into the elaborate Ziegler party sequence. The party scene contains many ideas and motifs that will be elaborated throughout the course of the film. During the scene, the golden hues of the downstairs public spaces are contrasted with the colder grey/blue and green tones of the private space of Ziegler's bathroom, the place of Mandy's apparent drug overdose. The cooler tones of the bathroom space are associated with a cold, tawdry view of sexuality and contrast with the elaborately lit and decorated space of the ground floor below, where the old-world seduction of Alice continues as party guests dance to the melodies of the big band.

Part of the effectiveness of the color scheme is a result of specific cinematographic and lighting strategies. In an *American Cinematographer* article,[8] Larry Smith, the film's cinematographer, discusses Kubrick's desire to use as much available light as possible to shoot the film, as he had done in both *Barry Lyndon* and *The Shining*. This necessitated unusual decisions about set design as well as force-development of the film stock in the laboratory, both contributing to the surreal, heightened quality of the filmed reality.

The artifice so theatrically presented in the orgy scene—with its preponderance of blue, black, red and golden hues—extends to the precise use of color and decor such as the reds and greens of the Christmas decorations and the excessive lighting, with the thousands of tiny lights, of the Ziegler party space. These color schemes are reworked in subsequent locales such as: Domino's apartment, which has many Christmas decorations, a tiny Christmas tree and walls lined with masks; the careful color scheme of the Soho/Village streets where Bill wanders; and the Nathanson apartment, with its luxuriant golden hues. The Nathanson bedroom where Bill encounters Marion contains muted greens and also features the deep blue background so strongly felt in Alice's confession scene and in the sequence where she recounts her dream. The color blue is also a strong feature of the Sonata Café decor, which also features deep reds and, once again, an overabundance of decoration and lighting. The jazz club itself seems less like a club in New York City at the end of the nineties than one of the intimate clubs that jazz afficionados and maybe Kubrick himself would have frequented in the 1940s and 1950s. Many of the other public spaces in the film such as Sharkey's Café, with its overabundance of decorations, strike the viewer as fantasy spaces that have little to do with the reality of present-day New York City and more to do with Bill's state of mind.

The Somerton mansion itself and the staged events that occur in both its ornate interior and imposing exterior offer excellent illustrations of the significance of decor, color, costume and lighting to the film's conception of subjectivity. The blue, wrought-iron gates, the black-clothed guardians who frequently emerge out of black limousines, the deep red of the lush carpets, Red Cloak's crimson outfit, the black cloaks of most of the participants/observers and the ornate decor of the rooms with their appropriately excessive gold paint often lit with gold and blue filtered light all contribute to the idea of a fantasy space fabricated from Bill's unconscious. The orgy scene is crucial as well in the use of masks that hide the identity of each individual and invoke the notion of public and private selves, revelation and deception. The theatrically staged ritual with Red Cloak and the circle of near-naked women that begins the orgy scene is once again immensely enhanced by Jocelyn Pook's mesmerizing composition ("Masked Ball"), which is highlighted by electronic distortions and allusions to medieval or pagan rituals. The scene is reminiscent of a Hammer film from the 1960s—Terence Fisher's *The Devil Rides Out* (1968), a film set in 1930s England involving cults, ceremonies and witches' covens, starring Christopher Lee, immediately springs to mind. The cinematic references to horror films continue during Bill's trial scene with the quick zoom into the mysterious woman who offers to "redeem" Bill. The self-conscious allusion to nameless, cheesy horror films marks the moment as something more than a simple ironic reference; it is another clue that the scene is being filtered through Bill's imagination. The scene is simultaneously compelling and a little preposterous. We are captivated by the proceedings, yet can't quite believe our eyes.

The many scenes of Bill roaming the streets of Manhattan, with their over-determined decor and color scheme, also contribute to the heightening of the fiction and the notion of a waking dream. One of the most striking uses of color occurs during Ziegler's lengthy explanation scene, when the intensity and prominence of the red-covered pool table takes center stage. In fact, it is so conspicuous that one could jokingly claim that it is the main character in the scene. The color red, of course, has been extensively used throughout the film, especially in the Somerton scenes, and recalls both the decor of the mansion and Red Cloak's costume.

Other important uses of color and decor include the use of blue and gold during Alice's confession and the recounting of her dream, the blue and red of the Sonata Café, the excessive Christmas decorations at the Ziegler party and their insertion into many later spaces such as the Sonata Café and Sharkey's Café, and, as noted above, the golds, blues, reds and blacks at the Somerton orgy. These elements of decor, color, costume, cinematography and lighting are continually reworked throughout the film and allude to each other. They reinforce the reading that much of the film is a poetic rendering of Bill's consciousness and often stand in for his emotions.

This emphasis on the visual (and aural) also strengthens the argument that Kubrick is primarily a nonverbal filmmaker. Although his screenplays are always carefully crafted, dialogue often takes a back seat to the emotional force and conceptual ideas his films communicate without language. He is an intellectual filmmaker, yet he is mistrustful of words. *Eyes Wide Shut* is a wonderful illustration of how language can mislead the viewer and is often superfluous to the meaning of a scene. One brief illustration is a shot that frames Bill's stalker standing beside a STOP sign intercut with Bill holding a copy of the *New York Post* that carries the headline "Lucky to Be Alive." The shot composition, shot montage and use of the Ligeti extract from *Musica Ricercata II* communicate the thematic ideas, ironies and notion of a fantasy space much more convincingly than any dialogue. The Ligeti extract is first heard in the orgy scene, and again when Bill goes to Somerton and is handed the note by a mysterious man on the other side of the blue-gated mansion— a color that by this point in the narrative has significant associations. We hear it again in Sharkey's Café when Bill reads the newspaper account of Amanda Curran's death. It contributes a menacing, emphatic note each time it is heard and resonates long after the scene ends.

In thinking about the centrality of the use of color and decor and its relation to dreams and poetic states, I am reminded of Federico Fellini's remark about the use of color and its connection to dreams in *Juliet of the Spirits* (1965), his first color film. He stated:

I don't think I would have done it in black and white. It is a type of fantasy that is developed through colored illuminations. As you know, color is a part not only of the language but also of the idea and the feeling of the dream. Colors in a dream are concepts, not approximations or memories. . . . In a dream color is the idea, the concept, the feeling, just as it is in truly great painting.[9]

Many other elements of the narrative construction, of course, contribute to the feeling that Bill is experiencing something like a waking dream, or at least that what we view is a projection of the character's interior world. For example, Bill frequently refers to his position as a doctor to gain secret information or entry into a difficult situation. He shows his "doctor's card" to Milich at Rainbow Fashions, he shows it again to the hotel clerk to gain confidential information about Nick Nightingale, and at the coffee shop he mentions that he is a doctor as he attempts to obtain the piano player's address. He shows his card again at the hospital when he attempts to visit Amanda Curran. This is another way that Bill's sense of identity and self-importance are tied to his status in society. The fact that he uses his doctor's card as if it were a secret mantra (and a policeman's badge) suggests that these scenes are not meant to be taken as realistic. Other fantasy elements include the deserted space of the New York City hospital/morgue, which has virtually no people in attendance and lovely abstract artwork on its corridor walls—rather than the drab institutional reality one would expect to find, it is a fantasy projection of a yuppie professional who lives a privileged existence.

As a way of concluding this discussion, I'd like to point out one unusual and deeply embedded example of the film's subjective presentation. It occurs during the scene of Bill reading the newspaper report of Amanda Curran's death, at Sharkey's Café. Bill has ducked into the café to hide in a more public space after being menaced by the man who is trailing him in the streets of Soho. The idea of a dream has already been invoked by the deserted streets, the sense of menace, Bill's failed attempt to get a taxi and many aspects of the decor and shot composition. He buys a copy of the *New York Post* with the headline "Lucky to be Alive" on its cover, which invokes the irony of the previous scene with Sally that is concerned with Domino's HIV results as well as the more immediate threat of the stalker. When Bill enters Sharkey's, the room is congested with murmuring customers and the air is filled with the majestic music of Mozart's *Requiem*. He sits at the one empty table and proceeds to read the story of Amanda Curran's death from a drug overdose. A slow zoom towards Bill cuts to a POV zoom into the newspaper revealing the startling news of Mandy's death. The image of the newspaper account is on the screen for only a few seconds. There is then a cut to Bill's reaction in a slow zoom into a large close-up of his face. The Ligeti piano motif is heard throughout the three-shot sequence, intensifying the mood of the scene.

A close look at the newspaper image reveals that the article contains numerous sentences that are repeated. Phrases such as "hotel security personnel after her agent asked them to check on her," "at the time she ingested the drugs" and "she has many important friends in the fashion and entertainment world" are all printed twice, emphasizing the nonnaturalistic, dream landscape of the film and Bill's subjective experience of the events. Kubrick has designed the sequence in such a way that the shot is not on the screen long enough for most viewers to spot the repetitions—it is only ten seconds long. This is another example of how mysteriously the film operates. The repetitions can only be discovered by freezing the shot and carefully observing the image. It's another way for the director to articulate the film's themes through an element of form that can only be observed by digging below the film's surface. The scene illustrates that Kubrick intends his images to operate on different levels, depending on how hard we look. A casual viewing of a Kubrick film is never sufficient to discover its deeper meanings.

More could be said about how subjectivity functions in *Eyes Wide Shut*, and certainly the use of color, decor, music and sound is more complex than we can illustrate in this brief discussion. It is to be hoped, however, that the discussion has at least pointed the way to avenues of thought that might unlock some of the film's complexities. Ultimately, the challenge of the film is to communicate in a strikingly original and compelling cinematic way how Bill and Alice Harford emotionally feel the world. The challenge for the viewer is to grasp the intricacy of that compelling vision.

Along with *The Shining* and *2001*, *Eyes Wide Shut* is Kubrick's most open filmic text, offering the spectator an almost endless array of interpretive possibilities. It demonstrates that the director maintained and enriched a line of inquiry that ran from his earliest work to the present. More than a line of inquiry, the combination of subjectivity within an objective presentation and objectivity within a subjective presentation ultimately became a necessary component of his vision. One of the great accomplishments of Kubrick's final masterwork is its significant contribution to Kubrick's project of forcing viewers to rethink their understanding of both cinematic realism and filmic subjectivity.

SUBJECTIVITY VERSUS OBJECTIVITY

To end this discussion, I'd like to offer some observations about the concept of subjectivity and its relation to the idea of objective presentation. When cinematic material is said to be presented objectively, this does not mean, of course, that it is done with complete neutrality or without bias. Certainly a different process of filmic narration is involved than the one described in our discussion of subjectivity. Objective presentation implies a more impersonal narration that does not privilege an individuated character's subjectivity. This necessarily involves different narrative and stylistic choices.

Apart from third-person commentary, many details of organization and presentation of narrative material in Kubrick's work can be considered within the category of objective or nonsubjective presentation. *2001* is notable in this regard, primarily because it begins fairly objectively and then shifts to a subjective mode in its final movements. The film originally had a voice-over narration to accompany the opening "Dawn of Man" section, which now contains no dialogue. The voice-over was ultimately rejected after a cut of the film had been screened. Gene Phillips has said that this version's voice-over contained "explanatory narration" and that the director "appended a ten-minute prologue to the film, consisting of edited interviews with several scientists about their speculation on extraterrestrial life elsewhere in the universe."[10] Phillips has stated that most of the eliminated narration was part of the "Dawn of Man" prologue.[11]

It is understandable that Kubrick might originally have wanted to include scientific data to support his filmic speculations. One can certainly understand his initial reluctance to begin the film with the wordless twenty-minute "Dawn of Man" sequence. The use of carefully constructed landscapes in this section—involving a complicated front projection system rather than the more typical rear projection—is another instance of the director's commitment to the notion of a detailed presentation. And, of course, the fact that this section presents only apes instead of human characters makes it an even more daring beginning.

The aesthetic decision to eliminate the semidocumentary material and voice-over was correct, I believe. There are enough details in the visual presentation of the film to convince viewers of the accuracy of its presentation. It is the manipulation of details of reality that is one of the central tenets of the director's work. The dialectic of presenting details rooted in reality within a stylized, distanced presentation is a key element in Kubrick's aesthetics.

2001's presentation of details in the "Dawn of Man" and the later space travel scenes is done with complete conviction. The viewer believes that the world might have looked like this several million years ago, and the depiction of space travel is similarly convincing. The impeccable model work, the use of a specially designed front projection system, the slow editing patterns and the camera work are tools to achieve a more complete illusionism. The nature of that illusionism rests on the belief that the audience accepts what is placed before the camera for what it claims to be.

As I discussed earlier, the detailed presentation largely depends on carefully thought-out camera and editing strategies. Kubrick's objective presentation depends, to a great extent, on the attenuation of the film's temporality. This is not to say that scenes are presented in real time, for that would be absurd in a commercial narrative film. Individual sequences are carefully edited with scrupulous attention to their internal rhythms. The rhythmical fades to black that punctuate the "Dawn of Man" sequence are an example of this commitment to editing rhythm. The sequences in space and in the opening landscape scenes, however, are edited to take the necessary amount of screen time for the viewer to marvel at their details of presentation. Rapid editing does not intrude on their gracefulness. Montage would call attention to itself and distract the viewer from the object on view.

The depiction of space travel, with all the attendant details of weightlessness, decor, docking procedures and movement of different bodies in space, is one of the film's strongest aspects. There is a sense of documentary reality about many of these scenes. This sense of reality is a necessary prelude to the movement toward the more subjective presentation of Bowman's journey in the later stages of the film.

Kubrick's careful attention to details of presentation is no doubt related to the possible reception of the film. *2001* is clearly invested with a seriousness in all its aspects, and it would be natural to expect the film to be received in a similar way. This serious reception might have been compromised if the film had been viewed as merely another science-fiction film, albeit a superior one. Kubrick's film is such an ambitious project—aesthetically, technically, and philosophically—that if too much of its presentation were unbelievable, the whole work might crumble under its inflated ambitions. As it is, the film is scientifically solid, within the confines and limitations of a commercial narrative (art) film. Its speculations and details of presentation, including the meticulous depiction of weightlessness, are entirely plausible and convincing.

This concern with the particulars of cinematic presentation should not surprise those familiar with Kubrick's obsessive attention to detail, an obsessiveness that can be discerned in all his work. It was evident as early as *Paths of Glory*. Gene Phillips has stated how concerned Kubrick was in preparing the battlefield that was to be the sight of the battle to take Ant Hill:

Prior to shooting this sequence, Kubrick spent several days preparing the landscape for the assault by planting explosives, creating bomb craters, placing tangles of barbed wire all over the terrain, and making it look like what one critic called "the rim of hell." On the day that the battle was filmed, the director had six cameras placed at strategic points along the attack route, while he himself used a hand-held camera with a zoom lens to zero in on Kirk Douglas and record his reactions to what was happening to him.[12]

A similar attention to detail can be found in *Dr. Strangelove*. One of the film's most impressive achievements is its sense of reality within an absurdist, almost surreal context. This sense of reality is the result of several aesthetic decisions. From the beginning of its credit sequence, over the visuals of the refueling of a B-52 in midflight by another aircraft, one can sense the dialectic of realism and artifice at work in the film. Here is an event depicted in a way that might indeed occur in reality. B-52 aircraft must be refueled in mid-air because their effectiveness rests on their constant readiness. The images that represent this procedure have a documentary feel to them. But the editing and musical accompaniment ("Try a Little Tenderness") transform the event into something like a sexual act. Not only does this sequence prepare the audience for the sexual associations to come in the film, it also implies that any piece of reality can be manipulated to become a fiction.

The element with the strongest verisimilitude in *Dr. Strangelove* is the reconstruction of the interior of the B-52. Although it was actually constructed in a studio, it is apparently authentic in almost every detail.[13] The exterior attack scenes against Burpelson Air Force Base are likewise shot in a *cinema verité* reportage style. The grainy texture of the film stock, the use of a hand-held camera, the editing patterns and the image composition all contribute to this verisimilitude.

Other interior sets have an equally high degree of verisimilitude, particularly the Burpelson interiors and General Ripper's office. The Pentagon War Room with its Big Board is slightly more fantastic, in keeping with the surrealistic quality of events depicted there. The room could conceivably look like this in reality, of course, but the set design consciously emphasizes the cramped, architecturally oppressive atmosphere of the space. The expressionism here contrasts with some of the film's other spaces. There is no contradiction, however, between the realism of certain elements of the film's design and the expressionism of others. This kind of blending or meshing of opposites is in keeping with the absurd yet truthful aspects of the narrative events. The characters *are* caricatures, but still plausibly drawn. A character like Ripper is ridiculous, but not outside the realm of possibility. Kubrick evidently had this idea in mind and has stated: "I'm not entirely assured that somewhere in the Pentagon or Red Army upper echelons there does not exist the real-life prototype of General Jack D. Ripper."[14]

The effective presentation of the film's caricatures depends, to a large extent, on its conception of psychological plausibility. If the presentation of character were so absurd as to be unbelievable, the film could not sustain its critique of the military. Viewers would be left with an excellent farce and little else. But the believable presentation of realistic details on all levels (decor, character psychology, workings of the military and government) ensures a viable critique. The inclusion of this critique lifts the film above the level of farce. For the film to work effectively, both as farce and as social critique, the viewer must have faith that its fictional world is grounded in reality. The film's attention to detail is a key component in creating that sense of reality.

Kubrick's other major foray into the world of the military, *Full Metal Jacket*, contains a meticulously detailed re-creation of war-ravaged Vietnam. An unusual aspect of the film's look makes the locale seem like a realistic portrayal of Vietnam, but at the same time, it feels unreal. An abandoned concrete city (Beckton-on-Thames) and gasworks were demolished, and thousands of plastic trees were imported to lend verisimilitude to the film. Despite this accuracy, the film achieves a kind of hyperrealism because of an almost over-aestheticism in the decor and production design. The inferno of war has never seemed so accurate and yet so removed and distant.

One of the most startling aspects of verisimilitude is the film's use of language. The audience's first encounter with the brutal drill instructor offers an interesting example of a performance that relies tremendously on the character's use of language and mode of delivery. The performance apparently involved a good deal of improvisation. In an interview, Kubrick claimed that Lee Ermey, the actor who plays the role of Hartman, the drill instructor, created half of his dialogue based on personal experience at Parris Island.[15] His performance and its attendant dialogue provide the film with one of its strongest aspects of authenticity. The performance feels real, yet it could also be described as stylized and excessive. The constant stream of abuse the character spews forth certainly feels exaggerated and excessive. But what precisely makes it feel excessive to the audience? Is the excess located in the characterization or the performance style? Or are viewers simply uncomfortable with the lack of naturalism that often forms a part of such acting? And what role does language play in audience response to the characters?

In fact, the film's use of language is astonishing. It communicates a strong sense of realism and unreality simultaneously. The graphic, explicit nature of the drill instructor's abusive harangues against the raw recruits is an example of the film's accurate depiction of the verbal interplay among the Marines. Hartman's speeches often have a sense of unrehearsed, illogical word juxtapositions that seem true to life. His rhythmical delivery also adds a level of stylization. The most obvious examples of rhythmical speech are the numerous cadences ("I love the Marine Corps"), but Hartman's normal tirades also contain a similar use of rhythmical language:

If you ladies leave my island, if you survive recruit training (pause), you will be a weapon. (pause) You will be a minister of death, praying for war. (pause) But until that day you are pukes! (pause) You're the lowest form of life on Earth. You are not even human fucking beings! (pause) You are nothing but unorganized, grabasstic pieces of amphibian shit!

Some of Hartman's outbursts are humorous in their graphic descriptions: "You had best unfuck yourself or I will unscrew your head and shit down your neck." The use of this kind of language has an obvious shock quality, a directness rarely encountered in a combat film. The macho, bullying and humiliating behavior of the Marines has never been depicted with such precision.

The language also emphasizes how cut off from the outside world the military is, with its own laws of behavior and language system. It is a secret world, where speech consists of a constant stream of invective and references to the human body, including many references to excrement.

The depicted realism and unreality of the second part of the film, set initially in Da Nang and moving to Hue City, owes much of its power and accuracy to the way characters communicate with each other. The film faithfully captures the rhythms of daily speech of men in combat. The scene of the editorial meeting of "The Sea Tiger" at the Quonset Hut illustrates how the military communicates its ideology by using simultaneously sanitized and obfuscating language. It is not the propaganda function of the military press that is surprising here, but the discovery of the cryptic codes of this secret world: "If we move Vietnamese, they are evacuees. If they come to us to be evacuated, they are refugees." The audience also sees that language is an important tool in controlling the way the outside world perceives the war and U.S. involvement: "In the future, in place of 'search and destroy,' the phrase 'sweep and clear.' Get it." The sanitized language is meant to diminish the brutality of the action.

There is also plenty of humor in the language. Some of it is sexual, such as the kinds of photographs expected from a USO visit by Ann-Margret ("morning dew"), and some of it is simply obscure, such as "where's the weenie?" referring to the absent "kill" of Joker's story: "Joker, I've told you before, we run two basic stories here. Grunts who give half their pay to buy gooks toothbrushes and deodorants—winning of hearts and minds, okay? And combat action that results in a kill—winning the war."

The ideology expressed in the official Marines' newspaper must conform, not surprisingly, to the ideological position of U.S. involvement in the war. It is less important to tell the truth than to tell the official version of that truth: "You rewrite it and give it a happy ending" refers not so much to Joker's story but the feelings of many war veterans, who often voiced similar thoughts about the war itself. Many did want to rewrite the history of the war with a happy ending—one of the few accuracies in jingoistic films like the *Rambo* cycle.

The sense that the military is a hermetic, secret world, open only to the initiated, can also be seen in the new names handed out to the recruits: "Animal Mother," "Payback," "Touchdown," "Rafterman," "Cowboy," "Joker"—all anonymous and casual. The names refer to one salient characteristic of each individual, since the military world is a world where the complexity of human behavior must be distilled and simplified. This is due partly to the impermanence of wartime camaraderie and partly to the fact that no one can be encouraged to scrutinize the world too deeply. The war exists and it must be won. That is the only view that can be advocated. *Full Metal Jacket* illustrates that the language system of the military world is an important factor in accomplishing this military objective.

Typically for Kubrick, the presentation of character and the careful attention to performances are crucial to the film's power and success. The way characters interact and communicate with each other feels accurate. But when they talk to each other, there is also a sense of absurdity and surrealism that correlates with the absurdity of the war. This is not, of course, an inconsistent strategy, but adds layers of complexity to a film that clearly has many levels of meaning.

Much of Kubrick's work revolves around dialectical operations such as the use of details from reality to produce artifice and the use of artifice to reveal reality. This has been evident in several films throughout this analysis. The most complex working out of these ideas can be found in *Barry Lyndon*, Kubrick's masterpiece of objective presentation.

In terms of *mise-en-scène*, Kubrick has gone to great lengths here to ensure a high degree of historical accuracy. The costumes, decor, make-up, wigs and architecture are inspired by representative paintings of the period. The film was shot entirely on location in England, Ireland and Germany, and the use of real locations adds an important element of realism to the film. Finally, the use of appropriate music from the period (all compositions, save the Schubert, were composed during the years depicted by the film's events) adds another element of accuracy to the film. These elements from reality provide an appropriately faithful historical and aesthetic context for the narrated events.

Because the film takes the art and culture of the period (painting, music, architecture and fashion) as its starting point, its view of the eighteenth century is largely determined by its aesthetic view of the period. Additionally, on the level of character psychology, the film displays a strong sense of reality. But saying that the film displays a high degree of reality in the details of its presentation does not mean that the film is without artifice or stylization. The combined use of available light (candles), the extensive use of the zoom lens, the placement of characters in frozen gesture within the frame and the creation of painterly images combine to create an extremely stylized and distanced presentation. There is no subjective, controlling point of view here—as in *A Clockwork Orange*—to account for the stylization of the image. The film operates in a seemingly neutral and objective mode.

Even though no character subjectivity mediates the proceedings, *Barry Lyndon* has a degree of mediation in the person of the omniscient narrator. He often serves as the *voice* of the eighteenth-century aristocratic class depicted in the film. At times, he serves as an authorial device through which the film articulates many of its ideas.

How then is *Barry Lyndon* an objective presentation if it is, indeed, so stylized, distanced and mediated? It is clear that the notion of objectivity does not mean that the depiction is completely neutral, unbiased or purely factual. There are significant differences between a subjective presentation such as the one in *A Clockwork Orange*, and a more objective one with no overtly subjective point of view such as in *Barry Lyndon*. The subjective mode represents the view, on some level, of a character or organizing consciousness from within the fiction. Elements of the image and cinematic space are used to represent this personalized view. An objective presentation does not include such a construct, and the view is not filtered through an individual character. Even when an omniscient narrator mediates the fictive world, he or she is not the film's controlling consciousness. The commentary acts as another voice in the film, albeit one with a privileged point of view. This point of view is not infallible. The represented fictional world may still exhibit characteristics that differ from the perceptions of the impersonal narrator.

Barry Lyndon's visual stylization and distanced presentation are combined with the device of an impersonal narrator to mediate its objective view. The impersonal narrator exhibits a distinct point of view. This mediation is a key characteristic of Kubrick's conception of filmic objectivity. The precise nature of this mediation helps distinguish the director's more objective presentations from his subjective ones.

Both kinds of filmic organization are complex and highly determined, and it is not always clear where to demarcate the line that distinguishes them. It is apparent that both are at the service of a larger ambition: that of finding the most appropriate form to depict the lives of the characters and the world of the film. Kubrick's conception of narrative became so intricate that such categorizations as "subjective" and "objective," though helpful in understanding the formal operation of the films, may ultimately prove inadequate to account for his accomplishment.

NOTES

1. Jonathan Culler, *The Pursuit of Signs: Semiotics, Literature, Deconstruction* (Ithaca, N.Y.: Cornell University Press, 1981), 169–70.
2. Edward Branigan, *Point of View in the Cinema: A Theory of Narration and Subjectivity in Classical Film* (Berlin, Germany: Mouton Publishers, 1984), 73.
3. Ibid.
4. Ibid., 76.
5. Stephen Heath, *Questions of Cinema* (London: Macmillan, 1981), 46–47.
6. Ibid., 47.
7. I was first introduced to the term "mythopoeia" as it relates to cinema through reading (and studying with) P. Adams Sitney, whose brilliant book on American experimental film, *Visionary Film: The American Avant-Garde* (New York: Oxford University Press, 1979, 2nd edition) remains the best analysis of the avant-garde yet written. Many of the filmmakers discussed by Sitney such as Maya Deren, James Broughton,

Stan Brakhage and Bruce Baillie represent a particular strain of the American avant-garde that incorporated specific references to mythology in their films. This tendency seems to have reached a peak in such films as Brakhage's *Dog Star Man* (1961–1965), which incorporates the Sisyphus myth to create a complex and dense multilayered abstract film that functions almost like a waking dream. Kubrick's relationship to the avant-garde is most apparent in *2001*, whose visual abstractions in the Star-Gate sequence in particular owe much to their experiments. Readers might also want to consult Gene Youngblood's book, *Expanded Cinema* (New York: Dutton, 1970) for another excellent analysis of the "visionary" strain of the American avant-garde.

8. Larry Smith quoted in Stephen Pizzello, "A Sword in the Bed," *American Cinematographer*, 80:10 (October 1999), 28–38.

9. Federico Fellini, quoted in Peter Bondanella, *The Cinema of Federico Fellini* (Princeton, N.J.: Princeton University Press, 1992), 299.

10. Gene D. Phillips, *Stanley Kubrick: A Film Odyssey* (New York: Popular Library, 1975), 134.

11. Ibid.

12. Ibid., 49.

13. Ibid., 109.

14. Quoted in ibid., 114.

15. Tim Cahill, "The Rolling Stone Interview: Stanley Kubrick," *Rolling Stone* (27 August 1987), 36.

6

Character and Performance

The creation of character in Stanley Kubrick's films is complex and intimately linked to the various thematic and stylistic operations at play. Performance and how to communicate meaning through character have consistently been crucial components in Kubrick's aesthetics. I will focus my remarks here on *A Clockwork Orange*, *Barry Lyndon* and *The Shining*, concentrating for the most part on each film's main character. These particular characterizations involve some of the more distinctive performances in contemporary film acting and reveal much about Kubrick's conception of character and his inventive direction of actors.

A CLOCKWORK ORANGE

The opening shot of *A Clockwork Orange* presents Alex as its main performer and declares that his "performance" will be the focal point of the film. Violence will be his "creative act." The elements of fantasy and theatricality are clearly evident in the first HOME sequence where Alex performs his first "star turn." Alex's "dance" involves an impersonation of a freaked-out Gene Kelly. He moves with great flair and his violent actions become his creative release. Carefully choreographed movements and gestures punctuate his actions. There is little wonder that the film's violence is in some ways attractive. Not only is it presented with great imagination and skill, but it is also performed by the only character in the film with any degree of charm. This may present some viewers with a moral dilemma. If the film criticizes the violent world it presents, why is violence presented with such imagination? Further, if Alex is not meant to be sympathetic, why make him so charming and everyone else so unappealing?

Alex is not presented with complete sympathy, but the film does argue that there is something admirable in the way the character channels his creativity.

It further argues that the fascistic solution of the Ludovico treatment that produces the character's loss of free will is not an acceptable alternative to Alex's violent, anarchic behavior. In the director's world view, the ability to make choices is a primary component of our humanity. Can the world really be a better place if we all become less human in the process? The aestheticization of the film's violence contributes to the articulation of this idea. This choice may complicate the film's argument, but it makes for a more interesting and serious work.

In the ensuing attack on the couple, Alex continues to play a role as he enters the apartment. He carries a cane and wears a distended, phallic mask and a bowler hat. He kicks and jumps on the writer, with the camera recording much of the scene in hand-held, distorted views from ground level. The gang begins its attack in a kind of frolic around the space. Alex gets the attention of his gang members by whistling, giving orders and generally orchestrating the action. Again, Alex takes control of the situation—he is the star performer. He begins his performance by shoving a ball in the mouth of the writer's wife, taping it shut, and performing a soft-shoe dance to "Singing In the Rain." He kicks the writer and brutally slaps the woman. His choreographed movements include kicks for added punctuation. He bends to one knee (like Al Jolson) and stuffs a ball in the writer's mouth. Then he jumps on the writer's table and continues his dance of destruction, flipping over the desk and toppling an entire bookcase. The camera shifts points of view by alternating eye-level shots of the action with shots of Mr. Alexander from floor level with eyes bulging.

The sexuality of the attack (and the performance) becomes more pointed as Alex uses scissors to cut holes out of the clothing covering the woman's breasts and slits her jumpsuit up the middle. The suave, stylish Alex is a striking contrast to the brutish Billy Boy and his gang's abuse of their naked victim in the previous scene.

The elements of fantasy and play that figure in these brutal acts relate to the subjective presentation emphasized by many elements of the film's design. These include point-of-view shots, the use of distorting wide-angle lenses, character voice-over and aspects of lighting and editing. They convey the impression that the world is filtered through the consciousness of Alex.

The world that Alex inhabits takes on an air of fantasy. Alex is not a violent thug in this world but one of its stars, at least in his own mind. He views himself perhaps as a rock star or performance artist and does not associate viciousness or brutality with any of his actions. He makes little distinction between the real world and his fantasy life. The drug-induced violent acts give Alex his sense of identity, allowing him to escape the drab existence of his home life in the dilapidated projects where he lives with his parents. The visual style of the film is critical to maintaining the film's subjective point of view.

The subjective presentation continues, first in a high-speed sexual escapade with two teenage girls, then in a slow-motion sequence of Alex as he attacks his gang of droogs at the Flatblock Marina. Both sequences emphasize the theatrical exaggeration and stylization. In something of a reversal of expectation, the scene of sexuality is illustrated in fast motion while the sequence of violence is temporally elongated. Alex finds his pleasure in violence while sex becomes a mere mechanical act. Both actions illustrate the performing aspect of the character.

Alex's violent ballet at the marina is the more interesting of the two scenes. Not only does it contain a wider array of cinematic expressiveness, such as rhythmical editing, varying shot size, different angles of view and slow motion, but it also illustrates again how Alex transforms violent actions into creative acts.

As the sequence begins, Alex and his gang are shown in long shot, full view as they walk along the marina in slow motion. In voice-over, Alex declares:

But suddenly, I viddied that thinking was for the gloopy ones, and that the oomny ones used like inspiration and what Bog sends. For now it was lovely music that came to my aid. There was a window open, with a stereo on, and I viddied right at once what to do.

The ensuing violent ballet is comprised of sixteen shots. Alex disposes of the gang members by sending them into the water and, as the music crescendos, he pulls a knife from his club and coaxes Dim out of the water in an extreme, low-angle shot. He then cuts Dim's wrist as he feigns a helping hand. The use of different film speeds acts to stretch out the time and distort the visual presentation. It is the heightening of a moment of creation. Alex's actions and speech at this point are the clearest indication that he views his entire life, especially his acts of violence, as an artistic creation. He is "inspired" by the music emanating from an open window. The sequence is brilliantly edited to the music, and Alex's graceful movements have balletic overtones. In Alex's mind, there is a clear distinction between the "artist," who acts instinctively and spontaneously (divinely inspired by "Bog"), and the individual, who relies on thinking (the critic, the intellectual). Although Alex is very intelligent, he is certainly not an intellectual. He sees himself instead as a creative artist.

The aestheticizing of violence and the creative aspect of Alex's violent actions are also notable in the Cat Lady sequence. The woman is first shown contorting her body in a yoga position reminiscent of the painting over Alex's bed. Her physical position is also similar to those in the paintings that hang in her elegant home. The eccentric and unflattering presentation of the woman is another indication of the deterioration and decadence of this society.

The sequence emphasizes the class distinctions between Alex and his victims. Alex comes from a disadvantaged social stratum and lives in a decayed, debris-strewn housing project. He is portrayed as one more victim of an uncaring and decadent society. Although it would be wrong to sympathize with him, the film clearly views him as a symptom of society's problems rather than their cause.

The Cat Lady is surrounded by *objets d'art* that echo the sadomasochistic subtext of the sequence and illustrate how the wealthier classes have appropriated the violence around them into their art. The entire sequence is shot through a distorting wide-angle lens. The woman is surrounded by dozens of cats. Her voice has a deep, masculine timbre that adds a quality of "drag" or cross-dressing to her presentation. Her house is filled with wall paintings that place women in fetishistic positions such as licking boots and breasts. The space also contains a giant sculpture of a penis that Alex will shortly appropriate as his murder weapon. This presentation illustrates how the decadence of this society has reached such an extreme that the upper classes can afford to concentrate on their bodies, surround themselves with decadent art and lead an altogether eccentric existence. Art and life have merged to the point that human sexuality has been displaced by art work.

Alex enters the apartment, again wearing his phallic mask, and seems genuinely surprised by what he sees. He strikes the penis sculpture with his hand, and its movement metaphorically stands in for his unbridled sexuality. The sculpture becomes a kind of exteriorization and extension of his character. The woman fends him off with a bust of Beethoven. As Alex continues his dance steps, the hand-held camera alternates views of the two characters. The woman finally hits Alex with the Beethoven bust. The camera is placed directly in the middle of the mayhem as Alex picks up the penis sculpture and, in an extremely low, oblique angle shot, prepares to penetrate the woman with his monstrous member. An overhead camera zooms into the woman's face several times and cuts away at the moment of impact to several shots of the wall paintings.

This chaotic, anarchic world is represented through spatial distortion, camera movement and a fragmented editing style. There is no symmetry here. The world is irrational. Inserted fragments from the wall paintings (a mouth within a mouth, a hand, a breast, a hand masturbating) act as objectifications of the woman's sexuality. The woman achieving orgasm in a painting is perversely brought to life by the sexually charged attack on the Cat Lady. The merging of pleasure with pain and sexuality with violence perfectly illustrates the distorted values of this society. The sexual symbolism and inversion of pain and pleasure continue as Alex achieves his orgasmic release a moment later outside the mansion, when Dim flamboyantly and in slow motion smashes a milk bottle over his face.

The Cat Lady sequence raises disturbing questions about the role of art in society, and the exciting, in some ways attractive, presentation of its violence may make some viewers uneasy. This is one of the strongest sequences in the film, exciting, brilliantly handled and flamboyantly presented. This does not necessarily make the violence pleasurable, but it is intensely watchable. One can legitimately ask whether the violence is not presented too attractively to support the critique it aims for. If the sequence is an attack on modern art, is all modern art suspect? Certainly, Kubrick does not intend a blanket condemnation. If the film is a cautionary tale about where modern society is headed, why dazzle the audience so completely that the critique gets blurred?

The second HOME sequence begins immediately after Alex has been brutalized by the gang of derelicts and the police (his former gang members, Dim and Georgie). Alex stumbles in the night toward the shelter of HOME in the midst of a drenching thunderstorm. This beginning makes clever allusions to the horror genre, especially for viewers familiar with some of actor Patrick Magee's earlier roles. The hand-held camera follows Alex as he crawls up the walkway to the writer's house. The following interior shot begins similarly to the first HOME sequence. Mr. Alexander is seated at his desk facing the camera. "Who on earth could that be?" he asks. As the camera tracks right, it reveals a body builder companion in place of Mrs. Alexander from the earlier sequence. Alex falls through the front door in exhaustion and is picked up and cradled by the body builder in a composition that slightly resembles the *Pietà*. This continues the film's religious symbolism and is taken directly from the Burgess novel.

Magee's performance style is extremely exaggerated, as he recognizes Alex from the newspapers as the "poor victim of this horrible new technique." The actor modulates his voice into its upper registers. He shakes and trembles. He blinks his eyes rapidly, bites his fingernail and rapidly sucks in his breath. It is a comic, literal interpretation of the "lunatic" left. The exaggerated performance recalls some of Magee's work in earlier films in which he often played depraved characters (as in *Masque of the Red Death* [Roger Corman, 1964] and his quintessential role as the Marquis de Sade in *Marat/Sade* [Peter Brook, 1967]). As the scene progresses and Mr. Alexander hears fragments of "Singing in the Rain" coming from the upstairs bathroom, he is sent into a fit of recognition. The camera films him in an extreme low-angle, distorted shot with his hands on his knees, eyes rolling, mouth open and body shaking. The sounds of Alex singing now are equally distorted, continuing the subjective presentation.

Magee continues his exaggerated performance in the next scene. He loudly declaims his lines ("*Food* all right? Try the wine"), emphasizing and shouting individual words, altering the pitch of his voice. The hysteria continues as the character invokes his wife ("*My wife* [trembles] used to do everything for me, and leave me to my writing. . . . No, she's *dead!*"). Magee continues his exaggerated performance, as he blinks quickly, alters his facial expressions rapidly, smiles uncontrollably and exhibits pain and pleasure simultaneously. The sequence ends with Alex's suicide attempt (illustrated by an optical point-of-view shot). Although the sequence reverses the roles of victim and aggressor from the first HOME sequence, it continues to highlight the performance aspects and theatricality so prominent throughout the film.

Alex continues his performance and his role of victim in the next few scenes at the hospital, where government officials try to amend their past mistakes. Enormous music speakers are wheeled in accompanied by a bevy of photographers to capture the next phase of the propaganda campaign. These scenes continue to stress aspects of the film's theatricality: frontality, audience and role-playing. Even Alex's chewing of food is presented as a performance. The Beethoven music blasts from the speakers, and the audience sees Alex roll his eyes upward in an ecstatic reverie. This leads directly to the final, dreamlike sequence of him and a woman in a naked sexual frolic, shot in slow motion. The couple is being applauded by an upper-crust audience decked out in fine clothes. Alex remains the star performer, whether in real life or in his fantasies.

It is difficult to separate the "real" Alex from his impersonations. Whatever identity the character has is derived from the different roles he plays: sadist, victim, dandy, model prisoner, gang leader and versatile musical comedy performer. Alex has transformed his violent urges and brutal behavior into his creative act. His life has become his art.

The exaggerated performance styles, the use of direct address through voice-over and the ironic language counteract the possibility of audience identification or empathy that such extreme subjectivity might normally elicit. The film's distancing precludes any identification with Alex. Although a kind of intimacy is created through the voice-over and other details of the subjective presentation, Alex remains at an emotional remove because of the extreme artifice and theatricality of Kubrick's presentation of him.

This is not to say, of course, that the viewer's relationship with Alex is unimportant; it is of crucial significance to the film's main argument. The film must strike a delicate balance between involvement and distance. Alex may elicit the viewer's sympathy. The audience may even admire his creativity and survival instinct, but if it gets too close to the character emotionally, the film's main critique will be undercut. A degree of emotional distance must be maintained, which is why the internal tensions, performance strategies and visual style are of such importance.

The film's ending suggests that Alex will revert to his original character ("I was cured all right") and anarchistic behavior. For many viewers, this will seem no worse a prospect than the totalitarian world created by the Ludovico treatment. Despite the ending's jocular tone, it is not a happy prospect. The narrative closure is tentative for, in Kubrick's bleak view, there seems no way out.

BARRY LYNDON

This grim world view continues to unfold in *Barry Lyndon*, the director's most aesthetically ambitious and emotionally satisfying film. The strategies of long takes, long shots, elaborate *mise-en-scène*, slow zooms, camera and character placement are elements in a complicated formal design that help articulate many of the film's thematic concerns. The creation of Barry's character is inextricably bound to such strategies.

A key component of the depiction of Barry's character is his placement within the frame, frequently in a frozen gesture with a blank facial expression. These shots typically communicate Barry's powerlessness and the fact that he has little will or identity of his own. Viewers come to know Barry primarily through strategies of *presentation* rather than more typical character-building conventions. Many of the film's visual and temporal strategies are designed to elaborate Barry's character. In fact, the radical nature of the film's stylistics extends to its articulation of character. Thus, viewers come to know Barry through frozen gestures, placement within the frame and severe restriction and limitation of the frame edge. This effect is achieved in part through the use of the slow zoom, static long takes and strategic uses of camera movement. The visual presentation of Barry and the look of the entire film are paramount to its ambitions and the realization of his character.

Barry is essentially a prisoner, both of the frame and of his society. The two-dimensional, lifeless, orderly individual he becomes is largely the result of his style of presentation. In sequence after sequence, the audience sees Barry in similar poses. He often looks directly ahead but not *at* anyone. An example of this can be found in a scene with Barry in the role of a German spy. He stands in front of Captain Potzdorf (Hardy Kruger), who is seated with his uncle, the chief of police. Barry speaks but not *to* anyone, nor does he direct his gaze at either man. When he does speak, it is in an unthinking manner, as if he were a machine.

Many scenes find Barry in situations where his physical movements are deliberately slow, artificial and stylized, or else where he is completely immobile and locked in a frozen gesture. Barry is most frequently seen in medium or long shots, presented frontally. He is often shown walking or standing in a pose, with arms folded behind his back and head bent downward, or looking straight ahead with a far-off look in his eyes. The film uses many such distancing devices and maintains them throughout.

The film bears some similarities to *A Clockwork Orange*. For example, the main character's role-playing is always in the foreground. Like the earlier film, *Barry Lyndon* does not blame its protagonist for his character flaws. Barry's downfall is portrayed sympathetically. Throughout the film, Barry takes on a succession of different roles. By the end, he has little identity of his own left. What identity he has is in relation to others: his wife, his son, the chevalier, his mother and the aristocratic society around him.

The pattern of role-playing and occasional victimization is established early in the film. In an elaborately staged duel, Barry is manipulated by his cousins to persuade Captain Quin (Leonard Rossiter) to marry into their family. Barry is forced to leave home and is immediately robbed by highwaymen on the road to Dublin. He enlists in the English army and then is forced into the Prussian service. These episodes reinforce the impression that Barry's will is not his own. His energy and vitality are being drained from him. Experiences that might normally broaden his outlook on life and enrich his character serve, in fact, only to rob him of his youthful ideals and naïve belief in love. They are crucial in shaping the cynical, opportunistic individual the audience comes to know in the second half of the film.

At various points in the narrative, Barry pretends to be an English officer, a Prussian spy, a valet and his own gambling partner, the chevalier. This is the more obvious sort of role-playing in the film. Less obvious are the roles that society forces on Barry. He eventually plays the role of husband, lover, father and an English gentleman, the role he aspires to most. There is little difference between these two types of role-playing, for both gradually divest Barry of his identity and innocence.

Barry spends much of the first half of the film falling into situations over which he has little control. His one ambition in life is to attain wealth and position. The years spent touring the European courts as a gambler with the chevalier (Patrick Magee) instill in Barry the desire to be wealthy. If Barry is made to strive for wealth and status, it is because he is convinced that society values this way of life above all others. When marrying into a great family fortune inevitably proves unsatisfying, Barry foolishly believes that he must direct all his energies and considerable wealth to the pursuit of a peerage. It does not occur to him that there could be something other than wealth, position and the pursuit of pleasure in life. But then, Barry can only reflect the values of the society that has created him.

This idea—that Barry must aspire to wealth, property and title at the expense of his youthful ideals—provides one of *Barry Lyndon*'s harshest critiques. The film argues that love, passion and emotion may be appropriate in a young boy, but they have no place in the adult world. Barry plays one role after another and assumes one pose after another until all he has left is the pose. By the end of the film, what was genuine and authentic in his original character has been lost. The film's fatalistic narrative argues that as people become more experienced, they inevitably lose the innocence of youth. The film goes further, however, in arguing that people also lose their energy, their will power and all that is vital, even a sense of identity. There is never any notion that experience can enrich and make one wiser.

The film does not always resort to the same temporal and/or visual strategies to articulate the complex thematics centered on Barry's powerlessness, his loss of ideals and his imprisonment in the eighteenth-century aristocratic value system. Early in the film, Kubrick offers an excellent example of the way in which the static long take combines with long-shot framing to communicate such notions. The exterior long shot begins with Barry and Nora, who are in the extreme background of the shot, walking hand in hand toward the camera. They stroll along a path lined with huge trees. The conversation revolves around the fact that Nora has repeatedly danced with Captain Quin, an older military man. Barry, who is only sixteen at this point, cannot contain his jealousy at being slighted by his flirtatious cousin. They end their walk in a medium shot with Barry screen left and Nora screen right. They face each

other in center frame in the foreground. The conversation ends as Barry an-
grily tells his cousin to "best have your Englishman take you home" and exits
the frame, screen left behind the space where the camera is positioned. Nora,
left alone in the frame (in a 3/4 shot), turns and walks back down the road
into the background. The shot lasts 82 seconds, and the camera remains immobile throughout.

Although the youthful Redmond Barry displays emotion in the scene, the
immobility and spatial, emotional distance in the shot hint at the powerless,
ineffectual life he can expect to lead. It is a subtle use of a static long take, and
it illustrates how important space and framing are in communicating the
film's ideas. Throughout the shot, the camera is immobile except for a slight
reframing and tilt-up to frame Nora as she moves back down the road; it
holds until Nora reaches the spot, in depth, where the two characters had
begun their walk. The formal arrangement and length of the shot emphasize
the codified rigidity of the characters' world, while the framing alludes to
their inability to operate outside the constraints of their class structure. They
are bound to the value system of the aristocracy as rigidly as they are bound
within the limits of the frame. This is one example of a tableau-like strategy
that creates a kind of theatrical space. Highly studied in its arrangement, the
scene emphasizes the rules and structures of the regimented society that im-
prisons the characters.

Many of the film's visual and editing strategies illustrate Barry's mechanical, mannequin-like nature. In some shots, Barry is shown ceremoniously
marching with his troops or standing erect, gazing straight ahead to emphasize the frontality of presentation and the shallow space he inhabits.
These scenes are generally shot in similar ways, either in long or medium
shot, and often employing a slow zoom into or out of the subject. Many
present Barry as almost lifeless, merely going through the motions. The audience rarely has a sense that Barry gives thought to any action or has much
of an interior life. Rather, viewers get the impression of a character acting
out his various assigned roles.

The blank facial expression and lack of interiority are readily apparent in the
sequence in which Barry contemplates escaping from the English army. The
scene begins with Barry walking to a stream to collect water. He overhears
two gay soldiers bathing in the stream. Their conversation indicates that one
of them must carry important papers to an army general, which will afford
Barry his chance for escape. The camera slowly zooms into Barry's face, and
the voice-over explains what Barry will do. The information conveyed by the
commentary is impossible to decipher from Barry's facial expression, which is
essentially blank. The audience must take the narrator's word that this is what
Barry is thinking. There is little conventional drama to the scene. The plot has
been advanced primarily through the device of voice-over.

The shot illustrates that notions of character in the film are frequently
conveyed not by Ryan O'Neal's performance but by other formal devices.

Through such devices as voice-over narration, blank facial expressions and stiff presentation, slow zooms and other framing strategies, the film creates an essentially dedramatized style (and space) of presentation. There is a clear relationship between Kubrick's formal, flat presentation and the flat, shallow character of Barry. The limitations imposed on Barry through framing and other formal strategies echo the limitations and restrictions imposed on him by his society. The film thus shifts the weight of character development and narrative information away from the naturalistic or dramatic acting of the central character to other elements of the film, resulting in a more complex and ironic work.

As the narrative unfolds, Barry becomes more and more unfeeling and superficial. In his life as a gambler, it is the fine clothes, make-up, style and fashion that are central. One senses the emptiness of Barry's life very sharply in these scenes with the chevalier. Barry increasingly abandons control of his destiny. It is the chevalier who decides what course their lives will take, and these lives seem both precious and decidedly unhappy. Barry seems bereft of pleasure throughout much of the film. The only exceptions are the scenes with his son Bryan.

In the scenes with the chevalier, the audience has a sense that Barry has simply stumbled into another situation. Notions of happiness or satisfaction do not seem to enter into his thinking. Barry does not know what to expect of life, but he gradually creates a set of expectations and ambitions centering around material goals: title, wealth and property. This leads to Barry's courtship of Lady Lyndon and to his next role. (It is perhaps significant that, after Barry's seduction of Lady Lyndon, the narrator says "to make a long story short, six hours after they met, her ladyship was in love." Not only is this admirable narrative compression, but, crucially, the narrator does not mention Barry's feelings. Love is clearly not part of his scenario.)

As I have argued, the creation of Barry's character is intimately connected to the film's style of presentation, which includes many visual and editing strategies. It is not mere coincidence that Kubrick's most profound filmic character is found in his most radical aesthetic experiment. In fact, it is the very radicality of the film's stylistics that accounts for the profundity of characterization.

Barry begins life with a certain innocence and a naïve world view, and he appears connected to his natural environment. Nonetheless, he is a prisoner of his aspirations as surely as he is imprisoned within the film's rigid frame constructions. The open spaces that are predominant in Part 1 of the film are no less confining than the enclosed spaces of Castle Hackton in Part 2. Barry's fate is predetermined from the moment he is forced to flee home after the duel with Captain Quin. The rigid frame and the two-dimensional flatness of the image, emphasized by the zooms, foreshadow the shallow, callous, lifeless society Barry eventually inhabits. The film's style of presentation is essential in communicating this formal environment and the kind of individual Barry becomes.

The strongest impression viewers have of Barry in the film's early scenes is physical. He is presented as passionate, stubborn, idealistic and naïve. This impression is formed essentially through the audience's awareness of his body—its robustness and its beauty. What the audience admires most about young Redmond Barry is his youthful vitality. He is not especially thoughtful but more of a presence on the screen. Although the audience occasionally sees Barry in reflective moments, these moments become fewer as the film progresses. It is a sad realization that, with a few exceptions, it is only in these early scenes that the character is allowed to be genuinely emotional. The older and more experienced Barry grows, the more mannequin-like and less given to emotion he becomes. The major exception in Part 2 is the sequence in which Barry brutally attacks his stepson, Lord Bullingdon, at a music recital. In most other scenes, the film shows Barry in various poses, marching with his troops or simply standing, watching or playing at the gaming tables. These scenes emphasize the lifeless quality of the character.

It is appropriate that at his wedding to Lady Lyndon, Barry is arrayed in the finest clothes, wearing thick make-up and lipstick and with coiffed and powdered hair. Viewers have the impression that, besides his new name, Barry is adopting a new identity. Although he is still a relatively young man at this point in the narrative, the strapping youth of the early scenes has disappeared. He has been replaced by an opportunistic, shallow and lifeless dandy. There are scenes filled with genuine feeling in the second half of the film, in which the audience can see traces of the young Barry. But they are mere traces. Barry Lyndon is no longer Redmond Barry; he is an artificial creation of a decadent society.

The creation of character, the performance style and the stylistic system are so interconnected that *Barry Lyndon* is the most powerful example of Kubrick's melding of form and thematics. The character of Barry could not possibly exist outside the world of the film. The audience's understanding of Barry depends on many components, including elements outside the film itself. Viewers will, of course, relate in their own ways to this fictional character. Each of us brings a different world view to the experience of watching a film, and responses to characters are bound to be different. As a film with a radical conception of both character and style, *Barry Lyndon* has, not surprisingly, provoked the most wide-ranging set of responses. It remains one of Kubrick's most compelling and audacious experiments.

THE SHINING

The Shining differs so greatly from *Barry Lyndon* partly because the former film features a wildly inventive and emotionally charged performance by Jack Nicholson in the leading role. The performance is notable for its physicality and expressiveness, the very qualities underplayed in Ryan O'Neal's performance in *Barry Lyndon*. Although the styles of acting are quite different, each film places its main performer in unusual spaces. My understanding of *The Shining* and of many of its abstract ideas is directly connected to the placement and presentation of its main character.

As in *Barry Lyndon*, notions of character here are intimately connected to spatial strategies, including the idea that *The Shining* creates a kind of metaphorical mental landscape. Jack Nicholson's characterization is crucial in communicating many of the film's thematic and formal ideas. The exploration of space (and the relationship of Nicholson's performance and characterization to that space) is a key concern of *The Shining*.

Nicholson's performance is one of the most frequently noted aspects of the film. It is wild and extreme, verging on the hysterical. At times, the actor gives the impression of being out of control. The performance relies heavily on the physical and the comic for its effect. It is not a very "respectable" performance and may strike some as overbearing, vulgar and just plain "too much." In fact, it is precisely these risky, over-the-edge qualities that make the performance and the film so invigorating.

One of the film's most intricate strategies involves dualities, oppositions and the notion that things operate on more than one level. The concept of duality can be detected in Nicholson's characterization of Jack Torrance as well as in other aspects of the film's stylistic and narrative construction. *The Shining* seems to have been conceived with the possibility of multiple interpretations.

When the audience first encounters Jack Torrance, he is about to be interviewed for the caretaker job by Mr. Ullman, the hotel manager (Barry Nelson). As the camera follows Jack into Ullman's office, viewers get an immediate sensation that they are eavesdropping on a rather private conversation. Perhaps the slight wavering of the Steadicam contributes to this impression. There is also a stiff and staged atmosphere about the sequence. The audience feels like a silent presence in the room. This is an impression it will have many times in the film, and it results from the idea that the film operates on more than one level of discourse: the private and the more public. There seems to be a level of discourse that does not depend on language at all, but on gesture, reaction shots, glances and symbolic imagery (the "elevator of blood" shots)—in other words, on things that are not overtly stated. If there are evil forces at work at the Overlook, they are not immediately apparent. Likewise, if Jack has an evil side, it is not instantly visible (although it is hinted at from the beginning). The film continually intimates such dualities.

In this early scene with Ullman, viewers have the feeling that something is not quite right about Jack and his presentation of self. He seems to be posing for Ullman and has a kind of "phony" exterior. It is evident in the way he tries so hard to be affable and accommodating. It is apparent in his grim reaction as Ullman describes the 1970 Grady axe murders. Clearly, the important elements in the scene are not the banal information that Ullman communicates to Jack but the interaction between the two characters. The intensity in Jack's expression as Ullman describes the axe murders indicates that he is taken aback by the revelations. Although Ullman describes the murders almost lightheartedly, Jack looks genuinely stunned by the revelations. In moments like these, one senses the dark side of Jack's character lurking below the surface.

There is a complexity and thoughtfulness in Nicholson's playing of the scene that is remarkably subtle. Kubrick's skill as a director and editor lies in bringing out shades of meaning in what appears, on the surface, to be a rather ordinary scene. There is a layer of deceptiveness in Jack's character that is not immediately apparent. It can be detected, however, in many aspects of the narrative, as well as in Nicholson's performance. Things clearly are not what they seem in *The Shining*. The audience must dig below the surface to discern its meanings.

In the scene with Ullman, viewers sense that the stories told to Jack are not simply for his amusement or edification, but for some as yet unknown reason. Perhaps some part of Jack understands that he has a role to play in the drama/comedy about to unfold. There is a quality to Nicholson's acting in *The Shining* that is at once exteriorized and interiorized, revealing and mysterious, obvious and subtle. Nicholson's skill as an actor is evident in the way he so effortlessly articulates different aspects of his character, opening up many possible interpretations. His performance is very physical, highly comic and hammy. It reflexively ridicules itself and the conventions of the genre. At the same time, his acting is somewhat interiorized, elusive and thoughtful, and it does not reveal itself so obviously.

Nicholson elaborates his character by giving the impression that he has a dual nature: a "normal" side and an "evil" side. Viewers are presented with this duality often in the film. One particularly forceful and amusing example comes early in the scene that shows Jack driving to the Overlook with his wife and son. This sequence is interesting not only for what it reveals about Jack's character and Nicholson's performance, but also because it is the only time in the film that the audience will see the Torrance family alone and together in the frame. The framing reinforces the idea that the Torrances are a typical American family, an idea that becomes subverted as the film proceeds. The semblance of normality begins to fall apart almost immediately. These characters will never share the frame as a family unit again.

The intense expression on Jack's face as this shot begins is in marked contrast to the effusive, happy exterior seen in the earlier interview scene. Now Jack seems determined and preoccupied, apparently disturbed about something. The closer he gets to the Overlook, the closer his other (darker) personality comes to the surface. When Danny innocently mentions that he is hungry, Jack's response has a cruel edge to it. When the boy asks about the Donner party, Jack takes perverse glee in answering his son's question. Nicholson rolls his eyes upward, arches his eyebrows—one of his more familiar facial expressions in the film—and gives a very knowing smile to the camera, as if sharing a private moment with the spectator.

Many scenes continue the exploration of Jack's duality. One such scene shows Wendy serving Jack his breakfast in bed. The scene begins as a mirror shot of Jack lying in the bed eating his food. The reversed shot is maintained throughout much of the scene, formally hinting at the notion of duality through the framing. The dialogue is banal but revelatory. When Wendy tries to explain how simple the creative process is, Jack replies condescendingly. Wendy's reaction shots emphasize her role as a dutiful housewife. Her character is fearful and uncomprehending in the face of Jack's cruel remarks, and she generally communicates a quality of submissiveness.

Halfway through their conversation, the scene shifts to a normal, nonmirror shot. Jack discusses his feelings of *déjà vu* and the sensation that he has been at the hotel before. The scene becomes more comic as Jack playfully manipulates his food while he speaks. He makes light of his feelings, treating them as a joke. This is a small but effective example of how Nicholson uses a prop or creates a piece of "business" to add meaning to a scene. Coupled with the use of the mirror and the reversed framing, the scene takes on added complexity. The sequence creates more tension and a sense of uneasiness through the framing and the static long take. At the same time that viewers are amused by Nicholson's playing of the scene, the character's treatment of his wife is disturbing. The film often creates such feelings of disquiet and discomfort, especially during the later, intense sequences.

In a similar scene, Danny discovers his father seated on his bed staring straight ahead as though in a trance, not really looking at anyone. The image includes the real character and his mirror image. This is another example of how the framing reveals the dual nature of Jack's character. The framing of Jack and his mirror image indicates perhaps that Jack's two personas are merging. Jack and his alter ego, the public and the private, are becoming less and less distinguishable. By including Jack's mirror image and the real Jack in the same frame, the film formally indicates that both "Jacks" are equally present. Jack has noticeably deteriorated by this point in the film. He seems dazed and detached from his surroundings.

The conversation here is revealing. Danny asks his father if he likes the hotel. Jack responds that he loves it. In fact, he would like to stay at the Overlook "forever and ever and ever," echoing the words of the Grady daughters of an earlier scene. Danny asks, "Dad, you would never hurt mommy and me, would you?" Jack continues, "I love you, Danny. I would never do anything to hurt you." This time, the inflection of his voice is like that of an old man. By taking on different voices in the scene, Nicholson not only communicates the breakdown of his personality but allows for the possibility of more than one personality.

Occasionally, the idea of duality is emphasized by the order or sequencing of different scenes, each contrasting and commenting on the other. An example of this begins with a shot of Jack's typewriter on his writing table, surrounded by a few pencils and a burning cigarette in an ashtray, signaling

Jack's creative stagnation. The meaning of the shot is intensified by the loud, pounding sound of Jack throwing a ball against a wall. The use of sound here amplifies what is implied in the image. It adds an oppressive heaviness to the scene that complements the meaning of the props on Jack's writing table. It also carries an additional metaphoric connotation—that Jack is unable to break through his creative wall. Moreover, Jack throws the ball against one of the hotel's murals decorated with a maze motif, adding another potential meaning—that the hotel itself is responsible for Jack's creative block.

What is equally important in the scene is the way Nicholson uses his entire body. His movements are shown in long-shot as he throws the ball with full force against the wall in long, sweeping gestures. This physicality is the most crucial aspect of Nicholson's performance, and it involves a subtle manipulation of every part of the actor's body.

This interior sequence is immediately followed by and contrasted with shots of Wendy and Danny running playfully in the snow as they explore the maze outside. They are having fun and releasing their energies in a healthy, liberating way, in contrast to Jack's stagnation and repression inside the hotel. It is clear that Jack's "reality" is very different from the world inhabited by his wife and son. A shot of Wendy outside dissolves into a shot of Jack inside, linking the two worlds. Jack's world is now exclusively that of the hotel itself. He continues to play with the ball, throwing it down with great force. His energy is all wasted and uncreative. As the film proceeds, the sheer physical presence of Jack's body dominates each scene more and more. He jumps as he throws the ball down with ever greater force. His hulking movements are slow, heavy and brooding.

Almost every scene after this point illustrates the physicality of Nicholson's acting and shows how inventive he is in using his whole body to create his performance. A few examples will suffice to illustrate this point. Jack's first visit to the Gold Room comes immediately after his "nightmare" and Wendy's accusation that he is responsible for injuring Danny. As he walks down the corridor to the room, the audience sees Nicholson has momentarily taken on the persona of a crazy person, a bowery bum. Nicholson's movements, especially the way he flails his arms and talks to himself, closely approximate the gestures of a demented derelict. The long-shot framing allows viewers to see his entire body. The camera moves backward as Nicholson walks down the corridor. He punctuates the air with his fists, lost in his hermetic universe. Nicholson communicates the madness and seething anger of the character by the insistent thrusting of his arms down the sides of his body and into the air, as if striking at some unknown assailant.

This sequence leads to Jack's first encounter with Lloyd, the bartender in the Gold Room. Jack sits at the bar lined with mirrors, which again hints at notions of duality and the double. The scene is notable for its humorous parody of the horror genre, a parody that reaches its climax later in the film as Jack, axe in hand, drags his injured leg in a clear homage to earlier horror films. In this scene with Lloyd, the parody is played mostly at the level of language. Jack begins by exclaiming, "God, I'd give anything for a drink. I'd give my goddam soul, just for a glass of beer," a jocular reference to the Faust legend. Lloyd himself undoubtedly hints at vampire films with his manner of dress and lack of expression. His slicked-back black hair, unemotional facial expression and the lighting that gives him a bloodless quality all refer to the undead. The sequence is filled with verbal clichés, such as "women . . . can't live with 'em . . . can't live without 'em," "white man's burden" and "hair of the dog that bit me," all used with obvious irony. The sequence becomes particularly funny, albeit cruel, when Jack describes his problems with Wendy and an incident several years earlier when he dislocated Danny's shoulder. Nicholson plays the scene for comedy. A lovely moment occurs when Jack takes his first drink of bourbon. He drinks the alcohol as if it were some precious elixir, slowly savoring it and rolling his eyes in ecstasy. The actor shifts his body around, arches his eyebrows and manipulates his fingers.

The sequence illustrates one of the most important and surprising aspects of the film. In scenes like this, and many others, the film strikes a delicate balance between the truly frightening and the comic, between a genuine horror film and a comedy. This is especially noticeable later when Jack's mugging reappears in the most violent and frightening scenes as he menaces Wendy and Danny. In the scenes with Wendy in particular, the audience is often torn between the enjoyment of Nicholson's performance and revulsion at the cruelty he displays. This does not stop viewers from being fascinated by their scenes together, but they are unsettling.

Jack's cruelty and insensitivity to Wendy are especially harsh in a scene in which Wendy casually interrupts Jack at his writing table. The scene begins with Jack intensely typing while music by Bartók (*Music for Strings, Percussion and Celesta*) plays ominously on the soundtrack. Wendy innocently walks in and says, "Hi, hon. Get a lot written today?" Jack is extremely upset by her interruption, and Wendy accuses him of being grouchy. Jack's response is very extreme. He rolls his eyes upward, rips the typing paper, pounds his forehead, arches his eyebrows and sweeps his hair back as he shouts insults and obscenities at Wendy. He is condescending and completely insensitive to her feelings. Although Jack is very cruel to Wendy, it is a fascinating scene to watch. It highlights both the physicality of Nicholson's acting and the audience's ambivalent feelings about scenes containing complex and sometimes contradictory elements.

Occasionally Nicholson's characterization is most effective when it is least agitated. One such moment is a remarkable shot of Jack that clearly indicates that the character's descent into madness is now complete. The shot is a slow zoom into Jack's unshaven face. He is totally frozen and immobile, completely lost in his mental landscape. What is unusual is the lack of empathy the spectator feels with his character, even though the close-up is so privileged. There is a disengagement and distance created by the shot that seems the opposite of what such a moment might normally reveal. The shot serves to objectify the character, negating any possibility of spectator identification.

The camera zooms in to a big close-up of the actor's face and holds the shot for some time. Rather than creating intimacy with the character, the shot emphasizes Jack's isolation. The close view does not bring the audience any closer to understanding the character. The animated, gesticulating Jack of the earlier scenes is well on his way to becoming the frozen statue in the snow at film's end. Jack is now ready to do the hotel's bidding. He has shed his "normal" persona and allowed his "evil" side to surface.

At the end of the shot, Jack offers a faint smile. It is a curious moment. At whom is Jack smiling, and for what reason? Jack takes secret pleasure from some mental image or from a feeling he cannot possibly share with the spectator. Still, the shot also hints at the possibility of complicity between Jack and the viewer, implying that he and the viewer know what must be done. The drama (or comedy) must be allowed to play itself to its bloody conclusion. The elusive ambiguity and complexity of the shot are the results of both the brilliant formal orchestration of the moment and Nicholson's underplaying of the scene.

The film's narrative is played out at such a level of abstraction and unreality that the notion of character empathy is virtually impossible. The spectator is at once distanced from the proceedings because of the level of parody and irony, and totally absorbed because of the film's momentum and intensity. Although it is difficult to sympathize with Jack, the audience is taken up with enjoying Nicholson's performance. The last hour of the film, in particular, is played out at such an absurd, abstract level, that it precludes any kind of sympathy or moralizing by the spectator. The film is nonnaturalistic, extreme, grotesque and very funny.

There are many instances of verbal humor in the last half of the film that add to the overall effect. When Jack crashes through a door with his axe, he exclaims with mocking humor, "Wendy I'm home," saying the line like a "dad." Nicholson is also very funny in his impersonation of the Big Bad Wolf ("Little pigs, little pigs"). Jack mugs and limps his way through many scenes, in contrast to the genuine terror and piercing screams emanating from Wendy. There are, of course, many psychosexual implications that resonate throughout these scenes. Jack's use of the axe is not arbitrary. Its phallic connotations are obvious, such as when it rips through various doors where the terrified and helpless Wendy waits, mouth wide open, on the other side. The violent attacks on Wendy substitute for Jack's repressed sexuality and his creative stagnation.

The film contains not only an interesting mix of moods but also a real contrast in acting styles. Shelley Duvall plays her scenes in a very convincing and naturalistic way. She seems to be directed to perform as if she were in a genuinely scary and more conventional horror film. She acts truly terrified and often appears physically exhausted. Nicholson plays his role in a different way.

He is a nonnaturalistic comic, a self-knowing parodist of the menacing figure in horror films. The mix of acting styles and the shifts between comedy and horror are genuinely surprising and unconventional. Consequently, the spectator must shift his or her responses from one moment to the next. Are viewers to take the film seriously? Are they meant to laugh? How can they laugh at what Jack is trying to do? And yet, how can they not laugh?

As the film nears its climax, Jack's limp becomes more pronounced and his mugging—"Here's Johnny"—more outrageous. The film often seems on the verge of becoming so comic that its horrific moments will be dissipated. In fact, this does not happen. Whenever the audience feels that the film cannot possibly be scary, there is a genuinely frightening moment. For example, Halloran's (Scatman Crothers) gruesome murder comes in the middle of Nicholson's mugging.

What is perhaps most audacious about the film is precisely the way it keeps shifting in tone without losing its bearings, giving Jack laugh lines at just those points when he is most murderous. Jack is quite clever in his use of language, though shortly he will be unable to utter a single word. Very few filmmakers or actors could carry this off so successfully. Nicholson's great comic and dramatic talent is crucial to the film's success. I cannot think of another actor who can so effortlessly shift from comedy to drama. Nicholson's particular history as an actor, for many years outside the Hollywood system but now very much a star of that system, also invests the role with additional meaning. The role demands a recognizable star who can parody the genre and himself.

The film culminates with the technically brilliant sequence of Jack pursuing Danny through the maze. Jack becomes the personification of every child's nightmare (and one of the most common dream forms): a nameless, unstoppable, evil force, even more terrifying because it is Danny's "daddy." As Jack shouts and slurs his words, he becomes less and less capable of verbal articulation. He skulks and howls, finally collapsing in exhaustion. The transformation is now complete. Jack has become a deformed maniac incapable of uttering an intelligible word and barely capable of making any sound at all. This final sequence is no longer comic; rather, it recalls the nightmare quality of fairy tales or dream imagery. Nicholson's physicality and use of his voice, coupled with the intensity of the montage, the brilliant use of the Steadicam, the involving music and the harsh blue lighting, combine to create one of the most unforgettable sequences in contemporary film.

The film creates much of its meaning through the presentation of Jack (both Torrance and Nicholson) and his interaction with the camera, other actors and the space around him. The various narrative and thematic dualities touched on here—subjective/objective, interior/exterior, expansive/compressed, the idea of the double, fantasy/reality, movement/stasis, surface/depth—are often articulated through the presentation of this complex character.

Although lacking the degree of character sympathy achieved in *Barry Lyndon*, the characterization of Jack Torrance in *The Shining* represents a new level of complexity for Kubrick in his experiments with character. The director has found inventive ways to articulate and connect his stylistic concerns with thematic and structural organization. The characterizations of both Barry and Jack represent a level of experimentation that has tended to remove the director's work even further from the narrative mainstream. An appreciation of Kubrick's late work demands that one appreciate ironic, distanced and reflexive filmmaking, which are hardly the qualities that will endear him to a mass audience.

I stated earlier that in *The Shining* Kubrick reaches a new level of exploring space in cerebral ways. But this exploration of space is not merely a formalistic exercise divorced from narrative or thematic considerations. *The Shining* represents an interesting and unusual exploration of performance and space. It is concerned, among other things, with how to communicate and present an actor within a variety of spaces and how to create additional meanings through this presentation.

Kubrick has always been interested in exploring formal and narrative parameters in the construction of his films. With the creation of characters such as Jack Torrance and Barry Lyndon, one senses an attempt to find new relationships involving characterization, the formal arrangement and spatial presentation of actors, and experiments with performance and acting styles.

This discussion also illustrates the inadequacy of words to describe how many aspects of films operate. The experience of viewing films is very different from reading (or writing) about them. One cannot duplicate the film experience through language but only summarize some of a film's characteristics or outline ways that films may function. Language can teach us much about how art operates, but what it can't do is stand in for the experience of art. The relationship an audience creates with filmic characters or an artwork cannot be reduced to an exercise in pure description. What the viewer feels and thinks about the world keeps intruding. Viewers often create their own characters when they watch films. Ultimately, they make films their own when they view and internalize them.

7

Final Thoughts

Throughout this analysis I have explored issues related to narrative organization, style and how meaning is generated in Stanley Kubrick's films. It is clear that many formal operations contribute to the creation of Kubrick's artistic vision. I now propose to take up some thematic interconnections and consider how they are often inscribed within a film's discourse.

When I describe aspects of the director's style or fictional world as "Kubrickian," the term refers not only to consistencies of style that can be traced from film to film but also to ways in which the filmmaker inscribes himself in the work. When I say that Kubrick is the author of his films, I am speaking primarily of the creative decisions and logistical organization involved in their making. I am not claiming that Kubrick is the only creative artist with significant input into the final film. I am arguing instead that Kubrick's overall contribution is the most significant and that his creative input essentially guides the other contributions. This is how I have always understood the idea of a film auteur.

In earlier discussions of editing and camera strategies, I argued that a particular aesthetic decision (for example, shot length) was an important element in the director's style. My contention was that, through an analysis of such formal organization, it was possible to describe aspects of the director's style and detect the presence of a Kubrickian "voice." This term refers neither to the narrative function of an implied author nor to the author's second self as formulated by such literary critics as Wayne Booth. I am speaking of something more basic to the notion of creating art—the ways in which a work of art represents creative expression and the artist's being in the world.

The following thematic speculations should be viewed in combination with other claims made about the films throughout this analysis. A film obviously communicates its various ideas through many aspects of its discourse. Thematic interconnections are an important element in how a film generates meaning and how the artist communicates ideas. Because thematic discussion has dominated much of the Kubrick literature, I have tended to underplay it in my analysis because I believe that meaning is almost always connected to form and style.

It is often difficult to separate the views and function of a fictional character from the beliefs of the filmmaker. Thematic interconnections run consistently through most of the films, and these thematic ideas are often communicated by cinematic characters. How can viewers discern Stanley Kubrick's views and voice in a finished film? This final discussion will explore the nature of these thematics and how they may reveal aspects of the filmmaker's voice. What can thematic interconnections reveal about the operation of the films, their maker and the creative process?

Moving more specifically to Kubrick's characters, one can reasonably argue that the director frequently presents flawed and unsympathetic characters and often displays an ironic attitude towards them. Even when his characters are more sympathetically drawn (as in the case of Barry Lyndon, Humbert Humbert, or Alice Harford), Kubrick still eschews the identification devices common to classical film. Kubrick's conception of character operates on a more cerebral, less emotional level. Characterization in a Kubrick film is an important strategy; it helps to create the film's meaning and offers a medium through which the filmmaker's voice can be heard. Characterization is as important as any editing, camera or *mise-en-scène* decision. Kubrick's characters naturally have a particular function within the fiction, but they are also called upon to help articulate the director's world view.

Turning to a specific example, how can one describe the critique of the military in *Paths of Glory* as Kubrickian, when its antiwar message clearly has its source in Humphrey Cobb's novel? In translating the novel into a screenplay, Kubrick made a crucial decision that helps audiences locate his voice. In the film, the role of Colonel Dax is amplified from the marginal character depicted in the book to the central character. Colonel Dax, in some ways, is the device through which the director's presence will be most prominently felt. When Dax delivers his sentimental and emotional speech to the court, it is a direct plea to the viewer. The film presents Dax's views sympathetically. The positive presentation is intensified by the negative portrayal of the generals in the film. This kind of negative character functioning operates in *A Clockwork Orange* as well. Because Dax and the enlisted men are surrounded by detestable characters in positions of authority, the film makes viewers sympathize more with the men.

When Kubrick's hand-held camera zooms into Dax (Kirk Douglas) during the battle to take Ant Hill (and it is, literally, the director holding the camera in most of those shots), the act of privileging the character in this particular way is related to the film's sympathetic presentation of him. The visual strategy helps communicate and position the character's views in a more positive light. I would also argue that the film's presentation of Dax is a way to detect the director's presence. The cinematic privileging of Kirk Douglas in precisely *this* way, the use of direct address in the courtroom scene (and elsewhere) and the particularly ironic tenor of the characterization are ways in which Kubrick makes his views known. The film asks the audience (through several privileging devices) to pay particular attention to the character of Colonel Dax. It asks viewers to attend to his ideas and physical presence above all others.

It could be argued that the characters of Johnny Clay and Maurice in *The Killing* have very specific functions that are not always related to the film's plot. Apart from their more obvious function within the narrative, there is a philosophizing tone in much of their dialogue. I would argue that in certain select moments, primarily through the creation of particular subtexts, Kubrick is making a specific intervention to communicate his personal point of view. Here is Maurice talking to Johnny in a scene at a chess club:

You have not heard that in this life you have to be like everyone else, the perfect mediocrity, no better, no worse. Individuality is a monster and it must be strangled in its cradle to make our friends feel comfortable. You know, I often thought that the gangster and the artist are the same in the eyes of the masses. They are admired and hero worshiped. But there is always present an underlying wish to see them destroyed at the peak of their glory.

This crucial dialogue begins ironically, but one senses the filmmaker's voice at the center of Maurice's argument. The dialogue is delivered casually, in an off-hand way. The speech is not critical to the main narrative but functions as a kind of philosophical subtext. Maurice is not only a relatively minor character, but his lines are difficult to understand because of the actor's speech patterns. If Kubrick is using this minor character to communicate his personal view about the role of the artist in contemporary society, why state it in such a half-hidden voice? Why not have it resound through a major character in a pivotal scene?

It may be that the director is experimenting with the possible ways in which he can speak through his characters. In his next film, *Paths of Glory*, Kubrick has no difficulty speaking directly through a major character. Indeed, Kubrick's early development as a filmmaker contains numerous instances of such experimentation. Although it is a consistent feature of his work, here it sounds like the effort of a youthful director still learning how to construct an intricate narrative. Maurice's dialogue, in fact, sounds a little out of place, though not necessarily out of character since this scene is the viewer's only real exposure to him. His only other scene involves the diversionary brawl staged at the racetrack during the heist. Maurice's character is opaque, and his real function in the film seems to be to deliver this piece of philosophizing.

The manner in which Johnny Clay's character allows the audience to hear the director's voice is a little more complicated. It is not so much *what* Johnny says that is important but rather his role in the fragmented narrative process in which Kubrick's views may be located. I argued earlier that the impersonal narrator in *The Killing* could reasonably be described as fallible, if the errors in the film's time structure were significant. The one character in the film who possesses the most knowledge is, in fact, not the commentator but Johnny Clay. He organizes every detail of the heist and tells each gang member only the necessary minimum to successfully carry out each assigned task. Johnny deliberately fragments the information he gives to each character (and to the viewer). He tells some more than others but never tells any single character all the details of the robbery. This fragmentation includes Johnny's relationship with Fay, who seems particularly in the dark about Johnny's world and never seems to question any of his actions.

The fragmentation of information involving Johnny and the other characters is related to the fragmented time structure of the film. The viewer's attention is continually shifted from one detail or character to the next and from one time frame to the next. The audience never sees any action carried out to completion. Thus, two very deliberate strategies of fragmentation seem to be operating parallel to one another.

Both the process of fragmenting information and the film's nonlinear time structure reflexively comment on the process of filmmaking. The complicated structure makes viewers more aware of the importance of temporal ordering in film, forcing them to reflect on the organizing function of the filmmaker and the manipulation that goes into creating a film's narrative. By continually shifting the viewer's attention from one action to another and by frustrating conventional expectations of closure, Kubrick has constructed a more modernist narrative.

In some ways, the character Johnny Clay appears to be a stand-in for the filmmaker. The director organizes the act of making a film as Johnny organizes the heist. Each member of the crew has an assigned task; no one person has all the information. A director such as Kubrick is the only individual involved in the entire process from beginning to end. He is privileged with the most knowledge in the process of making the film. Johnny's organization and manipulation of the heist can be viewed as analogous to the act of film directing. Both procedures involve crews, fragmentation of information, organization and precise timing in many different areas. Thought of this way, the film's subtext of reflexiveness is more apparent and intriguing. It becomes a way for Kubrick not only to speak through a character but also to insert himself, somewhat obliquely, into the film.

Maurice's comments about the analogous social roles of the artist and the gangster also make more sense. His remarks help articulate the reflexive subtext of the film. If one takes Maurice's comments and applies them to the role of the narrative filmmaker who is engaged in making what she or he considers to be art, the speech becomes revelatory. The pressures of satisfying a mass audience, the expectations engendered by genre and other aesthetic or historical considerations and the economic exigencies of making a commercial feature film are all sharply felt by most filmmakers. The artist who tries to be audacious and original will almost always be consumed by the monster of mediocrity—the mass audience. It is not inconceivable to argue that Kubrick's voice is speaking through Maurice's dialogue. Every Kubrick film, on some level, contains an internal tension between familiar and unfamiliar filmic rhetoric, between classical storytelling and a less classical narrative mode.

In *The Killing*, Kubrick's experiments with the time structure, voice-over commentary, static long takes, generic conventions and the insertion of subtexts are all clear attempts to insert an original voice into his filmic discourse. Even as a young man, Kubrick no doubt keenly felt the pressures of creating a more original film while satisfying the Hollywood system and his financial backers. Maurice's dialogue and the specific ways in which Johnny functions as a character are examples of how the filmmaker speaks directly (and not so directly) to the audience. They have less to do with the film's plot and everything to do with the film's creator.

An example of how a subtext can communicate the director's world view is perhaps most elusively felt in the way Quilty is inscribed in *Lolita*. By structuring the film so that Quilty's appearances and traces of those appearances are in the foreground, Kubrick speaks, if rather indirectly, to the way his film generates meaning. A large part of the pleasure of watching *Lolita* has to do with the game analogy, and one of the most interesting games concerns these elusive appearances and the main character's obliviousness to them.

The viewer of *Lolita* is in a privileged position. He or she has much more information than the main character. An attentive viewer understands the significance of the dolly movement into Quilty's picture on Lolita's wall (at least, in retrospect) and of the ever-present car trailing Humbert and Lolita after they leave Beardsley, Ohio. The audience can always see through Quilty's impersonations, while Humbert always remains in the dark.

Why should Kubrick structure his film around these imperatives of presence and absence and around the main character's lack of information? It is not enough to claim that the film is more interesting or playful or enjoyable this way. It is also unsatisfying to claim that the original novel restricted the film's conception of Quilty's character. Once again, my speculation is related to the notion of cinematic reflexiveness. The "Quilty game," and all that this game implies, can be read as another way for the film's organizer of meaning, its creator, to speak (indirectly) to the viewer. One could relate this level of discourse to the notion that much of a film's meaning lies embedded. As in any valuable work of art, the attentive viewer must reflect and dig below the surface for the layers of complexity that an artwork can yield.

The perceptive viewer has the reasonable expectation that many layers of a film's meaning will not reveal themselves on first viewing. The subtext that I relate to the film's structural insertion of Quilty and also to the process of generating meaning in the film is certainly elusive. It does not represent the most common thematic form in Kubrick's work. Kubrick's body of work is intriguing precisely because his films encourage this kind of speculation. Their thematic operation is often as complex as their formal organization, and inextricably connected to it.

Based on my reading of *2001*, I would contend that Kubrick is ambivalent about the uses, potential and promise that technology holds for humankind. On the one hand, the attention to detail in scenes such as the space ballets indicates to me that Kubrick admires a great deal of what machines can do. Their graceful presentation is a way to humanize them. The banality of the human characters is meant to contrast with this graceful and attractive technology. The character of HAL offers an instance of a machine taking on human characteristics and contrasts with the banal presentation of the human characters.

On the other hand, the film's narrative presents a cautionary tale. Its thesis about the evolution of the species might profitably be interpreted in conjunction with *Barry Lyndon*. Both films are concerned with the suppression of human instinct and the capacity to display emotion. The potential conflict between humanity's irrational, chaotic urges and the rational control evident in many areas of human endeavor (art, science, ideas) is a persistent and central concern in the director's work.

The military structure that controls the fate of the world in *Dr. Strangelove* is threatened by a chaotic force from within. The character of Ripper is the logical outcome of Cold War paranoia, only slightly exaggerated for purposes of farce. There is little doubt that Kubrick believes that such madness could actually occur. Like all good satire, the presentation of extreme characters and situations in *Dr. Strangelove* is not so far removed from reality as to appear completely ridiculous. The humor is a way of commenting on the military under the guise of entertainment.

HAL's madness in *2001* is not unlike Ripper's crack-up in *Dr. Strangelove*. Both are paranoid responses to critical situations by characters in a privileged situation. Bowman's visionary journey is guided by forces outside his control. On its own, the film seems to argue, humankind is incapable of proceeding to the higher level of development that its technological sophistication would warrant. Human beings have developed their rational faculties at the expense of their intuitive, emotional side. The apes in the "Dawn of Man" episode are more in touch with their primal drives than are the scientists of *2001*, who seem not far removed from the atrophied aristocracy displayed in *Barry Lyndon*. Barry's primitive eruption of violence against Lord Bullingdon is an example of that urge to violence evident among the apes of *2001*. This primitive display is unacceptable to Barry's aristocratic society.

Alex's violent urges and freedom of choice are also expunged by society in *A Clockwork Orange* through the drug therapy of the Ludovico treatment. The fascistic state that reduces Alex to a whimpering, sick tool of the government is fearful of the very qualities that specifically make Alex human. Rather than attempting to harness Alex's creativity by first admitting its complexity and attempting to channel it positively, the state admits its failure. Its fearful response to the monster of Alex is to eliminate all vestiges of his humanity, even though his violent desires might have been released through some creative outlet. In the sick society portrayed in *A Clockwork Orange*, the notion that violence or aggressive behavior could be creative is an impossibility, except to Alex. It is one reason that viewers are drawn to Alex's creative activity. The film argues not that man's rational side is overdeveloped but that his primitive urges are out of control. The connections one finds in *Dr. Strangelove*, *2001*, *A Clockwork Orange* and *Barry Lyndon* help articulate this Kubrickian thematic.

Barry Lyndon is an historical piece, but it is also concerned with contemporary issues related to aesthetics, male/female relations, the amassing of wealth and the loss of one's instinctual self. With the possible exception of Colonel Dax and Bill and Alice Harford, the character of Barry Lyndon is as close as Kubrick gets to presenting a sympathetic character. The film illustrates how an essentially noble individual is made to act ignobly. When this basically decent person is made to act in a way that represents the worst aspects of his society, Kubrick is surely making a personal comment about contemporary society. The character of Barry is an extension of Alex, in the sense that both characters are corrupted by their society.

Kubrick is not necessarily comparing the eighteenth century with the world of *A Clockwork Orange*, but, in some ways, both societies are portrayed as being responsible for the corruption of the individual. Although the two societies seem to be at opposite ends of a spectrum, Barry and Alex share certain affinities. They both lose their identities and the qualities that make them most human. They are both incapable of a loving relationship, and both reflect the distorted values of the society that created them. An analysis of these two seemingly dissimilar characters well illustrates that the director's films deal with personal issues.

Aesthetically, both *Barry Lyndon* and *A Clockwork Orange* share similar concerns. *Barry Lyndon* holds that the eighteenth-century aristocratic society has integrated and subsumed its idealistic world view into art. An appreciation of art and of all things beautiful is the mask behind which this society hides. The film argues that the more horrible aspects of society's view of the individual can be repressed and idealized through painting and by surrounding the individual with material comfort. Money, property, art and an appreciation of other fine things are attempts by the eighteenth-century aristocracy to cover up its failure in terms of the individual. This particular society has reached the summit of its development yet cannot tolerate an emotional outburst. It cannot deal with the irrational or chaotic. It fears the instinctive, primal self that is a necessary part of humanity. The destruction of Barry's humanity is no less brutal than the Ludovico treatment of Alex, although it is different. It is not as overtly fascistic and comes blanketed in the material comfort of the landed aristocracy. It also has the sanction of both state and church. But the world of *Barry Lyndon* is no less bleak, alienated or depressing than the world of *A Clockwork Orange*. The deterioration of society in Alex's world is a logical outcome of the useless and decadent world portrayed in *Barry Lyndon*.

The response to the threat of the individual in *A Clockwork Orange* is dissimilar but no less extreme than in *Barry Lyndon*. The aestheticization of violence by the upper classes, particularly in the Cat Lady sequence, is a paranoid, decadent response to the reality that these same classes have helped create. They believe that they can tame the libido by making it the subject of their decadent artwork. This is an ineffectual response to the threat represented by Alex's unbridled sexuality and violent urges.

The Cat Lady sequence in *A Clockwork Orange* also criticizes the worst tendencies of modern art, although I doubt that Kubrick is against the idea of modernism in art; his films themselves argue against such a limited view. Nonetheless, he is, no doubt, attacking the undisciplined, infantile rejection of the great achievements of the artistic past and the aesthetic amnesia one associates with the most superficial trends in popular culture. Kubrick's work confirms that he appreciates classical music and the many achievements of Western art. The pop-art and abstract expressionist influences on *2001* and the pop-art influences in *A Clockwork Orange* indicate that he values elements of twentieth-century visual art. The brilliant use of Bartók in *The Shining* and of Ligeti in *2001* also argues that the director appreciates the achievements of twentieth-century music. Further, Kubrick's experiments with narrative illustrate that he shares an affinity for the open narrative mode of contemporary art films. To claim that the Cat Lady sequence in *A Clockwork Orange* attacks all modern art would be a superficial reading.

Full Metal Jacket further confirms the claim that Kubrick's art is firmly planted in a modernist, perhaps postmodern, mode. From the film's abstracted soundscape to its hyperreal visuals and other elements of ironic discourse, almost every aspect of the film demonstrates its affinities with contemporary art. On a thematic level, the film explores many ideas that have cropped up in the director's other films. *Full Metal Jacket* challenges notions about the human potential for violence in the modern world. The ethical complication and moral dilemma faced by Private Joker at the end of the film give it an added moral seriousness. The brutality of Joker's action in killing the sniper is tempered by the fact that he is only completing and making certain of her already inevitable death. Is Joker's action an act of mercy or brutality? In fact, it is both. Joker's peace symbol button and the words "Born To kill" scrawled on his helmet are emblematic of the film's position regarding the complicated, at times contradictory, nature of human action.

Full Metal Jacket's reluctance to analyze American involvement in Vietnam and the nation's conflicted feelings over it may disappoint those who expect films such as this to be analytical and essayistic in nature. The film may also disappoint viewers unfamiliar with Kubrick's ironic and distanced aesthetic or those who expect a combat film to aim for a cathartic release. Although there is a kind of catharsis by the end of the sniper sequence, *Full Metal Jacket* is generally cool in tone and always aware of itself and its effects. The film is tightly controlled and never succumbs to the worst excesses of melodrama. On its own terms, *Full Metal Jacket* is a coherent and complex film that ranks with the best work of the director and the best films in the genre.

One of the more controversial aspects of Kubrick's work is how to take his representation of women. Kubrick has often been attacked because his films either eliminate women almost entirely (*2001, Paths of Glory, Dr. Strangelove, Full Metal Jacket*) or create caricatures ranging from the black widow or harpy (Sherry in *The Killing*, Charlotte in *Lolita*) to sex objects (Miss Foreign Affairs in *Dr. Strangelove*, many women in *A Clockwork Orange* and *Eyes Wide Shut*, and Lolita in *Lolita*).

It is true that the most fully rounded and sympathetic character in Kubrick's work is a man (Barry Lyndon), that the most privileged mythic journey is taken by a man (Bowman in *2001*), and that several films have virtually no major female characters. It is also true that certain women in Kubrick's films have been his most interesting, humorous and strong-willed characters (Charlotte Haze, Alice Harford, Sherry Peatty) or his most competent (Wendy Torrance). Conversely, some of his most monstrous characters have certainly been men (Jack Torrance, the generals in *Paths of Glory*, General Ripper, and Alex). Bowman may be the savior of the species in *2001*, but, along with the other scientists in that film, he is portrayed as banal, numb and lacking in humanity. Humbert Humbert's victimization is not really by Lolita but is a result of his own obsession. Although Kubrick's sympathy is with Barry Lyndon, he is no less a mannequin than Lady Lyndon. He may aspire to her position in society, but both are products of their time and both are its victims. And certainly Kubrick's final legacy, *Eyes Wide Shut*, is as penetrating a look at male-female relationships as he has ever given us. It is a sympathetic portrait, though laced with melancholy. Still, it can be viewed as an ultimately hopeful view that the rewards of marriage are worth the suspicion, jealousy and difficulty placed along the road, both by human nature and our individual foibles.

The issues of character and meaning are too complicated and too dependent on their particular contexts to enable facile observations about Kubrick's portrayal of women. Kubrick's male characters are generally as negative, weak, flawed, monstrous or victimized as his female characters. If Kubrick's view of humankind—male and female—is negative, it is not a selective view; everyone is in trouble. Everyone bears some responsibility for arriving at this point in evolution. Kubrick's world view indicts good and bad, male and female alike. The female sniper in *Full Metal Jacket* is no less or more a monster than the drill instructor in the same film. The fact that she is a woman may surprise some viewers, but it indicates that Kubrick views all members of society as capable of the worst forms of human behavior. Everyone—male or female, adults or children—has the capability to perpetrate the worst crimes, and also to save the planet and renew the species.

In this analysis, I have tried to show that the films of Stanley Kubrick are extraordinarily coherent in terms of their structure, formal and stylistic organization, narrative patterns and thematics. They represent one of the most illustrious, if at times problematic, bodies of work in all of cinema. One may disagree with Kubrick's ideas about the world, but one would be hard pressed to claim that his views were inauthentic or not articulated with great cinematic power. Kubrick's films are rigorous in their operation and function in complex ways, both formally and thematically.

This book has been an attempt to describe what I feel are some of the key aspects of Kubrick's cinematic universe. It has also been an excursion into the speculative nature of cinematic art and the possible meaning films can generate. It has never been my claim that these readings are exhaustive, and certainly there are other ways to think about the films. I also don't claim that Stanley Kubrick is beyond criticism. If I have tended to focus on what I take to be most interesting about his work, it is because I believe that a positive approach to art criticism is ultimately more illuminating than a negative one. To my mind, it is more fruitful to accept Kubrick's work for what it is than for what it might have been. And what it is, as I hope my analysis has convincingly argued, is one of the formidable achievements of cinematic art.

Kubrick's films were made with great artistry and craftsmanship, and the director was profoundly committed to the uniqueness of the film medium. His films challenge our understanding of the world and sometimes force us to think in ways we would prefer not to. If we are, at times, made uncomfortable when we view a Kubrick film, we are just as often exhilarated by the experience. It is my fervent hope that the reader will want to rediscover the films since without them, there would be no need for this book. In this era of digital videodisc and other forms of new media, Stanley Kubrick's cinematic legacy will continue to provide pleasure, provoke controversy and contribute to a better understanding of both art and human nature. Now, more than ever, we need Stanley Kubrick's films to make us think about who we are and how to live in the world.

Appendix

NARRATIVE SEGMENTATIONS

The Killing

1. Marv Unger (Jay C. Flippen), Mike O'Reilly (Joe Sawyer) and George Peatty (Elisha Cook) are introduced at the racetrack, which will be the scene of the heist later in the film. Time is 3:45 P.M. Saturday. Voice-over.

2. Officer Randy Kennan (Ted De Corsia) meets a loan shark in a bar. Time is 2:45 P.M., same day. Voice-over.

3. Gang leader Johnny Clay (Sterling Hayden) is at his apartment with his "girl," Fay (Coleen Gray). Time is 7:00 P.M., same day. Voice-over.

4. Mike is at home with his sick wife. Time is 6:30 P.M., same day. Voice-over.

5. George is at home with his wife Sherry (Marie Windsor). Time is 7:15 P.M., same day. Voice-over.

6. Sherry meets her lover (Vince Edwards). No precise time is established, although viewers know it is later than segment 5. No voice-over.

7. The gang meets and discovers Sherry, who is listening in another room. George is roughed up. No precise time is given, although viewers know it takes place after segment 6. No voice-over.

8. George is at home with Sherry. No precise time is given, but it is still Saturday night, and so it must come after segment 7. No voice-over.

9. Johnny talks to Maurice (Kola Kwariani). It is the Tuesday following the previous Saturday of sequences 1-8. 10:15 A.M. Voice-over.

10. Johnny talks to Nicky (Timothy Carey). The time is unclear, but probably after segment 9. No voice-over.

11. Johnny rents a motel cabin. The time is unclear, but probably after segment 10. No voice-over.

12. Sherry and George are at breakfast. The time is 7:30 A.M. the following Saturday (all the following actions take place on this, the day of the heist). Voice-over.

13. A view of Red Lightning, the horse to be shot in a planned diversion at the racetrack. The time is 5:00 A.M. Voice-over.

14. Johnny talks to Marv at his apartment. He mentions that he will be back at 7:00 P.M. The time is 7:00 A.M. Voice-over.

15. Johnny arrives at the airport. The time is 7:00 A.M. Voice-over.

16. Johnny at the motel cabin. The time is 8:15 A.M. Voice-over.

17. Johnny at the bus station. The time is 8:45 A.M. Voice-over.

18. Johnny slips a key in Mike O'Reilly's mail box. The time is 9:20 A.M. Voice-over.

19. Mike O'Reilly is at home with his sick wife. The time is 11:15 A.M. Voice-over.

20. Mike takes a key out of the mail box and goes to the bus station where he takes a flower carton (containing a rifle) out of a locker. He hops on a bus to the racetrack, where he works as a bartender. He arrives at the racetrack at 11:29 A.M. Voice-over.

21. Mike arrives at the track and puts the flower carton in his locker. Viewers see George take the rifle from the locker. The time is 12:10 P.M. Voice-over.

22. Mike pours beer for a customer. Marv appears drunk. The time is sometime after the first race. Voice-over.

23. Officer Randy Kennan makes a call to the police chief to say that his car radio is out of order. The time is 3:32 P.M. Voice-over.

24. Randy drives to the track and positions himself under the window. The seventh race begins approximately at 4:00 P.M. Voice-over.

25. Maurice is at the chess club. Viewers learn that he is to be in position at the track at 4:00 P.M. The time is 2:30 P.M. Voice-over.

26. Maurice begins his diversion at the track. Viewers hear that it is the start of the fateful seventh race. Johnny is in position. Maurice is dragged out at 4:23 P.M. Voice-over.

27. Nikki leaves his farm at 11:40 A.M.; he arrives at the track at 12:30 P.M. The film stays with Nikki until he shoots Red Lightning during the seventh race and is himself shot dead at 4:24 P.M. Voice-over throughout all of Nikki's actions.

28. Johnny buys a briefcase and positions himself for the robbery at the start of the seventh race. The time is from 2:15 to 4:00 P.M. Voice-over.

29. In the racetrack money room, George opens the door for Johnny and gets the gun out of the flower carton. The roles of the various gang members become clear, except for Randy Kennan. Johnny throws the money bag out the window. No voice-over.

30. The gang members wait for Johnny to arrive. They sit listening to a radio announcer describing details of the robbery. The radio announcer voices puzzlement about how the duffel bag containing the money was removed from the track. Viewers see the bag come out of the window in a flashback. George announces the time. It is 7:15 P.M. He notes that Johnny was supposed to be at the

apartment at 7:00 P.M. The two hoods (Vince Edwards, Joseph Turkel) break in. The sequence ends with the climactic bloody massacre. No voice-over.

31. Johnny reaches the motel cabin "40 minutes earlier" than the previous scene and takes the duffel bag of money out of the cabin. The time is 6:25 P.M. according to the voice-over. However, if we take George to be correct in the previous scene, it would make the time 6:35 P.M.

32. Johnny arrives at the meeting place at 7:29 P.M. The police arrive. Johnny notices that something is wrong and drives away. Voice-over.

33. Johnny buys a large suitcase at a pawnshop and stuffs the money into it. The time is 7:39 P.M. (10 minutes later). Voice-over.

34. Sherry is at her apartment. George walks in covered in blood and shoots Sherry. The time is unclear but it is after segment 32. No voice-over.

35. Johnny meets Fay at the airport. He is informed that his bag is too big to be carried onto the plane. He is forced to check the suitcase and it is placed on a small loading van. A small dog runs toward the plane on the runway. The baggage van swerves to avoid hitting the dog. Johnny and Fay look on in horror as the suitcase full of money flies open. They begin to leave, but Johnny resigns himself to his fate and decides to give himself up. The time is unclear, but it is after segment 33. End of film. No voice-over.

Lolita

1. After opening credits, Humbert Humbert (James Mason) wanders through Clare Quilty's (Peter Sellers) mansion and shoots Quilty. Several transition shots (aerial/car shots, etc.) follow and a title announces, "Four years earlier." Character voice-over by Humbert begins after this first scene.

2. Humbert is introduced with some background information. Charlotte Haze (Shelley Winters) and Lolita (Sue Lyon) are also introduced.

3. Humbert, Charlotte and Lolita watch a horror film at a drive-in movie.

4. Humbert teaches Charlotte how to play chess.

5. Humbert observes Lolita as she plays with her hulahoop in the garden.

6. Humbert, Charlotte and Lolita are at a school dance; Quilty is there in the company of Vivian Darkbloom.

7. Humbert is at home with Charlotte after the school dance. Lolita interrupts them while they are dancing.

8. Humbert is writing in his diary the morning after segment 7. This is the second sequence with Humbert's voice-over.

9. Charlotte and Lolita are at the breakfast table. Lolita takes breakfast up to Humbert's room where the two briefly discuss the diary. Humbert reads an extract from Edgar Allan Poe to Lolita.

10. Humbert and Charlotte are at the dinner table. Charlotte informs Humbert that Lolita will be going to summer camp (Camp Climax).

11. Lolita gets in a car to go to camp and gives Humbert a goodbye kiss. Humbert walks into Lolita's room and cries on Lolita's bed. Humbert reads Charlotte's letter. Camera ends scene on Quilty's picture on the wall in full frame.

12. After Humbert's wedding to Charlotte, Humbert is writing in his diary. This is the third voice-over in the film. Humbert and Charlotte discuss God. Charlotte takes out a gun. She mentions her plans for Lolita who will be sent away to school, allowing Charlotte and Humbert to live alone. He contemplates murder; they argue. Humbert addresses the spectator. Charlotte discovers his diary. She is hit by a car, off-screen. Humbert discovers her body on the street outside their house.

13. Humbert is in the bathtub with his drink. Neighbors come in. They notice the gun and assume (wrongly) that Humbert wants to kill himself.

14. Humbert goes to Camp Climax to fetch Lolita.

15. Humbert and Lolita are in the car. Humbert tells Lolita that her mother is ill and in the hospital. The odyssey begins!

16. Quilty and Vivian Darkbloom are at the hotel. Quilty talks to Mr. Swine, the night manager. Quilty notices the arrival of Humbert and Lolita at the hotel.

17. Humbert and Lolita are in a hotel room.

18. Humbert is in the hotel lobby but does not notice that Quilty is also there. They go outside; Quilty impersonates a policeman ("just a normal guy" speech). Humbert does not recognize Quilty.

19. Humbert and a bellhop try to open a folding cot; Lolita is asleep in bed. Humbert is thwarted in his attempt to consummate their relationship.

20. Next morning Humbert and Lolita are playful. The implication is that their relationship is consummated here, off-screen.

21. Humbert and Lolita are in the car. He tells Lolita that her mother is dead.

22. In the motel room, Lolita is in tears. Humbert promises never to leave her.

23. Voice-over announces that they are in Beardsley, Ohio, six months later. Humbert paints Lolita's toe-nails (same action under opening credits). Lolita asks to be in the school play. Humbert refuses.

24. Humbert talks with Dr. Zempf, the school psychologist, impersonated by Quilty.

25. Backstage at the school play, Humbert discovers that Lolita has been missing piano lessons for weeks.

26. Lolita and Humbert have a tremendous argument. He proposes that they leave Beardsley. Lolita leaves the apartment.

27. Lolita is in a phone-booth, probably talking to Quilty.

28. Voice-over and car scenes as Humbert and Lolita travel across the country. A car follows them. Humbert notices he is being followed. They stop at a gas station. Humbert notices Lolita talking to someone in another car. They have a blow-out. The car behind them also stops. Both characters seem to be getting ill.

29. Lolita is in hospital. Humbert brings flowers. He notices a pair of dark sunglasses.

30. Humbert is in a motel room. The phone rings in the middle of the night. It is Quilty in another impersonation.

31. Humbert goes to the hospital and discovers that Lolita has been checked out to the care of her uncle. Humbert goes berserk and has to be restrained.

32. Typewritten page of a "Dear Dad" letter. It is much later in time since Lolita is now married and pregnant. She is badly in need of money.

33. Humbert drives to Lolita's house. He takes a gun out of the car's glove compartment.

34. Humbert and Lolita are in her house. Lolita explains everything about Quilty to Humbert. He gives Lolita money after one final attempt to have Lolita leave with him. Lolita's "nice" husband is introduced. Humbert drives away.

35. Humbert walks into Quilty's mansion, echoing the opening scene. The film ends with Humbert shouting the words, "Quilty, Quilty."

A Clockwork Orange

1. Alex (Malcolm McDowell) and his gang of droogs are at the Korova Milkbar. Alex introduces himself and his gang in what will be the film's consistent mode of narration: direct address to the spectator through the device of character voice-over.

2. Alex and his gang beat up an old man on the street. The time is after segment 1; Alex's voice-over continues the direct address.

3. Alex and his gang break up the attempted rape of a young woman by Billy Boy and his gang in a highly stylized, violent ballet. Voice-over continues. Time is linear and will remain so throughout the film.

4. Alex and his gang drive wildly on the road leading to the first HOME sequence, where they brutally beat the writer and rape his wife. Alex performs "Singing in the Rain" as he brutalizes them. Voice-over.

5. Alex and gang return to Korova milk bar after segment 4. Female opera singer sings an extract from Beethoven's *Ninth Symphony*, indicating Alex's great love for this music. Alex reprimands Dim, one of his gang members, for his boorish behavior. Voice-over.

6. Alex returns to his home, puts his loot for the evening into a drawer and listens to Beethoven. Alex is in an ecstatic (masturbatory) state shown by movie-like fantasy images that unreel in his mind. Voice-over.

7. Alex's parents are at the breakfast table. Mr. Deltoid, Alex's parole officer, speaks to him and makes a grab for his crotch. No voice-over.

8. Alex is at a record store dressed in a "dandified" outfit; he encounters two girls and takes them home for a quick sexual encounter (rendered visually through fast-motion photography). No voice-over.

9. Alex meets his gang members, realizes something is amiss and decides to assert his authority. Slow-motion scene of violence along a marina. Voice-over picks up again.

10. In the "Duke of New York" bar, the gang is as before. The insurrection has been put down. They plan their next caper (Cat Lady sequence).

11. Cat Lady sequence. Alex smashes an enormous penis sculpture onto the woman. Alex's gang turns on him, smashing a milk bottle in his face.

12. Alex is at the police station being interrogated and beaten by the police and Mr. Deltoid. No voice-over.

13. Aerial shots of the prison. Alex arrives at prison, strips and undergoes physical inspection. Direct address continues.

14. The prison chaplain delivers a sermon about hellfire; prisoners mock the sermon. Alex and other prisoners sing a hymn with the chaplain. The voice-over announces that it is two years after the time of segment 13.

15. Alex is in the prison library reading the Bible. He imagines himself as a Roman soldier at the time of Christ. Alex mentions to the chaplain that he has heard about the Ludovico treatment and would like to volunteer for it. Voice-over continues.

16. A government minister selects Alex for the treatment. No voice-over.

17. Alex is chosen for Ludovico treatment. No voice-over.

18. Alex is taken to the Ludovico Medical Facility. Voice-over picks up again.

19. Alex begins the Ludovico treatment. No voice-over.

20. Alex is strapped to a chair with his eyelids forced open and watches violent films. He notices that he begins to feel sick. Voice-over picks up.

21. Alex is in a hospital bed and a female doctor is near. No voice-over.

22. Alex watches more films that have Beethoven soundtracks. Alex screams in agony as he hears the music. Voice-over continues.

23. Alex "performs" for the prison audience. He is now cured, as demonstrated in two episodes involving actors on stage. The chaplain argues against the treatment. Voice-over.

24. Alex is released from prison and goes home to his parents. He notices a stranger has replaced him. He attempts to strike the boarder but is physically repulsed. Voice-over continues.

25. Alex walks along the Thames Embankment. He stares into the water and contemplates suicide. The old derelict from sequence 2 recognizes Alex as the youth who attacked him earlier and proceeds, with many of his friends, to attack Alex. Dim and Georgie (now police) chase the tramps away. Voice-over continues.

26. Dim and Georgie take Alex to the country and torture him. They place him in a vat of water and brutalize him. No voice-over.

27. The second HOME sequence is at the house of the same writer as sequence 4. Alex collapses at the front door. He is bloody from his various beatings and is taken to bed. Voice-over.

28. The writer proposes to use Alex for his political ends. Alex, in the bathtub, sings "Singing in the Rain." Memories of his earlier assault come back to the writer. No voice-over.

29. Alex eats a meal at the writer's dining table. He collapses (from the drugged wine) into his plate of food. Political friends of the writer arrive. No voice-over.

30. Alex is in the writer's home on the bed. Music of Beethoven permeates the air. Alex experiences revulsion and attempts to escape but the room is locked. Alex jumps out the window in a suicide attempt, rendered by a perceptual point-of-view shot. Voice-over picks up again.

31. Alex wakes up in a hospital bed. Voice-over.

32. Newspaper montage. The government is attacked for Alex's condition. Alex's parents visit him in hospital. No voice-over.

33. Alex is in bed. A psychiatrist gives Alex a psychological test. Voice-over.

34. Alex is eating in his hospital bed and visited by the government minister. Gigantic loudspeakers are rolled in and the Beethoven music is loudly played. Photographers come in and snap pictures of Alex. He rolls his eyes in ecstasy, leading to the final fantasy sequence. Voice-over.

35. Alex is rolling around with nude woman (dream-like sequence), applauded by group dressed in fine clothes, as if attending Ascot. The scene is rendered in slow motion. Voice-over. Credits roll.

SHOT DESCRIPTION: FRAGMENT OF *DR. STRANGELOVE*

Shot 1   *Exterior*, sky, daytime; long shot, B-52 flying in background, low over the landscape; cut to:

Shots 2–5   *Interior*, B-52, close-up, camera pans to Kivel (Glenn Beck) as he puts transparent screen into navigational aid; cut to radar screen; cut to Major Kong (Slim Pickens); cut to Ace (Shane Rimmer); cut to:

Shot 6   *Exterior*, sky; long shot B-52 flying; cut to:

Shots 7–12   *Interior*, B-52, low-angle close-up of Dietrich (Frank Berry); cut to Lieutenant Zogg (James Earl Jones); cut to shot of cockpit instrumentation panel; cut to Zogg; cut to switchboard; cut to hand on switch; tilt-down to panel marked: "Electronic Barometric Time Impact"; cut to:

Shot 13   *Exterior*, sky; long shot, high angle, B-52 flying; cut to:

Shots 14–18   *Interior*, B-52, low angle of Kong at controls; cut to switchboard; zoom in to panel marked "Fusing Circuits Test"; cut to Zogg; cut to Kong; cut to switchboard; zoom in to close-up "Arming"; cut to:

Shot 19   *Exterior*, sky; long shot, B-52 flying; cut to:

Shots 20–30   *Interior*, B-52, medium close-up of panel; zoom in to detonator altitude dial; cut to Kong; cut to panel; cut to switchboard; cut to Dietrich; cut to hands flipping switches; zoom in to switch marked "1st safety"; cut to Zogg; cut to Kong; cut to hand flipping switches; zoom in to switch marked "2nd safety"; cut to Dietrich's hand on switches; cut to switches marked "2nd safety;" zoom in to close-up of switch; cut to:

Shot 31   *Exterior*, sky; long shot, B-52 flying; cut to:

Shots 32–44   *Interior*, B-52, low-angle close shot of Kong at controls; cut to hand on switch; tilt-up to bomb door; warning light reads "CLOSED"; cut to Zogg; cut to open-bomb-door switch; fingers flipping switch; tilt-up to bomb door warning light reading "CLOSED"; cut to Zogg; cut to Kivel; cut to Zogg; cut to Kong; cut to Zogg; cut to bomb door

	warning light flickering and reading "CLOSED"; cut to Kong; cut to Kivel; cut to Zogg; cut to:
Shot 45	*Exterior*, long shot, B-52 flying; cut to:
Shots 46–49	*Interior*, B-52, close-up of bomb door warning light flickering and reading "CLOSED"; cut to Zogg; cut to Kong; cut to Zogg; cut to:
Shot 50	*Exterior*, long shot, B-52 flying; cut to:
Shots 51–53	*Interior*, B-52, close shot of hand trying "Firing Switch"; zoom in to close-up "Firing Switch"; cut to bomb door warning light reading "CLOSED"; cut to Zogg; cut to:
Shot 54	*Exterior*, long shot, B-52 flying; cut to:
Shots 55–57	*Interior*, B-52, close shot of Kong; cut to Kong who climbs out of seat and exits through hatch; cut to Kong coming down ladder; tilt-up to his face as he lands on floor; close shot of Kong as he crawls through hatch; cut to:
Shot 58	*Exterior*, long shot, B-52 flying; cut to:
Shot 59	*Interior*, B-52, low angle; Kong enters bomb bay; two bombs in position marked "NUCLEAR WARHEAD—HANDLE WITH CARE." Written on bomb heads are words "HI THERE" (left) and "DEAR JOHN" (right); cut to:
Shot 60	*Exterior*, sky; long shot, B-52 flying; cut to:
Shot 61	*Interior*, B-52 bomb bay; Kong walking on bomb doors; tilt-up to wire fusing; he climbs on top of bomb left, beats at sparks with his Stetson hat; cut to:
Shot 62	*Exterior*, sky; long shot, B-52 flying; cut to:
Shots 63–66	*Interior*, B-52, shot of Kivel looking into navigation scanner; cut to radar screen; cut to cockpit instrument panel; cut to Zogg; cut to:
Shot 67	*Exterior*, sky; long shot, B-52 flying; cut to:
Shots 68–70	*Interior*, B-52, medium-long shot, Kong astride bomb fixing wires; wires spark; cut to Kivel; cut to radar screen; cut to:
Shot 71	*Exterior*, sky; long shot, B-52 flying; cut to:
Shots 72–76	*Interior*, B-52, low-angle close shot of Zogg; cut to Kong working on panel of loose wires that flash; cut to radar screen; cut to cockpit instrument panel; cut to Zogg; cut to:
Shot 77	*Exterior*, sky; long shot, B-52 flying; cut to:
Shots 78–79	*Interior*, B-52; low-angle medium-close shot of Kong working in bomb bay; flashes from wires; cut to radar screen; cut to:
Shot 80	*Exterior*, sky; long shot, B-52 flying; cut to:
Shots 81–85	*Interior*, B-52, low-angle close shot of Zogg; cut to Kong fixing wires; cut to radar screen; cut to cockpit instrument panel; cut to Zogg; cut to:
Shot 86	*Exterior*, sky; long shot, B-52 flying; cut to:
Shot 87	*Interior*, B-52, medium-close shot of Kong fixing wires; cut to:

Shot 88   *Exterior,* sky; long shot, B-52 flying; cut to:

Shots 89–95   *Interior,* B-52; high-angle medium shot of cockpit instrument panel; track-in to ground target in background; cut to Kong who connects some wires, then looks down as the bomb door begins to open; cut to Kong astride bomb; bomb doors open below; cut to Kong shouting; cut to Kong astride bomb; cut to bomb with Kong sitting on top; bomb with Kong drops down through bomb bay; cut to Zogg; cut to:

Shot 96   *Exterior,* sky; medium shot of Kong astride H Bomb like a cowboy; cut to:

Shots 97–98   Extreme high-angle long shot of mushroom cloud as bomb explodes; cut to shot of mushroom expanding; cut to: *Interior,* War Room (Sequence ends).

Filmography

SHORT FILMS

Day of the Fight (1951)
Photography, Editing, Sound: Stanley Kubrick
Assistant: Alexander Singer
Music: Gerald Fried
Commentary: Douglas Edwards
Length: 16 minutes
Distributor: RKO Radio

Flying Padre (1951)
Photography, Editing, Sound: Stanley Kubrick
Music: Nathaniel Shilkret
Length: 9 minutes
Distributor: RKO Radio

The Seafarers (1953)
Direction, Photography, Editing: Stanley Kubrick
Script: Will Chasen
Narrator: Don Hollenbeck
Length: 30 minutes
Distributor: Seafarers International Union, Atlantic and Gulf Coast District American
Federation of Labor

FEATURE FILMS

Fear and Desire (1953)
Producer: Stanley Kubrick
Director, Photography, Editing: Stanley Kubrick
Screenplay: Howard O. Sackler

Music: Gerald Fried
Cast: Frank Silvera (Mac), Kenneth Harp (Corby), Virginia Leith (the girl), Paul
Mazursky (Sidney), Steve Coit (Fletcher), David Allen (Narrator)
Length: 68 minutes
Distributor: Joseph Burstyn

Killer's Kiss (1955)
Production Company: Minotaur
Producers: Stanley Kubrick and Morris Bousel
Director, Photography, Editing: Stanley Kubrick
Screenplay: Stanley Kubrick and Howard O. Sackler
Music: Gerald Fried
Choreography: David Vaughan
Cast: Jamie Smith (Davy Gordon), Frank Silvera (Vincent Rapallo), Irene Kane
(Gloria), Jerry Jarret (Albert), Ruth Sobotka (Iris)
Length: 67 minutes
Distributor: United Artists

The Killing (1956)
Production Company: Harris-Kubrick Productions
Producer: James B. Harris
Director: Stanley Kubrick
Screenplay: Stanley Kubrick, based on the novel *Clean Break* by Lionel White
Additional Dialogue: Jim Thompson
Photography: Lucien Ballard
Music: Gerald Fried
Editor: Betty Steinberg
Sound: Earl Snyder
Art Director: Ruth Sobotka Kubrick
Cast: Sterling Hayden (Johnny Clay), Coleen Gray (Fay), Jay C. Flippen (Marv
Unger), Marie Windsor (Sherry Peatty), Elisha Cook (George Peatty), Ted de Corsia
(Randy Kennan), Joe Sawyer (Mike O'Reilly), James Edwards (parking lot attendant),
Timothy Carey (Nikki), Vince Edwards (Val), Joseph Turkel (Tiny), Kola Kwariani
(Maurice)
Length: 83 minutes
Distributor: United Artists

Paths of Glory (1957)
Production Company: Harris-Kubrick Productions
Producer: James B. Harris
Director: Stanley Kubrick
Screenplay: Stanley Kubrick, Jim Thompson, and Calder Willingham, based on the
novel by Humphrey Cobb
Photography: George Krause
Music: Gerald Fried
Editor: Eva Kroll
Sound: Martin Muller
Art Director: Ludwig Reiber

Cast: Kirk Douglas (Colonel Dax), Ralph Meeker (Corporal Paris), Adolphe Menjou (General Broulard), George Macready (General Mireau), Wayne Morris (Lieutenant Roget), Richard Anderson (Major Saint-Aubain), Joseph Turkel (Private Arnaud), Timothy Carey (Private Ferol), Peter Capell (Judge), Suzanne Christian (German girl), Bert Freed (Sergeant Boulanger), Emile Meyer (priest), John Stein (Captain Rousseau)
Length: 86 minutes
Distributor: United Artists (Presented by Bryna Productions)

Spartacus (1960)
Production Company: Bryna Productions
Producer: Edward Lewis
Executive Producer: Kirk Douglas
Director: Stanley Kubrick
Screenplay: Dalton Trumbo, from the novel by Howard Fast
Photography: Russell Metty
Additional Photography: Clifford Stine
Process: Super Technirama, 70mm. Technicolor
Editors: Robert Lawrence, Robert Schultz, Fred Chulack
Second Unit: Irving Lerner
Music: Alex North
Music Director: Joseph Gershenson
Production Designer: Alexander Golitzen
Set Decoration: Russell Gausman, Julia Heron
Art Director: Eric Orbom
Titles: Saul Bass
Sound: Waldo Watson, Joe Lapis, Murray Spivack, Ronald Pierce,
Cast: Kirk Douglas (Spartacus), Laurence Olivier (Marcus Crassus), Jean Simmons (Varinia), Charles Laughton (Gracchus), Peter Ustinov (Batiatus), Tony Curtis (Antoninus), John Gavin (Julius Caesar), Nina Foch (Helena), Herbert Lom (Tigranes), John Ireland (Crixus), John Dall (Glabrus), Charles McGraw (Marcellus), Harold J. Stone (David), Woody Strode (Draba)
Length: 196 minutes
Distributor: Universal Pictures

Lolita (1962)
Production Companies: Seven Arts/Anya/Transworld
Producer: James B. Harris
Director: Stanley Kubrick
Screenplay: Vladimir Nabokov (Stanley Kubrick, uncredited), based on Nabokov's novel
Photography: Oswald Morris
Editor: Anthony Harvey
Art Director: Bill Andrews
Associate Art Director: Sid Cain
Music: Nelson Riddle
Lolita Theme: Bob Harris
Orchestrations: Gil Grau

Production Supervisor: Raymond Anzarut
Sound Recordists: H. L. Bird, Len Shilton
Cast: James Mason (Humbert Humbert), Peter Sellers (Clare Quilty), Shelley Winters (Charlotte Haze), Sue Lyon (Lolita), Marianne Stone (Vivian Darkbloom), Jerry Stovin (John Farlow), Diana Decker (Jean Farlow), Gary Cockrell (Dick Schiller), Suzanne Gibbs (Mona Farlow), William Greene (Mr. Swine), Cec Linder (physician), Lois Maxwell (Nurse Lord), John Harrison (Tom)
Length: 153 minutes
Distributor: Metro Goldwyn Mayer

Dr. Strangelove, or How I Learned to Stop Worrying and Love the Bomb (1964)
Production Company: Hawk Films
Producer/Director: Stanley Kubrick
Screenplay: Stanley Kubrick, Terry Southern and Peter George, based on the book *Red Alert* by Peter George
Photography: Gilbert Taylor
Editor: Anthony Harvey
Production Designer: Ken Adam
Music: Laurie Johnson
Art Director: Peter Murton
Special Effects: Wally Veevers
Sound Recordist: Richard Bird
Assistant Editor: Ray Lovejoy
Associate Producer: Victor Lyndon
Cast: Peter Sellers (Group Captain Mandrake, President Muffley, Dr. Strangelove), George C. Scott (General "Buck" Turgidson), Sterling Hayden (General Jack D. Ripper), Keenan Wynn (Colonel "Bat" Guano), Slim Pickens (Major T. J. "King" Kong), Peter Bull (Ambassador de Sadesky), James Earl Jones (Lieutenant Lothar Zogg), Tracy Reed (Miss Scott), Jack Creley (Mr. Staines), Frank Berry (Lieutenant Dietrich), Glenn Beck (Lieutenant Kivel), Shane Rimmer (Captain Ace Owens), Paul Tamarin (Lieutenant Goldberg)
Length: 94 minutes
Distributor: Columbia Pictures

2001: A Space Odyssey (1968)
Production Company: Metro Golwyn Mayer
Producer/Director: Stanley Kubrick
Screenplay: Stanley Kubrick and Arthur C. Clarke, based on Clarke's short story "The Sentinel"
Photography: Geoffrey Unsworth
Process: Super Panavision
Additional Photography: John Alcott
Production Designers: Tony Masters, Harry Lange, Ernie Archer
Editor: Ray Lovejoy
Special Photographic Effects Designer/Director: Stanley Kubrick
Special Photographic Effects Supervisors: Wally Veevers, Douglas Trumbull, Con Pederson, Tom Howard
Music: Richard Strauss, Johann Strauss, Aram Khachaturian, György Ligeti

Costumes: Hardy Amies
Cast: Keir Dullea (Dave Bowman), Gary Lockwood (Frank Poole), William Sylvester (Dr. Heywood Floyd), Douglas Rain (voice of HAL), Daniel Richter (Moonwatcher), Leonard Rossiter (Smyslov), Margaret Tyzack (Elena), Robert Beatty (Halvorsen)
Length: 141 minutes (originally 160 minutes)
Distributor: Metro Goldwyn Mayer

A Clockwork Orange (1971)
Production Company: Warner Brothers/Hawk Films
Producer/Director: Stanley Kubrick
Executive Producers: Max Raab, Si Litvinoff
Screenplay: Stanley Kubrick, based on the novel by Anthony Burgess
Photography: John Alcott
Editor: Bill Butler
Production Design: John Barry
Art Directors: Russell Hagg, Peter Shields
Electronic Music: Walter (Wendy) Carlos
Music: Ludwig van Beethoven, Edward Elgar, Gioacchino Rossini, Nikolai Rimsky-Korsakov, Henry Purcell, Terry Tucker, Arthur Freed, Nacio Herb Brown, James Yorkston, Erica Eigen
Costumes: Milena Canonero
Assistant to Producer: Jan Harlan
Cast: Malcolm McDowell (Alex), Patrick Magee (Mr. Alexander), Michael Bates (Chief Guard), Anthony Sharp (Minister of the Interior), Godfrey Quigley (Prison Chaplain), Adrienne Corri (Mrs. Alexander), Warren Clarke (Dim), Miriam Karlin (Cat Lady), Paul Farrell (tramp), Philip Stone (Dad), Sheila Raynor (Mum), Aubrey Morris (Mr. Deltoid), Carl Duering (Dr. Brodsky), John Clive (stage actor), Madge Ryan (Dr. Branom), Pauline Taylor (psychiatrist), Margaret Tyzack (conspirator), John Savident (conspirator), Steven Berkoff (Constable), David Prouse (Julian), Michael Tarn (Pete)
Length: 137 minutes
Distributor: Warner Brothers

Barry Lyndon (1975)
Production Company: Hawk/Peregrine Films for Warner Brothers
Producer/Director: Stanley Kubrick
Executive Producer: Jan Harlan
Screenplay: Stanley Kubrick, based on the novel *The Luck of Barry Lyndon* by William Makepeace Thackeray
Photography: John Alcott
Editor: Tony Lawson
Production Designer: Ken Adam
Art Director: Roy Walker
Costumes: Ulla-Britt Søderlund, Milena Canonero
Music: J. S. Bach, Frederick the Great, W. A. Mozart, G. F. Handel, Franz Schubert, Giovanni Paisiello, Antonio Vivaldi, traditional Irish music played by The Chieftains
Music Adaptation: Leonard Rosenman

Cast: Ryan O'Neal (Redmond Barry/Barry Lyndon), Marisa Berenson (Lady Lyndon), Patrick Magee (Chevalier de Balibari), Hardy Kruger (Captain Potzdorf), Steven Berkoff (Lord Ludd), Gay Hamilton (Nora Brady), Marie Kean (Mrs. Barry), Murray Melvin (Reverend Runt), Godfrey Quigley (Captain Grogan), Leon Vitali (Lord Bullingdon), Diana Koerner (Lischen), Frank Middlemass (Sir Charles Lyndon), André Morell (Lord Wendover), Philip Stone (Graham), Anthony Sharp (Lord Hallum), Michael Hordern (Narrator)
Length: 185 minutes
Distributor: Warner Brothers

The Shining (1980)
Production Company: Hawk/Peregrine Films (in association with The Producer Circle Company) for Warner Brothers
Producer/Director: Stanley Kubrick
Executive Producer: Jan Harlan
Screenplay: Stanley Kubrick and Diane Johnson, based on the novel by Stephen King
Photography: John Alcott
Steadicam Operator: Garrett Brown
Editor: Ray Lovejoy
Production Designer: Roy Walker
Art Director: Les Tomkins
Music: Béla Bartók, György Ligeti, Krzysztof Penderecki, Wendy Carlos, Rachel Elkind, Henry Hall
Costumes: Milena Canonero
Sound: Ivan Sharrock
Second Unit Photography: Douglas Milsome, Gregg Macgillivray
Personal Assistant to Stanley Kubrick: Leon Vitali
Cast: Jack Nicholson (Jack Torrance), Shelley Duvall (Wendy Torrance), Danny Lloyd (Danny Torrance), Scatman Crothers (Halloran), Philip Stone (Delbert Grady), Joe Turkel (Lloyd), Barry Nelson (Ullman), Anne Jackson (Doctor), Lia Beldam (young woman in bath), Billie Gibson (old woman in bath), Lisa and Louise Burns (Grady girls)
Length: 144 minutes
Distributor: Warner Brothers

Full Metal Jacket (1987)
Production Company: Puffin Films for Warner Brothers
Executive Producer: Jan Harlan
Producer/Director: Stanley Kubrick
Screenplay: Stanley Kubrick, Michael Herr and Gustav Hasford, based on Hasford's novel *The Short-Timers*
Lighting Cameraman: Douglas Milsome
Production Designer: Anton Furst
Editor: Martin Hunter
Original Music: Abigail Mead (plus songs: "Hello Vietnam," performed by Johnny Wright; "The Marines Hymn," performed by the Goldman Band; "These Boots Are Made for Walking" performed by Nancy Sinatra; "Chapel of Love," performed by the Dixie Cups; "Wooly Bully," performed by Sam the Sham and the Pharaohs; "Paint It Black," performed by the Rolling Stones).

Sound Recording: Edward Tise
Special Effects Supervisor: John Evans
Cast: Matthew Modine (Private Joker), Lee Ermey (Sergeant Hartman), Vincent D'Onofrio (Private Pyle), Adam Baldwin (Animal Mother), Arliss Howard (Private Cowboy), Dorian Harewood (Eightball), Kevyn Major Howard (Rafterman), Ed O'Ross (Lt. Touchdown), John Terry (Lt. Lockhart), Ngoc Le (V.C. Sniper)
Length: 116 minutes
Distributor: Warner Bros.

Eyes Wide Shut (1999)
Production Companies: Pole Star/Hobby Films for Warner Brothers
Producer/Director: Stanley Kubrick
Executive Producer: Jan Harlan
Screenplay: Stanley Kubrick and Frederic Raphael, inspired by Arthur Schnitzler's *Traumnovelle*
Lighting Cameraman: Larry Smith
Steadicam Operators: Elizabeth Ziegler, Peter Cavaciuti
Production Designers: Les Tomkins, Roy Walker
Art Director: John Fenner
Editor: Nigel Galt
Original Music: Jocelyn Pook
Other Music: György Ligeti, Dimitri Shostakovich, Chris Isaak, Wolfgang Amadeus Mozart, Franz Liszt
Costume Designer: Marit Allen
Sound Recording: Edward Tise
Original Paintings: Christiane Kubrick, Katharina Hobbs
Cast: Tom Cruise (Dr. William Harford), Nicole Kidman (Alice Harford), Sidney Pollack (Victor Ziegler), Marie Richardson (Marion Nathanson), Rade Sherbedgia (Milich),Todd Field (Nick Nightingale), Vinessa Shaw (Domino), Alan Cumming (Hotel Desk Clerk), Sky Dumont (Sandor Szavost), Fay Masterson (Sally), Leelee Sobieski (Milich's Daughter), Thomas Gibson (Carl), Julienne Davis (Mandy), Madison Eginton (Helena Harford), Leon Vitali (Red Cloak), Abigail Good (Mysterious Woman), Togo Igawa (Japanese Man 1), Eiji Kusuhara (Japanese Man 2), Gary Goba (Naval Officer), Phil Davis (Stalker)
Length: 158 minutes
Distributor: Warner Bros.

Selected Bibliography

Agel, Jerome, ed. *The Making of Kubrick's 2001.* New York: New American Library, 1970.

Alcott, John. "Photographing Stanley Kubrick's *Barry Lyndon*." In *Perspectives on Stanley Kubrick*, edited by Mario Falsetto. New York: G. K. Hall, 1996. First published in *American Cinematographer* (March 1976).

Anderegg, Michael, ed. *Inventing Vietnam: The War in Film and Television.* Philadelphia: Temple University Press, 1991.

Appel, Alfred, Jr., ed. *The Annotated Lolita.* By Vladimir Nabokov. New York: McGraw-Hill, 1970.

Baxter, John. *Stanley Kubrick: A Biography.* New York: Carroll and Graf, 1997.

Beardsley, Monroe C. *Aesthetics from Classical Greece to the Present: A Short History.* New York: Macmillan, 1966.

Bernstein, Jeremy. "How about a Little Game?" *New Yorker* (November 12, 1966): 70–110.

Bogdanovich, Peter. "What They Say about Stanley Kubrick." *New York Times Magazine* (July 4, 1999): 1–22.

Booth, Wayne C. *The Rhetoric of Fiction.* Chicago: University of Chicago Press, 1961.

Bondanella, Peter. *The Cinema of Federico Fellini.* Princeton, N.J.: Princeton University Press, 1992.

Bordwell, David. *Narration and the Fiction Film.* Madison: University of Wisconsin Press, 1985.

Bordwell, David, and Kristin Thompson. *Film Art: An Introduction*, 5th ed. New York: McGraw-Hill, 1997.

Branigan, Edward. *Point of View in the Cinema: A Theory of Narration and Subjectivity in Classical Film.* Berlin, Germany: Mouton Publishers, 1984.

———. *Narrative Comprehension and Film.* London, England: Routledge, 1992.

Brown, Garrett. "The Steadicam and *The Shining*." In *Perspectives on Stanley Kubrick*, 1996. First published in *American Cinematographer* (August 1980).

Burgess, Anthony. *A Clockwork Orange.* New York: Ballantine, 1965.

————. "Juice from *A Clockwork Orange*." In *Perspectives on Stanley Kubrick*, 1996. First published in *Rolling Stone* (June 8, 1972).

Cahill, Tim. "The Rolling Stone Interview: Stanley Kubrick." In *Perspectives on Stanley Kubrick*, 1996. First published in *Rolling Stone* (August 27, 1987).

Chatman, Seymour. *Story and Discourse: Narrative Structure in Fiction Film*. Ithaca, N.Y.: Cornell University Press, 1978.

Ciment, Michel. *Kubrick*. Trans. by Gilbert Adair. London: Collins, 1983.

Clarke, Arthur C. *2001: A Space Odyssey*. New York: New American Library, 1968.

Cobb, Humphrey. *Paths of Glory*. New York: Viking Press, 1935.

Coyle, Wallace. *Stanley Kubrick: A Guide to References and Resources*. Boston: G. K. Hall, 1980.

Culler, Jonathan. *The Pursuit of Signs: Semiotics, Literature, Deconstruction*. Ithaca, N.Y.: Cornell University Press, 1981.

————. *On Deconstruction: Theory and Criticism after Structuralism*. Ithaca, N.Y.: Cornell University Press, 1982.

Daniels, Don. "Skeleton Key to *2001*." *Sight and Sound* (Winter 1970/71): 28–33.

Deer, Harriet, and Irving Deer. "Kubrick and the Structures of Popular Culture." *Journal of Popular Film* 3: 3 (Summer 1979): 233–244.

Dempsey, Michael. "*Barry Lyndon*." *Film Quarterly* 30 (1976): 49–54.

Doherty, Thomas. "Full Metal Genre: Kubrick's Vietnam Combat Movie." In *Perspectives on Stanley Kubrick*, 1996. First published in *Film Quarterly* 42: 2 (1988–89).

Dumont, J. P., and J. Monod. "Beyond the Infinite: A Structural Analysis of *2001: A Space Odyssey*." *Quarterly Review of Film Studies* (Summer 1978): 297–316.

Falsetto, Mario, ed. *Perspectives on Stanley Kubrick*. New York: G. K. Hall, 1996.

Feldmann, Hans. "Kubrick and His Discontents." In *Perspectives on Stanley Kubrick*, 1996. First published in *Film Quarterly* 30 (Fall 1976).

Geduld, Carolyn. *Filmguide to 2001: A Space Odyssey*. Bloomington: Indiana University Press, 1973.

Gelmis, Joseph. *The Film Director as Superstar*. Garden City, N.Y.: Doubleday, 1970.

George, Peter. *Dr. Strangelove*. New York: Bantam, 1963.

Herr, Michael. *Kubrick*. New York: Grove Press, 2000.

Hoch, David G. "Mythic Patterns in *2001: A Space Odyssey*." *Journal of Popular Culture* (Summer 1970): 961–965.

Houston, Penelope. "Kubrick Country." *Saturday Review* (December 25, 1971): 42–44.

Jenkins, Greg. *Stanley Kubrick and the Art of Adaptation: Three Novels, Three Films*. Jefferson, N.C.: McFarland, 1997.

Kagan, Norman. *The Cinema of Stanley Kubrick*. New York: Holt, Rinehart, and Winston, 1972.

King, Stephen. *The Shining*. New York: Signet, 1977.

Kinney, Judy Lee. "Text and Pretext: Stanley Kubrick's Adaptations." Ph.D. diss., University of California, Los Angeles, 1983.

Kolker, Robert Philip. *A Cinema of Loneliness*, 3rd ed. New York: Oxford University Press, 2000.

Kubrick, Stanley. "Director's Notes: Stanley Kubrick Movie Maker." In *Perspectives on Stanley Kubrick*, 1996. First published in *The Observer* (London), December 4, 1960.

————. "Words and Movies." *Sight and Sound* (Winter 1960/1961): 14.

————. "How I Learned to Stop Worrying and Love the Cinema." *Films and Filming* 9: 9 (June 1963): 12–13.

————. *A Clockwork Orange: A Screenplay.* New York: Ballantine Books, 1972.

————, Michael Herr, and Gustav Hasford. *Full Metal Jacket: The Screenplay.* New York: Alfred A. Knopf, 1987.

————, and Frederic Raphael. *Eyes Wide Shut* (also includes Arthur Schnitzler's *Dream Story*). New York: Warner Books, 1999.

Lobrutto, Vincent. *Stanley Kubrick: A Biography.* New York: Donald I. Fine Books, 1997.

Lightman, Herb. "Filming *2001: A Space Odyssey.*" In *Perspectives on Stanley Kubrick,* 1996. First published in *American Cinematographer* (June 1968).

————. "Photographing Stanley Kubrick's *The Shining*: An Interview with John Alcott." In *Perspectives on Stanley Kubrick,* 1996. First published in *American Cinematographer* (August 1980).

Maland, Charles. "*Dr. Strangelove* (1964): Nightmare Comedy and the Ideology of Liberal Consensus." *American Quarterly* (Winter 1979): 697–717.

Mayersberg, Paul. "The Overlook Hotel." In *Perspectives on Stanley Kubrick,* 1996. First published in *Sight and Sound* (Winter 1980/1981).

Michelson, Annette. "Bodies in Space: Film as Carnal Knowledge." *Artforum* (February 1969): 54–63.

Miller, Mark Crispin. "Kubrick's Anti-Reading of *The Luck of Barry Lyndon.*" In *Perspectives on Stanley Kubrick,* 1996. First published in *Modern Language Notes* 91 (1976).

Milne, Tom. "Stanley Kubrick: How I Learned to Stop Worrying and Love Stanley Kubrick." *Sight and Sound* (Spring 1964): 68-72.

Nabokov, Vladimir. *Lolita: A Screenplay.* New York: McGraw-Hill, 1974.

Nelson, Thomas Allen. *Kubrick: Inside a Film Artist's Maze,* expanded edition. Bloomington: Indiana University Press, 2000.

Phillips, Gene D. "Interview with Stanley Kubrick." *Film Comment* (Winter 1971/ 1972): 30–35.

————. *Stanley Kubrick: A Film Odyssey.* New York: Popular Library, 1975.

Pursell, Michael. "*Full Metal Jacket:* The Unravelling of Patriarchy." In *Perspectives on Stanley Kubrick,* 1996. First published in *Literature/Film Quarterly* 16: 4 (1988): 218–25.

Rapf, Maurice. "A Talk with Stanley Kubrick." *Action* (January/ February 1969): 15–18.

Raphael, Frederic. *Eyes Wide Open: A Memoir of Stanley Kubrick.* New York: Ballantine Books, 1999.

Salt, Barry. *Film Style and Technology: History and Analysis.* London: Starword, 1983.

Schnitzler, Arthur. *Rhapsody: A Dream Story.* Translated from the German by Otto P. Schinnerer. New York: Simon and Schuster, 1927.

Sitney, P. Adams. *Visionary Film: The American Avant-Garde,* 2nd ed. New York: Oxford University Press, 1979.

Pizzello, Stephen. "A Sword in the Bed." *American Cinematographer* (October 1999): 28–38.

Spiegel, Alan. "The Kubrick Case." *Salmagundi* 36 (Winter 1977): 194–208.

Strick, Philip, and Penelope Houston. "Interview with Stanley Kubrick." *Sight and Sound* (Spring 1972): 62–66.

Switzer, Judith Anne. *Stanley Kubrick: The Filmmaker As Satirist*. Ann Arbor: University Microfilms International, 1983.

Thackeray, William Makepeace. *The Luck of Barry Lyndon*. Middlesex, England: Penguin Books, 1975.

Titterington, P. L. "Kubrick and *The Shining.*" *Sight and Sound* (Spring 1981): 117–21.

Todorov, Tzvetan. *The Poetics of Prose*. Trans. by Richard Howard. Ithaca, N.Y.: Cornell University Press, 1977.

Trumbull, Douglas. "Creating Special Effects for *2001.*" In *Perspectives on Stanley Kubrick*, 1996. First published in *American Cinematographer* (June 1968).

Walker, Alexander. *Stanley Kubrick Directs*, expanded edition. New York: Harcourt Brace Jovanovich, 1972.

————, with Sybil Taylor and Ulrich Ruchti. *Stanley Kubrick, Director: A Visual Analysis*. New York: W. W. Norton, 1999.

Waterhouse, E. K. *Painting in Britain: 1530 to 1790*. Middlesex, England: Penguin Books, 1953.

White, Lionel. *Clean Break*. New York: E. P. Dutton, 1955.

Wolfe, Gary K. "*Dr. Strangelove, Red Alert*, and Patterns of Paranoia in the 1950s." *Journal of Popular Film* (Winter 1976): 57–67.

Youngblood, Gene. *Expanded Cinema*. New York: E. P. Dutton, 1970.

Zucker, Carole. *The Idea of the Image*. Cranbury, N.J.: Associated University Presses, 1988.

Index

About the Author

MARIO FALSETTO received his Ph.D. in Cinema Studies from New York University. He is a Professor of Film Studies at the Mel Hoppenheim School of Cinema at Concordia University in Montreal, and the author of *Personal Visions: Conversations with Contemporary Film Directors* and the editor of the anthology *Perspectives on Stanley Kubrick*.